MY GREEK DRAMA

MY GREEK DRAMA

LIFE, LOVE, AND ONE WOMAN'S OLYMPIC EFFORT TO BRING GLORY TO HER COUNTRY

DISRUPTION
BOOKS

Proceeds from this book will go to support youth and education initiatives in Greece and abroad.

A hardcover edition of this book was published in 2013 by Greenleaf Book Group Press.

FIRST DISRUPTION BOOKS EDITION PUBLISHED 2018.

Distributed by Disruption Books. For ordering information or special discounts for bulk purchases, please contact Disruption Books at info@disruptionbooks.com.

Cover and interior design by Rodrigo Corral and Abby Kagan

The Library of Congress has catalogued the hardcover edition as follows:
(Prepared by The Donohue Group, Inc.)
Angelopoulos, Gianna, 1955-
My Greek drama : life, love, and one woman's Olympic effort to bring
glory to her country / Gianna Angelopoulos.—1st ed.
p. ; cm.
Issued also as an ebook.
ISBN: 978-1-60832-581-8
1. Angelopoulos, Gianna, 1955- 2. Olympic Games (28th : 2004 :
Athens, Greece)—Management. 3. Businesswomen—Greece—Biography. 4.
Olympics—Planning. 5. Autobiography. I. Title. II. Title: Greek drama
GV721.2 .A54 2013
796.48/092 2012956124

Print ISBN: 978-1-63331-XXX-X
eBook ISBN: 978-1-63331- XXX-X

TO MY FAMILY—FOR YOUR LOVE, FOR YOUR STRENGTH, AND FOR
GIVING ME A JOYFUL STORY TO WRITE

AND TO MY EXTENDED FAMILY—THE PEOPLE OF GREECE FOR
WHOM,
I BELIEVE, THERE IS A BETTER CHAPTER AHEAD

AS YOU SET OUT FOR ITHAKA,

HOPE THE VOYAGE IS A LONG ONE,

FULL OF ADVENTURES, FULL OF DISCOVERY.

—C. P. CAVAFY, "ITHAKA"
(EXTRACT TRANSLATED BY EDMUND KEELEY)

CONTENTS

FOREWORD

ACKNOWLEDGMENTS

I WISH TO WARMLY THANK ALL THOSE WHO HELPED so that this book exists. All those who encouraged me to start (and finish) writing it, and then to publish; all those who told me not to.

Evidently I am no writer; in fact, I am far more a person of the spoken word—and a person of action. So, I feel in deep debt to Holly Sargent; to Jeff Nussbaum, Raphael Sagalyn, and Mark Starr, who labored along with me through drafts of this book; as well as to Lefteris Kousoulis, Michalis Zacharatos, Andonis Papagianidis, and Lena Zachopoulou, who believed in me and in this venture.

To my husband, Theodore, and my children—Carolina, Panagiotis, and Dimitris—who once more had to bear with me while I was immersed in yet another venture, thanks will never be enough, but neither would be other forms of expressing my gratitude. So thanks, *Efcharistó!*

PROLOGUE

AUGUST 29, 2004. After seventeen days of competitive cycling, running, diving, wrestling, and my own personal race, after a helter-skelter of emotions—mostly extraordinary highs but a few painful lows—I arrived at the Closing Ceremony of the Summer Olympic Games enveloped by a serenity that I hadn't felt since leaving London more than four years before to answer my nation's call.

I knew that Greece had triumphed. Greeks knew in their hearts and souls our achievement would cement our Olympic legacy.

And on this final day, I was secure in my own personal legacy.

My eye had always been on the dream of my childhood: to do something great for Greece. And we had delivered "unforgettable dream games!" Greece had shown the world a nation so unlike the stereotypes—lazy and backward—with which it had saddled us, a modern Greece that, by dint of hard work and sacrifice, could deliver on its promise and compete on the same playing field as all the other leading nations of a new Europe.

My heart was surprisingly light. My Valentino outfit—a silk blouse over peach-colored slacks, accentuated with a sash—was simple yet chic, comfortable, and celebratory. And I *was* ready to celebrate. To join in what my friend Dick Ebersol had characterized as a "party for Greece."

Indeed, the night was lost to revel. At some point, as the festivities— if not the musicians and dancers—wound down, most of the VIPs around me began to make for the exits. But I simply wasn't ready for the party to end. Greeks throughout the stadium were enveloped in a frenzy of joy. And alone in the VIP box, I felt a visceral connection with my country's people. So I surrendered heart and soul to the impassioned rhythms of the night.

Somebody later told me that what I experienced next reminded him of certain moments in the nineteenth-century novels of Leo Tolstoy. They occurred when a character acted without conscious thought, completely immersed in the passions of the moment. During my Tolstoyan moment, I began to dance the *hasapiko*, closing my eyes and extending my arms to the heavens where, no doubt, all the Greek gods were smiling. As I swayed to the music, lost in the exuberant joy of my people, I felt all the cares, anxieties, and pain of my long Olympic struggle flow out of my body. My happiness was truly transcendent.

Mine is a story of life and love, success and failure, betrayal and redemption.

It is a story of how the lessons and legacy of our Athens 2004 Summer Olympics were abandoned.

And it is a story that suggests paths Greece could follow today in its efforts to solve the serious problems it is facing. A memoir that is as much about Greece's journey as it is my own.

It is, in every sense, a Greek drama. My personal Greek drama, and the drama of Greece today.

MY GREEK DRAMA

Chapter 1

PHILOXENIA

OLIVE TREES, majestic as the sun plays on their leaves in the breezes coming off the Aegean Sea. The spicy taste of herb tea infused with fresh-picked thyme and *diktamos*. (This rare, expensive herb from Crete is believed to have medicinal virtues. In Virgil's *Aeneid*, for example, Venus heals Aeneas with a stalk of "dittany from Cretan Ida." My family too grew *diktamos* to brew for tea, a powerful potion that assured longevity. The locals call this herb *erondas*, meaning love.) The aromas of *melitzana* (eggplant), tomatoes, and lamb cooking over an open flame in summer, the time when it never rains. These are my memories of the place where I was born, the magical, historic island of Crete.

Greece is a country of islands. At present, four of the eleven million inhabitan ts of Greece live either in the capital city of Athens on the Attic Peninsula or in the mountainous northern provinces that extend to the borders with Albania and Bulgaria. But the soul of Greece lies in its twelve hundred to six thousand islands (depending on how you measure them) sprinkled across the Ionian Sea to the west, the Mediterranean Sea to the south, and the Aegean Sea to the east. Only about two hundred of these islands are inhabited, and of those merely seventy-eight have more than a hundred residents. Some of the islands are dry; they are covered in rocks, thyme, oregano, and white houses surrounded by blue sea and blue sky. Others are covered in pine trees. Rain, when it falls, falls in winter.

Crete lies three hundred miles south of Athens, in the southern Aegean. It is a true miniature of the flora and fauna of the entire Mediterranean. With more than three thousand square miles—twice as large as the state of Rhode Island—Crete is a large island, and its population exceeds six hundred thousand, rivaling that of such major US cities as Boston, Washington, Denver, and Seattle. It is the land of poets and artists. It is the birthplace of Nikos Kazantzakis, author of *Zorba the Greek*, who once wrote, "Happy is the man . . . who, before dying, has the good fortune to sail the Aegean Sea."

The city of my birth, Heraklion, is Crete's largest city. A place Lord Byron called "Troy's rival."

An ancient fortress built behind solid ten-foot-tall stone walls that remain standing today, Heraklion has witnessed a history of invasion and cultural assimilation as Crete's natural resources and strategic location have been a pivotal point of interest for generations.

In the thirteenth century, for example, the Venetian Empire seized control of Crete and ruled the island for more than four hundred years. Renaissance culture had a pervasive influence on the island and assured the development of rich literature and arts traditions. In the latter half of the seventeenth century, the Ottoman Empire drove the Venetians from the island and ruled Crete for two hundred years.

It wasn't until 1908, the year my father was born, that Crete declared its union with Greece.

Crete's economy has always been stronger than that of mainland Greece. The island boasts agricultural and tourist industries as well as a flourishing commercial port in Heraklion. Crete's natural beauty, along with its combination of cultural and economic riches, has bestowed upon many islanders a distinct sense of superiority. Cretans sometimes believe they are the super-Greeks—stronger, wiser, braver, and freer spirits who are blessed with more of all the virtues that are associated with the Greek people.

There has always been chatter on the island that Crete should break away from the rest of jealous Greece and become an independent nation.

For a long time I shared the feeling that we Cretans were a special people. At critical junctures in my life and career, my faith in the bonds of a shared heritage was rewarded. I always believed I could count on Cretans for assistance or, sometimes, a small miracle that I required.

Over the span of my life I have traveled extensively, meeting Greeks from across my homeland, all of whom seemed to subscribe to their own notions of regional exceptionalism. As a result, I have come to believe that while Cretans have been blessed and are, to some extent, a distinct culture, what we share with all Greeks is far greater than our differences.

As a young girl, I did not fully appreciate the heritage of Heraklion. I viewed my city as drab and unattractive. I did, however, appreciate aspects of Crete's ancient history. Beginning almost five thousand years ago and for almost thirteen centuries, Crete was the pinnacle of Western Civilization, home to the Minoans, who were renowned as the first palace-builders of Europe.

The most famous of those palaces is Knossos, the ceremonial center of a city built on the island between the seventeenth and fourteenth centuries BC. It was discovered and partially restored by the British archaeologist Sir Arthur Evans in the early years of the twentieth century.

I often visited Knossos during my childhood, biking there from my home, which was roughly three miles away. Most people think of antiquities as lifeless and colorless, your classic white marble structures. But Knossos was alive with color, most memorably lush red—*le sang de boeuf*. I marveled at the intricate architectural design that connected more than a thousand rooms, at the elaborate system of water and pipes that served to cool the palace and drain the sewage. I was dazzled by the sophisticated artistry, which included columns carved from cypress trees and stunning frescoes. But to a young girl from a conservative culture, nothing was more striking than the images of women decked out in elegant finery that left their breasts bared.

Years later, those images still resonated with me. When the director of the Opening Ceremony for the Athens 2004 Summer Olympics wanted to incorporate the beauty and sensuality of the ancient women of Knossos, I supported him. I only beat a diplomatic retreat after being warned that any nudity, no matter how deeply rooted in our heritage, might result in controversy.

However unprepossessing Heraklion's appearance, that was only a relatively minor concern of mine growing up there. I was far more distressed by what a cultural backwater the city was. I'm not talking about Minoan glories or Greek antiquities; rather, I'm talking about that 1960s and '70s youth culture—rock and roll, Hollywood movies, British fashion—with which I, like millions of young girls around the world, was totally infatuated. To be generous, I could say Heraklion gave me an appetite for life in a real city. And I would go on to spend my entire life living in major cities: first Thessaloniki, then Athens, and a decade in Zurich and London before, finally, a return to Athens.

I did not discover what it means to be truly Cretan—Cretan in heart and soul—in Heraklion. That transformation would occur in the countryside, in the tiny village of Embaros, nestled in a valley in central Crete.

When I was born, my paternal grandparents, Manolis Fazakis and Parthenia Daskalaki, had already lived in Embaros for some forty years, and it was there that they raised my father, Frixos, along with his older brother, Achilles, and sister, Ioanna.

My father viewed the family homestead in Embaros as the center of his universe. He insisted on taking my younger sister, Eleni, and me there as often as possible for vital infusions of the real Crete. So we visited during summer, during school vacations, and over holiday weekends. Sometimes my mother would entreat my father to let us stay in the city for a long weekend so that the family might partake of some more sophisticated social activities than another family dinner—but to no avail. My father felt it was essential that his daughters experience genuine Cretan life and that they embrace all the values inextricably bound up with his family, the land, and the village.

Although Embaros was merely thirty miles south of Heraklion, it was a world apart. Almost all the villagers had names from ancient Greece: The men were Achilles, Praxiteles, Epaminondas, and Pericles. All nine muses—Euterpe, Clio, Thalia, Terpsichore, Erato, Urania, Polyhymnia, Calliope, and Melpomene—were represented by the women there. Later, when I was taught Greek mythology in school, the names of the mighty heroes and the beautiful muses would conjure up for me the rugged and plain faces of the peasant folk in Embaros instead of those otherworldly creatures.

While Embaros may have been a short distance from Heraklion as the crow flies, it was a long journey. To get there, we traveled a rough, rutted, and overcrowded road on which cars were often stuck behind slow-moving vehicles, carts, and mules. My parents' may have been the slowest moving car of all.

My father refused to drive. He had been in an automobile accident during his World War II military service, but his reluctance may actually have had more to do with the damage his feet suffered traversing the rugged Albanian terrain during the war.

As a result, my mother always drove. And she always maintained a speed that rivaled the pace of your average mule. Make that your average mule carrying a heavy load. Mom insisted that her most important job was keeping us safe, not getting to the village quickly. And she was always totally focused on that task. She never seemed to hear the shouts—"Go wash some dishes, lady"—from the other travelers irked by her plodding pace. Nor did she appear to see their occasional vulgar gestures. I don't think she even heard my father's oft-repeated refrain—I *think* he was joking—that her driving would someday be the cause of his strokes. But she always got us there safely and he never required medical assistance. Any lingering distress from the long, boring trip would rapidly fall by the wayside as we felt the gentle embrace of the countryside—awash in color and redolent with exotic fragrances.

At the Daskalakis* homestead (I'll share with you in chapter 2 why it wasn't the home of Mr. and Mrs. Fazakis), vines crawled over the walls surrounding the huge open courtyard filled with pots of the island's various flowers. Crete boasts more varieties of herbs than in any other European country, and my grandparents planted pots of them as well, particularly basil. (Basil would play a major role in my later political life.) The door onto the courtyard was always left open, and occasionally a stranger would stumble inside, thinking he was on a path through

---

*Note that the addition of the suffix "s" in Greek surnames such as the author's maiden name does not signify the English plural form. Rather, the "s" at the end of Daskalakis is the masculine form of the family name.

the village. We Greeks embrace *philoxenia*, which translates literally as "love for strangers." Figuratively, *philoxenia* means that whoever comes to your house, friend or stranger, must be welcomed, made to feel at home, and offered a lot to eat. The value of a person's hospitality was judged by how generously he or she welcomed strangers. To fail that test was a family disgrace—and our family never failed.

If I close my eyes, I can summon many childhood memories of that magical place. Foremost among them are the olive trees that blanketed our fields. There is no more enduring symbol of Crete than these trees with their dark and silvery green shimmering leaves. For the Athens 2004 Summer Games, I chose to revive a custom to honor both my country's ancient Olympic traditions and the flowering beauty of Crete: a wreath made of olive leaves from the island's oldest tree in Chania was bestowed upon each of the medal winners.

I also remember the gentle burble of the streams where I would collect stones and catch crabs. I remember my sister and I in our garden trampling grapes in a vat (*patitiri* as we call it in Greek) to make the must that would ferment and become delicious wine. I remember the men climbing the walnut trees and beating the branches so that the nuts showered down for us to gather. (And I remember that a falling walnut can leave quite a lump on your head!) I remember a rainbow of plantings: tomatoes, eggplants, zucchinis, melons, and watermelons. I remember the orange and lemon trees too. And best of all, I remember the sweetest, most flavorful honey produced anywhere in the world.

A *klimataria* (an arbor) full of clusters of light and dark grapes and broad leaves extended from one side of the house, and we would gather for lunch in the cool shade of the perfect shadows it cast. In season, my father would pay my sister and me a half drachma—probably the equivalent of an American penny—for each basket of grapes we picked. I remember spreading grapes out in the sun to dry into sultana raisins. My aunt and grandmother taught us how to properly pick tomatoes and cucumbers in the garden. Eleni and I marveled at their ability to find in the abundant fields suitable wild leafy greens that they would later boil and dress with olive oil and lemon in a favorite dish called *horta vrasta*. Lemons and olive oil, salt and honey—our food was fresh, wholesome, and loved.

In the summer, we always cooked outside over an open fire. I recall the aromatic casseroles, stews, and lightly fried vegetables that my grandmother prepared not only for us but also for the people who worked our family's fields. My absolute favorite was the smell and, even better, the taste of the fried potatoes. My grandmother would use a flat knife to open the middle of each piece so that the potatoes simply bubbled over, almost as if they were filled with a thick soup. And long before the French made escargots an international delicacy, snails were a Cretan favorite, baked in the ashes of the fire and eaten with hard sea salt sprinkled over them. In Greece we have an expression that means, "Love comes through the stomach." That was true for my family then, just as it is today.

The men in our family would brew "raki," or *tsikoudia*, a powerful alcoholic beverage that was made from the leftover skins of the grapes after all the juice had been squeezed out. At night the adults would sit around the fireplace smoking, talking, laughing, and sipping raki. My grandmother insisted that if you mixed raki with a little honey and some dried figs it would cure any cough. It was also regarded as an excellent digestif.

I was told that as long as you ate potatoes and walnuts while you drank the raki you would never get drunk. I cannot testify to the truth of that prescription, however, because there was much raki yet to be consumed when Eleni and I were sent away to bed at nine o'clock each night. We never minded leaving because we were allowed first to go up to the roof, where we would try to count the stars. Because there was very little light from the village, the stars shone with extraordinary brilliance. We would quickly give up the count, of course, for there seemed to be billions of them shining down on us.

Beyond the comforts his home and family provided, my father believed that we belonged to a bigger family, the village. Each village in Crete celebrates its special saint's day with a large festive party, the *panigiri*. Relatives, friends, and acquaintances visit from other villages, lambs are cooked in the open, and raki and local wine flow freely. The music of the Cretan *lyra* is heard all over the village, and dancing—everyone from the very young to the very old joins in—goes on until the early morning hours.

Funerals, weddings, and, instead of birthdays, the celebration of our name days brought the whole village together. Years later I had the opportunity to meet Hillary Clinton, whose book *It Takes a Village: And Other Lessons Children Teach Us* was a celebration of an ethos I had lived. Later still I would be tasked with building a village of an entirely different kind, but possessed with a similar spirit—an Olympic village.

My father encouraged us to play with the children from Embaros, many of whom didn't have the same opportunities that we did in Heraklion, he explained. He also drummed into Eleni and me what was proper etiquette in the village. I can hear his voice to this day: "When you meet somebody, you greet them first, and when asked who you are, you reply, 'I am Gianna, the daughter of Frixos.'"

The daughters of Frixos were never to forget that, in Embaros, our every word and deed reflected on him and his good family name.

Chapter 2

FAMILY NAMES

ACCORDING TO GREEK MYTHOLOGY, Prometheus shaped man out of mud and Athena breathed the fire of life into his clay figure millennia ago. My personal "mythology" begins around the turn of the twentieth century with the courtship of my paternal grandparents (whom you just met in chapter 1).

Manolis Fazakis was the proverbial poor but honest man who scratched out a living from the rocky fields of Crete. His ambitions, it seems, were matched by his capacity for hard work. He chose to court the beautiful blond-haired, blue-eyed Parthenia Daskalaki—in appearance more Swedish than Greek—one of three daughters of a landowner in central Crete. My great-grandfather wasn't wealthy, but he was quite comfortable, which put him in an entirely different economic class from his would-be son-in-law. As they were in so many other places at that time, lines of class were drawn in Crete between farmers and merchants, the educated and the uneducated, city dwellers and country dwellers. So it is not entirely clear why this well-established landowner consented to his daughter's marriage to a hardworking laborer. It is likely that the two were so head-over-heels in love he feared they would defy him and elope.

Being a shrewd businessman, he decided it was preferable to marry off a daughter while he could exact a price for his blessing, and because Manolis Fazakis was poor and had little of material value, Parthenia's father demanded of her suitor a rather unusual one. Since my great-grandfather had no sons, he was distressed that his name would die out. He informed my grandfather that he would consent to the marriage only if Manolis would take the extraordinary step of adopting his wife's family name, Daskalakis, as his own.

This was truly a dramatic request. Greece has long been a male-dominated society in which a man's name is his most valuable asset. While the government has long discouraged dowries, it was customary at the time of my grandparents' courtship for a woman to leave her own family and become part of her husband's family, even transferring her wealth to her husband. In many parts of Greece today, there remains a strong custom that a woman's place is in the home. Although I would later serve in my nation's Parliament, when I was born, Greek women were still two years away from winning the right to vote.

In a bold decision, my grandfather accepted the proposition, pledging to adopt the name for himself and, more important, for his future children. His extremely radical decision may have signaled a subsequent disregard of conventionality that has run through our family ever since. The marriage agreement was not left to the vagaries of honor or chance, however. The two men traveled to the closest town with government offices and executed a contract to guarantee the pledge with the force of law.

And so, with the scrawl of a pen, my grandfather became Manolis Daskalakis-Fazakis and, very shortly thereafter, a husband. He would pass that name on to his children, including my father, who would, in turn, honor the pledge by passing it on to his daughters.

When I was eighteen years old, I decided to change my name, shortening it to Daskalaki by lopping off the Fazaki. That decision perplexed my father. I told him that, given the likelihood I would marry and eventually add my husband's name to my maiden name, Daskalaki-Fazakis seemed unnecessarily unwieldy. I wasn't sure how he would react, but he was sophisticated and, in certain matters, quite reasonable. He told me: "Okay, Gianna, I understand. It is too much." So, almost three-quarters of a century after my grandfather's name change, I too went down to the administrative office (though in another town) and changed my name.

Manolis Fazakis made one other pledge before he took Parthenia's hand in marriage. Confident that he would achieve financial success— "just you wait and see" are the words that have been passed down— he assured his father-in-law that he and his family would never be a financial burden. My great-grandfather no doubt was happy to hear this. After the wedding, he told the young couple, "Now you two are on your own."

My grandfather acquired some farmland and dedicated himself to building a life for his bride. But the land wasn't very fertile, and he soon found himself saddled with debts. The young couple's financial struggles only got worse, for they had three children in quick succession. After my father was born, my grandfather made the second most dramatic decision in his married life. He was certain that no matter how hard he worked his hardscrabble soil he wouldn't be able to provide for the many mouths he had promised to feed. His only hope was to go to America, where he could earn enough money to pay off his debt and, eventually, purchase more promising land.

He was not alone. Many Greek men of his generation faced the same choice—and sought the same opportunities on American soil. Like my grandfather, these young men left Greece with plans to return home one day. For those who stayed despite the unfamiliar places, language, and customs, America proved to be a land not of obstacles, but of opportunities. Today, the Greek-American community is a large and thriving part of American society. There are now an estimated 1.3 million Greek-Americans living in the United States.

No doubt my grandfather was drawn by the exaggerated stories of life in America, where there was lots of work and the salaries were high.

The reality was much different. Most of the Greek immigrants in America in the early 1900s were unskilled workers who wound up shouldering the hard labor that built the American industrial colossus. In 1907, for instance, approximately forty thousand Greeks were laboring on the railroads, on construction teams, or in factories.

My grandfather wound up in Indiana, where he worked long, physically demanding hours in the steel mills. Wages were good, but life was not easy. Nevertheless, America gave him what it had promised from across the Atlantic: success. He came to America in order to secure a better life for his family in Greece. And that is exactly what he did.

Once, when I was a little girl, I marveled at how smooth his skin was compared to my grandmother's wrinkled hands. He told me that his skin had been burned smooth by the searing heat of the steelworks. (In a strange twist of fate, my husband would one day inherit a steel mill in Indiana, not too far from where my grandfather once labored.) During my grandfather's American sojourn, he spent virtually nothing on himself, sending home enough money to feed his family and saving the rest for their future. He indulged only one passion: books. He would come home from work and spend the hours before exhaustion sank him into sleep reading everything he could get his hands on: history, mythology, geography, and religion. He certainly never thought of it as such, but he probably got the equivalent of a liberal arts college education at night in his tiny rented room.

Back home in Crete, his wife and three children subsisted on very little, and waited. Even as a very young boy, my father was acutely aware of their deprivation. When he ate lunch outside with his friends, for example, he knew that they all ate bread and cheese, but his mother could give him only bread. Aware of his embarrassment at his meager repast, Parthenia gave him two pieces and told him to pretend to himself that one was cheese. Instead, he boasted to his pals—with the food clenched in his fists—that he too had bread in one hand and cheese in the other. But he was humiliated when they pried open his hands, revealing only bread.

After working four years at the Indiana steel manufacturing plant, my grandfather decided that he had saved enough money to return home and rejoin his family. He paid off his debts and bought a modest home and a small parcel of land in Embaros. Eventually he made enough money from cultivating that land to afford a larger house with even more land. Today our family still owns that home and still farms the land.

Although my grandparents managed to make a living from their farm, life in Embaros didn't solve all their problems. There was a one-room schoolhouse in the village and a teacher who offered a curriculum that covered little more than the basics of reading and writing. Manolis and Parthenia did not regard this as adequate schooling for their children—certainly not with his passion for learning that my grandfather had nurtured in America. Our family has shared this passion for education ever since, by the way. Years later, while serving in Parliament, I would lead an effort to overhaul Athens's schools.

When Achilles, Ioanna, and Frixos were old enough, they were sent away to school in Heraklion. The three youngsters shared a single rented room, for their parents had little money to spare. Every few months my grandmother would load up a donkey and three mules with provisions— dried meat, potatoes, lentils, oil, vinegar, even firewood—for her children and make the long, slow trek to Heraklion. She probably traveled as fast walking as my mother did driving years later!

My Uncle Achilles inherited his father's love of books and became a top scholar. He went on to become an eminent professor of literature before, sadly, dying young. My Aunt Ioanna returned home rather than attend university. In doing so, however, she may have sealed her fate. Attractive, with the fair looks of her mother, sophisticated, and dynamic, she was not able to find an appropriate match in the small village.

My aunt never complained about her life, though. She was devoted to her family and the other families that lived in Embaros. When she got older, she took annual trips to the thermal baths in Edipsos, whose healing powers are legendary. Hercules supposedly bathed in those waters to restore his strength before undertaking each of his labors. My aunt lived a long and healthy life, maybe because of the waters of Edipsos.

My father's education fell somewhere between that of his older siblings. While he started out studying economics at the university in Athens, money was tight, and he interrupted his studies to return to Crete, where he took a job in Heraklion with the Union of Producers of Crete, an agricultural-marketing cooperative. He always intended to finish his studies and attain his degree after he saved up some money, but World War II disrupted his plans.

In October 1940, my father enlisted in the army and was sent to northern Greece and Albania to join the forces repelling Mussolini's advancing soldiers. When Italy was repelled, Hitler's Germany invaded Greece in April 1941. When mainland Greece fell, my father returned to Crete with the retreating troops to help with the defense of his home island.

On May 20, 1941, the Cretan sky was darkened with the thousands of German paratroopers who landed on the island and engaged the defending army in ten days of fighting. Out-trained and out-gunned, the Allied troops fought bravely, but German forces proved too strong. Many Allied soldiers hid throughout Crete after the battle, and many succeeded in escaping to rejoin the fight in other parts of Europe. That was my father's plan as well. He hid in a cave but was found by German troops. Along with the seventeen thousand Allied soldiers who were taken prisoner, on June 2, 1941, my father became a prisoner of war as well.

For my father, the fighting was over, though the war was only beginning.

He was held briefly on the island before being transferred to one of the many POW camps in Breslau, Germany, which is now Wroclaw, Poland.

Because he was educated, my father commanded the respect of the other Greeks being held in the German POW camp, and he became a leader among the prisoners. He organized some plantings—the land was not exactly the fertile soil of Crete, but white cabbage did okay— and tried to ensure that all prisoners got their fair share of rations. As Manolis Daskalakis-Fazakis had done throughout four lonely years of separation from his family, my father, during his long imprisonment, read every book he could get his hands on—many of them several times. He also tried to learn as much German, French, and English as possible, convinced that language skills would give him an advantage in business if he finally returned home.

My father wrote many letters from Germany but none reached Embaros. Nor was there any word about him from the Red Cross or other organizations. His family never heard a word about his fate, never knew that he had been taken prisoner.

Everybody in the village assumed Frixos was dead, everybody except my grandmother and aunt, that is. They defied convention by refusing to don traditional black mourning garb. People in the village thought they had lost their minds or that their minds were addled by grief. One Easter my aunt made herself a shawl decorated with red roses. When she wore it to church, she could hear the whispers: "The poor girl, she just cannot believe her brother is already dead." But the two women refused to surrender hope, and their steadfast faith was ultimately rewarded.

Allied forces liberated the POW camp on May 2, 1945, almost four full years after my father's capture, and it took him four months to make the long trek home to Crete. My father had endured an even harsher version of the life his father had experienced in America some three decades earlier and, in similar fashion, had seized opportunity amid extraordinary hardship. And like his father had done, Frixos Daskalakis-Fazakis would return to Crete and attain the success he had dreamed of as a younger man.

Chapter 3

"I DON'T NEED A SON.
I HAVE GIANNA!"

AFTER THE WAR, my father returned to Heraklion and reassumed a position with the Union of Producers of Crete. A private, nonprofit agrarian cooperative, the union helped its members market citrus fruits to buyers and consumers around the world. Most of the members were, like my grandfather, operators of small family farms who pooled their produce for better prices and better distribution. In my father's time, agriculture was one of the leading industries in Crete and in other parts of Greece.

My father held what would be regarded, at best, as a mid-level position with the union. He assisted in promoting sales of Greek goods abroad, mainly to Germany and other northern countries. He helped develop manufacturing facilities for preserving fruit. But he was bright, ambitious, and, having lost six years to the war, a man very much in a hurry. Intent as he was to advance his career, he was just as anxious to complete his university degree.

Shortly after resuming work, he sought permission to spend some time in Athens preparing for his final exams. The director of the cooperative considered university to be the province of the elite and regarded a degree as irrelevant to their business of buying and selling. As a result, he discouraged my father from concerning himself with academic matters. "What do you need with this university and this degree?" he repeatedly asked. But my father persisted and eventually received permission. He became a regular on the one-day boat ride from Crete to Athens and earned his reward: a coveted business degree from what was then called the Commercial University of Athens (now the Economic University of Athens).

He would rise to become head of the national board of collectives.

My father forged strong and lasting relationships with farmers, traders, and merchants all over Greece. This talent was one of his most important professional skills. He learned that keeping in touch with people was essential in running a successful business, just as it would be essential for me decades later when I launched my political career.

Although by every measure he was successful and we lived quite a comfortable life in Heraklion, my father never became wealthy like many men in comparable positions. When he retired, he didn't have much more than his pension to live on. He wound up building apartments on top of our home to rent and thus provide extra money for his and my mother's retirement years.

Marika Papadaki, my mother, was born to a prosperous Heraklion family. When her father, Yiannis Papadakis, was a boy, he worked for various merchants in town, impressing them with his intelligence, business savvy, and initiative. As a young man, he was able to capitalize on his experience and connections to secure bank loans that enabled him to start a business, and he became very successful exporting olive oil, raisins, and other Cretan products, primarily to Egypt. He became prominent in Heraklion social circles and was well known around the island. I recall a picture of my grandparents sitting with friends around a table full of roses playing a card game. My grandfather was quite handsome, with "brilliantine" on his hair and moustache. He wore what looked like a very expensive suit. My grandmother, Rodanthe, was also decked out in finery. Both were a vivid contrast to the modest country style of my paternal grandparents.

In 1936, my grandfather decided to venture just outside Heraklion to inspect some fields and to visit some of the farmers he worked with. He chose to walk the long distance back and worked up a considerable sweat. When he arrived home, he took a long drink from the well before thoroughly dousing himself with the cold water. Eight days later he succumbed to pneumonia. My grandmother was left a thirty-nine-year-old widow with three children to care for.

My mother was just four years old at the time. Her life changed dramatically. She remembers the interior of her once bright home turning black. Black cloth was draped over their elegant furniture, which is the traditional way Greeks mourn. Black cloth covered the full-length mirrors. Her mother, who enjoyed wearing stylish clothes, was herself dressed in black and wore no lipstick, face powder, or any other cosmetics. She dressed my mother in black as well and even tied a bow of black ribbon on her head. My grandmother wore black mourning clothes for decades, in fact, and as a widow, she never regained the stature she had enjoyed in her married life.

My mother was a good student and, having learned English in school, secured a job as the only administrative secretary at the only English-language institute in Heraklion. At about the same time, my father was looking to improve his skills in English, hoping to expand the markets for the cooperative's products. When he walked into the language school, he was instantly smitten by the attractive and charming young woman who greeted him. Apparently he was not alone. Years later he would tell his daughters that he always had to get in line at our mother's desk to see her. Literally! It seems that the male students always had some problem, a bill or paperwork that required urgent help—and only her help would do!

The courtship of my father and mother could not exactly be described as a whirlwind. Perhaps my mother was reluctant to commit to a man so much older than she was. But persistence was one of my father's strengths, and he earnestly pursued Marika for more than four years before she agreed to marry him. During that time, she came to recognize his many virtues. My father was not just older but also better educated and more worldly and sophisticated than the typical Cretan man. He traveled often, particularly to Germany, and regaled her with tales that seemed quite exotic. My mother envisioned a new life that would expand her horizons. She imagined herself accompanying him on business trips, where she would join him for dinners or at elegant parties. In January 1955, when he was in his midforties and she was half his age, they were wed.

That world of dinners, parties, and dances would remain in her imagination, however. Nevertheless, she did travel with my father a few times. She told me about one trip, for instance, to a trade show in Leipzig, Germany. My mother was freezing while she stood by my father at his cooperative's trade booth. After a few hours, she pointed out to her husband that the visitors to the booth were not interested in talking business. They were just interested in grabbing a handful of Greek pistachios.

After just a few months of marriage, she discovered she was pregnant—with me. She wasn't at all happy about it. She didn't tell my father or even consult a doctor. She had her own idea about how to handle this disturbing development. "Every day," she confessed to me years later, "I would jump rope about two hundred times, hoping maybe you were not strong enough and would just go away. I still feel guilty about that." But I was very strong (as I would prove—to her continued dismay—throughout my childhood). A month later she began to experience dizziness and nausea and the secret was out. The jump rope went into the closet. My official date of birth is Monday, December 12, 1955, at 23:55—or so my father insisted, because in Greece, Tuesday the thirteenth is considered bad luck. My sister followed in September 1958. My mother's destiny—at least until much later in life—was to lead the more traditional life of the Cretan wife and mother.

By Cretan standards, my family was very fortunate. My father's career was flourishing and we lived comfortably, if never ostentatiously. Inheriting my father's intellectual curiosity benefited me far more than did his business success. As a result of his travels, his extensive reading, and his keen intelligence, he was more open-minded than the typical Greek father of his day, and certainly of his generation—at least regarding certain matters. He encouraged Eleni and me to pursue higher education and to strive to realize our career ambitions, believing that we were every bit as entitled to pursue our dreams as any man's son. When, in classic Greek fashion, friends or colleagues lamented his lack of a son whose achievements might help support him in his old age, he abruptly dismissed their concerns. "I don't need a son," he would say. "I have Gianna!"

We went for family holidays to the beach, but there was nothing he loved more than taking us on trips to historic places. Obsessed with language, he would hold forth on history, mythology, and culture, and I hung on every mind-expanding word. Eleni was not as enchanted by the performances. She would complain, somewhat justifiably, that she not only had to hear the lectures from him at Olympia, the site of the ancient Olympics (and a place of great importance to me some years later), or Delphi, the site of the Temple of Apollo, but also again, after we returned home, when I repeated the lessons almost word for word.

Tales of the prophecies of the Delphic Oracle particularly enchanted me. It was said that when men asked her if they were destined to die in war, she would reply with such verbal dexterity that her prophecy, depending on the listener's interpretation, would always be right. I recall posing on a rock at Delphi, pretending to be the oracle—the priestess Pythia—and terrifying little Eleni with my fertile and less than gracious imagination: "You will be captured by the enemy and you will be tortured until . . . " (You see, I preferred a prophecy with only *one* possible interpretation.)

The enemy most likely to torture Eleni, at least through her early years, was naturally her older sister. We had opposite temperaments. I was outgoing, rambunctious, and quite willing to challenge and provoke authority (especially the authority of my mother). Eleni was shy and cautious. It made her very nervous when we flirted with trouble, almost always trouble of my making.

I once sneaked out of the house to get some cotton candy at a local festival, leaving my sister home alone. I promised Eleni I would return in a matter of minutes, but I had failed to anticipate the long line. The wait was getting so long that I panicked. I ran to the front of the line and said: "Sorry, there is an emergency with my grandmother and I have to leave. Can I please have one?" But the "emergency" occurred a little too late. I had taken only a few bites when my mother showed up and angrily disposed of my sweet treat.

I was never really chastened, however, and have, throughout my life, remained quick to challenge the established ways and the conventional wisdom. I have always been particularly contemptuous of silly rules that made no sense to me.

I'm not sure I can explain how, as a little girl, I developed such an outsized personality. But at a very early age I had a rather strong sense of self and an inflated notion of purpose. When I was just six years old,

I required a tonsillectomy. My father decided to entrust my care to a surgeon in Athens whom he knew from the army. That meant my first airplane flight. Just before walking out to the plane, I bent down rather dramatically and scooped up a handful of the earth. I wrapped it in a handkerchief that my mother always made sure I carried and tucked it away in my small handbag.

When my father puzzled over what I was doing, I told him, "I want to take some of the land with me because I am leaving." I had learned this symbolic gesture from "The Soil of Greece," a famous poem written by Georgios Drosinis, in which he wrote:

> Now that I am leaving and shall go to foreign lands,
> And we shall live apart for months and years,
> Let me take something from you too, my blue beloved homeland.

Everyone started to laugh because the narrator in the poem is departing on a long voyage and leaving everything—his country, his family—behind. He doesn't know if he will ever return to his homeland. Even though my tonsils wouldn't, I would be returning to Crete very soon.

While my sentimental gesture may have been over-the-top, theatrically speaking, it nevertheless reflected a genuine emotional undercurrent that has always remained at the core of my life. My father had hoped that I would be inspired to pursue a career as an archaeologist. But even as a youngster, I knew digging for ancient Greece wasn't my thing. I told my father I was far too impatient for archaeology. Always in a hurry, I would probably wind up dropping and breaking some of the country's most valuable treasures.

But the lure of history was not lost on me. I didn't just read books; I consumed them. I read history and realized how individuals could change the world. I began reading newspapers and following the shifting alliances among Turkey, Greece, the United Kingdom, the United States, and other nations. One word in particular caught my fancy: ambassador. Ambassadors were the critical players in deciding the fate of nations. They carried secret documents, negotiated treaties that altered the course of history. I decided that that's what I wanted to be. An ambassador.

Everyone with whom I shared this dream laughed at me. "Are you out of your mind?" the Greek chorus said. "This doesn't happen unless you belong to a wealthy family that already had somebody—a father, a grandfather, or, at the very least, an uncle—who was an ambassador. And in all your careful studies," the same chorus teased, "did you ever notice any women ambassadors carrying those documents or signing those treaties?"

History, in fact, supported their view. Greece didn't appoint its first female ambassador until 1986.

I felt that, like my father, I was first and foremost a patriot whose greatest joy would come from my service to the Greek people. I dreamed of achieving something monumental, something historic, for my country. And that remained my dream until it became a dream fulfilled. My father lived until 1991. He saw me elected to the Athens city council and then to the Greek Parliament. He was there when I married into one of our nation's most distinguished families.

I regret that he didn't live to witness the ceremony in 1998 when, after I led the successful campaign to bring the Olympics home to their birthplace, Greece honored me with the title of Ambassador.

Chapter 4

GROWING PAINS

AS I'VE SHOWN IN EARLIER CHAPTERS, my father had a modern outlook and was broadminded about certain societal trends. He supported his daughters' academics and career ambitions even when feminism was just in its infancy in countries far more progressive than Greece. My mother, on the other hand, was wedded to more traditional ways. Although those two perspectives may seem decidedly at odds, my sister and I perceived the divide this way: Embaros was all about play, while our home in Heraklion was all about work, duties, and responsibility.

My father, with his commanding personality, ruled the roost. But his long hours at work and frequent travel meant that far more often my mother was left in charge. She was, by nature, sweet and was totally devoted to her daughters. Yet she was unshakable when it came to the conviction that Eleni and I must be equipped to perform the traditional roles of Greek women. She made sure that we spent long, boring hours during our school holidays mastering the essential household duties: how to clean, how to sew, and how to cook. While other kids in our neighborhood were out playing, we'd be stuck in our master sewing classes. Fortunately, these tedious exercises were often held on the veranda, where we could look up from our needles and thread into our glorious garden. Lush with flowers—tuberoses, gardenias, roses, jasmine—and filled with herbs—always lots and lots of basil—our garden perfumed the air with fragrances so seductive that it surely compared favorably with the Garden of Eden.

I didn't do a very good job of masking my displeasure when my mother assumed the role of drill sergeant, though. I would vehemently deplore what I was certain was a waste of my precious time. "Someday I will have servants in my household and I will do none of this," I would say. She wouldn't even bother to challenge my fundamental assumption. Instead, she'd simply say, "Even if you have servants, you have to know how to control the household and how to check that they are doing their jobs well."

Indeed, some of the lessons my mother taught me proved to be very useful to me in the future.

In recent years, when visiting my children, I have taken great pleasure in surprising them by preparing home-cooked meals. "Surprise" may be a bit of an understatement. They were actually shocked, having no idea that I even knew how to cook. Despite these rare moments, when I have reflected my mother's notions of maternal duty, I was always my father's child, having spent almost my entire life on a path that, at least traditionally, was viewed as more the son's than the daughter's.

As I mentioned, growing up I clashed far more often with my mother than with my father. Unlike many Greek fathers of that era, he never raised a hand to us. Then again, he never had to. He would bristle with anger when either I or Eleni violated what he viewed as the essential standards of a civilized society, like respect for one's elders or modest dress. A glower from him was far more frightening than a scolding or a spanking could ever be. He had gorgeous gray-green eyes, but when he was angry, they turned into a wintry rough sea and delivered an unambiguous message.

Though my parents had enough money to send us to a private school for our grade school education, my father insisted that his daughters attend public school. His reasoning was virtually the same as when he encouraged us to play with the children in the village of Embaros. He didn't want us to slip comfortably into some elitist, upper-crust stratum of society; he preferred for us to mingle with a broad cross-section of real Cretans. He needn't have been that concerned. After all, we grew up between two classes. We learned how to be women both from my aunt, who worked on the farm in Embaros in her simple cotton dress and headscarf, and from my mother, who wore lipstick and small hats that were the rage in Europe. Though she is now in her eighties, my mother, once the city girl whose sister-in-law had to tell her to don plastic gloves when she cleaned the walnuts lest her hands turn black, tries to get back to Embaros once a month to ensure that everything is in order. I likewise try to return to Embaros every time I have a chance—along with my children—to get in touch with my roots. The ability to move between the world of the farm and the world of the city and to communicate with people across class and economic lines has proved to be an invaluable asset to me throughout my life.

Students in Greece attend elementary school through the sixth grade and then high school through twelfth grade before going to university.

After completing elementary school, I attended the First Heraklion District All Girls High School. There were about sixty girls in each class and the teachers treated us like numbers. We attended school from Monday through Saturday, enjoying no weekends at the time. We were required to pull our hair back and wear unattractive uniforms. I particularly hated the socks. Worst of all, the school was surrounded by high bars. The bars didn't stop the hundreds of young military reservists from ogling us, however, while they paraded past our school every week. Half of the love stories in Heraklion began on those fateful Friday afternoons.

And I did enjoy my courses. My favorite subject—no surprise—was history. My least favorite was math, though many years later, with my husband as mentor, I would prove more adept at it than I had ever demonstrated in school.

But if I had a singular talent during my early school years, it was for questioning things I did not understand. Questions such as why we used textbooks that had nothing to do with the lives we led on Crete. The books we studied had all been copied from French or English and were filled with pictures of things—snow, factories, trains—that couldn't be found on our island. My constant lament was, "Where on earth have I been born?" For me, cold and snow became a symbol of real civilization. Yet they seemed so distant from my life that they might as well have existed in another solar system.

Although I disliked our textbooks, I loved books more than almost anything else. Yes, like all little girls, I played with toys and dolls. I particularly liked the dolls my father brought home from Germany. But, just like my father, I devoured books of all kinds. Our house was filled with books, not only in Greek but also in English, French, and German. Remarque, Dostoyevsky, Mark Twain, and Victor Hugo. When I went to kiss my father good night, he was most often already in bed with a book in hand. I remember trying to imagine all the books he had read over the course of his life—as a schoolboy, as a prisoner of war, at college and, later, for work—and asking him, "Dad, are you never bored reading them?" "No," he told me. "Knowledge is very good for the spirit."

Despite our shared love of books, we would eventually bump heads over some of my choices in reading material. In school, I became friends with a girl whose father owned a bookshop. He was also a member of the Communist Party, and he gave me access to a whole range of books—from Marx to Jung—that would not normally have crossed the threshold of our home. My father disapproved, but I wanted to read books of every stripe so that I could voice an opinion on everything. And like so many young people of my generation, I saw knowledge as far more than just spiritual nourishment; I embraced it as an instrument for change in the world. When it came to my education, I refused to be constrained by convention, tradition, or middle-class values. For the first time in my life, I was openly challenging my father and his view of the world.

I would wind up defying him over more than books. As a young girl, I enjoyed the delicious foods my family lovingly served, perhaps a bit too much. I was a bit chunky, which caused my parents some concern. They didn't send me to ballet lessons like other girls in Heraklion, apparently anxious to spare me embarrassment. When I became a teenager, I slimmed down and morphed into an attractive young woman, and I was not the least bit concerned with sparing my parents any discomfort. The teenage years were marked by some titanic battles with my father and mother, battles that are likely familiar to teens and parents everywhere. We fought over clothes, makeup, music, magazines, indeed over all the critical trappings of the youth revolution that was sweeping the world (or at least the civilized world) and that I was desperate to join.

I took fashion tips from the Greek magazines. I hid a transistor radio in my bedroom and listened to the Beatles and the Rolling Stones played on the radio station at the local US Army base. I kept up with the popular hits of the day. I still remember the song "Parole, parole" by the French torch singer Dalida. My father refused to buy a television until I graduated from high school, so I had to go to the neighbors' to watch *Hawaii Five-O*, my favorite American program. And it was not even in color!

If the rest of the world was living in the age of mod dress and marijuana, little of the counterculture was evident in Heraklion. About all the city could boast by way of popular culture were a few movie theaters, where films were shown long after everyone else around the globe had seen them. I was thrilled to see *Love Story* and *Doctor Zhivago* and *Fiddler on the Roof*, and to imagine what life and love were like in the hip world of LA where movies were filmed—so distant from Crete. Just as it had been for my grandfather, America became my paradise, a dreamland of hope, opportunity, and success.

With legs that were finally worth showing off, I began wearing miniskirts—very mini—to noticeable effect. I was making men dizzy. Unfortunately, those dizzy men included our neighbors at the local coffee shop, where my father happened to be sitting one day when I strolled by. He stormed into the house in a rage, telling my mother, "I almost had a stroke looking at our daughter with her legs out and all the men staring at her with their greedy eyes." So my mother had a girl who helped out at home lower the hem of my skirt until it was below my knees. We warred over that hemline. Despite my reluctance during mom's sewing sessions, I had learned enough. When I was preparing to go out, I would slip into the bathroom and, with needle and thread and a little glue, turn my mother's maxi back into my mini.

All my parents' efforts weren't going to halt or hide what was, after all, a natural progression for any young woman.

My mother was as concerned about my soul as she was about my appearance. She was committed to her faith in the Greek Orthodox

Church. My father never really spoke to us about religion. Though he was always respectful of my mother's deep faith and her attachment to the church, he seldom attended Sunday services with us, always maintaining that he needed to catch up on his work. "Go with the children," he would usually say to my mother.

My sentiments about religion lie more with my father's. When I was not much more than six years old—during the excruciating boredom of the daily siesta my mother inflicted upon us—I remember getting all riled up on the subject of religion. I didn't like how my mother used God as her enforcer, warning us that God would punish us if we misbehaved. That made no sense to me, so I decided then and there to test God's punitive powers. I began to challenge the icon, the Virgin Mary with the baby Christ, on my bedroom wall. Nothing happened—no punishment manifested itself, not even a bolt of lightning descending from the heavens. My sister started crying, though, and I told her: "Shut up. If Mom comes, I will not let you play with me tomorrow."

Her crying stirred me up even more. So while she wept silently, I took my experiment with the deity a nasty step further. I began to direct certain hand gestures—ones I had seen irate drivers utilize to considerable effect—at the icon. Aware of the threat that "God will cut off your hand," I hedged my bet by using my left hand. But when nothing bad happened, I went at the icon with both hands. I remember saying to myself, "So that's the way it is: Whatever they tell you is most likely untrue." At a very tender age, I had decided that I would never fear the unknown nor substitute faith for proof.

My mother was very active in our church and involved in a lot of charity work. When I began butting heads with my parents, she decided it would be helpful if I talked to a priest. And she knew just the one, a younger priest with whom, she believed, I would identify because of his work with the poor. Unlike priests in the Roman Catholic tradition, priests in the Greek Orthodox Church are allowed to marry, although Bishops in the church cannot.

When I went to meet the priest, he wasn't interested in discussing my problems with my parents or even his good works with the poor. Instead, he began to lament his marital difficulties and how he could no longer approach his wife. He suggested that, as I was a very smart young woman, it would be good if we could develop a closer relationship. But because I was a very smart young woman, I knew exactly what he had in mind. I literally fled the church—running all the way home to my mother. When I told her what had happened, she was furious at my blasphemy. "I'm sure you misunderstood," she said. But I was sure that I hadn't, and I refused to attend that church ever again. So did Eleni, one of the first times I can recall that we forged an alliance rather than fought. In later years, my opinion of the clergy would change somewhat, as two of my most trusted associates turned out to be sons of Greek Orthodox priests.

Despite all the teen drama, I continued to do very well academically. Even though I was unwilling to become what we then called "a grind," I was always in the top of my class. But I was also eager for the fun to begin in my life. I wanted to model myself after my cousin Lena, who was seven years older than me and had gone off to study law in Athens. Lena was smart, but she was also beautiful and stylish, always wearing the latest fashion in clothes and makeup. She even knew the words to all the Beatles songs. Boys were streaming by her house to take her to parties or dance clubs. I understood her popularity, but what was truly amazing to me was her parents' permissiveness. They never seemed to say no to her.

My parents always said no. They didn't approve mixing young women and young men in social environments. I tried every argument I could think of to convince them that these parties were harmless. I chided them for listening to silly gossip from people who had nothing better to do and who knew nothing about us. In desperation, I resorted to classical quotes to buttress my case: "Pay attention to the right people when they say something about you." But my father could always trump me when it came to a battle of wit and knowledge. Without hesitation, he responded: "Caesar's wife must be above suspicion."

The fights continued to escalate, and my challenges to parental authority, particularly my mother's, became more brazen and outrageous. On one occasion, when I was sixteen, the family took a vacation in Athens. We were supposed to go shopping the first morning, and my parents and sister were already waiting when I emerged from my room looking like an extra out of the musical *Hair*. My hair was huge, teased way out, and I was wearing a maxiskirt with a slit that ran a long way up my leg. Worst of all, at least in my parents' eyes, I wasn't wearing shoes, intent on frolicking barefoot through the streets of Athens. Visibly stunned and completely at a loss for words, my mother stepped up to me and slapped my face. I didn't cry and I didn't make any smart remarks. Indeed, I didn't say anything at all. I knew I had crossed a line. But I sure do remember exactly what I was thinking: "Very soon I will be out on my own and then there will be no way for anybody to control me."

Chapter 5

ESCAPE FROM CRETE

MY LONG-ANTICIPATED ESCAPE FROM CRETE, my first major step on the path to independence, would be university studies.

In the early 1970s, the government ran all of the universities in Greece. A university degree was a near necessity for anyone who wanted to work in the civil service or pursue a professional career. The college application process differed from the process in the United States. In the Greek system, students had to choose a course of study and to list colleges in their order of preference before taking an exam that would determine where, and if, they would attend.

First I had to choose a course of study. Unfortunately no degree programs were directed toward my becoming an ambassador. And while I loved history, I wasn't interested in a staid academic career. I considered myself more of an activist, less interested in explaining past events than in solving future problems. I decided to study law, convinced that it offered the most career options.

The other critical decision was where to study law. All students take national exams, after which they are assigned a spot at a university—hopefully one of their top choices. I was an excellent candidate and was confident I would fare well in the competition for placement. So I limited myself to two choices: the University of Athens and Aristotle University in Thessaloniki in northern Greece, the country's second largest city.

The announcement of university placements was such a big deal in Crete that it was broadcast on local radio. Everybody could hear how you fared at exactly the same moment you learned your fate. I was playing tennis the afternoon the placements were announced. (Even today, I can't explain why I went to such lengths to appear indifferent when I was anything but. Perhaps I wanted to see myself as above it all. Or maybe I was simply too nervous to endure the long wait at home, to hear my name in the company of my mother.) Though I wasn't much of a player or even, truthfully, much of an enthusiast, the tennis club provided me with a good excuse to get out of the house. And it was one place I was allowed to go where I could meet my peers, particularly young men. (Remember, that wasn't easy for me while attending an all-girls school.) My tennis game ran late and I missed the radio announcements.

When I got home, there were no lights on in the house—something unusual—and I found my mother sitting in the dark, crying. I felt a stab of panic. Was it possible that I hadn't been accepted at either university? Somehow through her sobs, my mother managed to blurt out the distressing news. I had not been accepted to the university in Athens. I would be going to school in Thessaloniki, which, she gasped, was twice the distance—*two plane rides*—from Crete. Though Athens had been my top choice, the advantages of being in Thessaloniki were suddenly apparent. At "two plane rides" away, the city and campus would not be convenient for spur-of-the-moment parental visits. I would really be out on my own. I comforted my mother, feigning distress over the distance that would soon separate us. But it was all I could do to keep from leaping up, pumping my fists, and shouting joyously: "Yaaaaayyyy! Thessaloniki, here I come!"

The summer before I left for university seemed one of infinite possibilities—for me as well as for the entire country. I had been chafing under the tight supervision of my parents and frustrated by life on Crete. I felt that the options there for a young person of wide-ranging interests and serious ambitions were severely limited. I was ready, indeed eager, to expand my horizons. I wanted to abide by my own rules and to make my own decisions, and I was prepared to live with the consequences.

At the same time, Greece was making a great escape. In 1967, military leaders had seized power in a coup, ostensibly to prevent a Communist takeover of the government—"a revolution to save the nation" was what the junta called it. The Prime Minister and other political leaders were arrested. Democracy was suspended, as were critical constitutional rights. Dissenters could be arrested without a warrant and tried before military tribunals rather than in civilian courts. Martial music replaced Western music on the radio.

In 1974, after nearly seven years of "The Regime of the Colonels," the military dictatorship was tottering, weakened by internal discord and by nationwide protests (led by a student uprising at the Athens Polytechnic).

I confess that as a teenage girl preoccupied with her own parental oppression, government oppression hadn't seemed particularly acute or the most pressing matter on our island or on my mind. Nor was politics a subject my father discoursed on at home, unless it was the politics of

ancient times. But my reverence for Greek's illustrious traditions, rein-
forced by all my reading, aligned me with classic democratic values. So
the summer of 1974, when the military government fell and democracy
was restored in Greece, I celebrated in the streets with true enthusiasm.
As I left Crete for university, there was a palpable sense of excitement
and change in the air. The American press celebrated the fall of the junta
with headlines that read on July 25, "Greece: The Old Fire Rekindled,"
and on July 28, "A Breath of Freedom Sweeps Through Greece."

In November, parliamentary elections were held, the first free elections in a decade, and Constantinos Karamanlis, who had served as
Prime Minister in the late '50s and early '60s before going into exile,
was swept back into office with a huge majority of voters supporting his
new conservative party, New Democracy. Democracy had been restored
in its birthplace. And a month later, in an extraordinary national plebi-
scite, Greeks voted against restoring the monarchy.

To be honest, given my reverence for Greek history, I wasn't
entirely sure of my feelings about the monarchy. But I did believe the
country needed wholesale change more than reflexive obeisance to past
traditions. For the people of Greece, not its military, to cast off what
the monarchy represented was, at the very least, a monumental, historic
change. I didn't hesitate to join the raucous celebration in the streets of
Thessaloniki.

To me, the city of Thessaloniki was charming and very congenial—
quite likely a better choice for me than Athens would have been. In
Athens, the university is sprawled all over the city and has no real campus center. When Eleni studied law in Athens, she said she sometimes
felt more like a worker than a student because she spent so much time
commuting to various parts of the campus. The university in Thessaloniki is smaller—seamless and quite intimate—and when I arrived,
it was abuzz with student activity, making it easy for me to plunge into

campus life. Moreover, in contrast to Athens, which seemed ancient and pointed back toward history, Thessaloniki seemed modern and decidedly pointed toward the future. There was lots of contemporary music, art, theater, and film. The city even boasted its own movie festival. Perhaps the surest sign to me that I had scaled new heights of modern civilization was that there were seasons, and at last I got to experience the cold and snow that had once seemed so otherworldly.

Still and all, it would be hard for me to characterize my first year at university as a total success—except for my genuine belief that you often learn a great deal from your mistakes. Employing that standard, I learned a whole lot that year. I was totally engaged in campus intellectual life, but mainly those parts that occurred outside the classroom. I met all kinds of people, from working class to wealthy, and read all kinds of books. I was a regular among large groups of students that would pile into small apartments late at night for intense discussions of politics, education, psychology, and sociology. We broached radical ideas and concocted new ways to address old problems. Like many university students of that era around the globe, we wanted to change the world. In the meantime, we would show up to protest any and every righteous cause. I even marched with the leftists, and I firmly believe even now that if you're eighteen, nineteen, or twenty and you're not a leftist, it's unhealthy. I was almost too busy to attend classes; there was always a rally or protest underway.

My mother had arranged for me to share an apartment with two other girls from Crete. Both were attractive: Thalia was dark, with an exotic tropical look, and Stella was fair and blond. Friends liked to joke that we were the "Three Graces," and amid our scruffy, working-class neighborhood, that was certainly true. We got the feeling that everyone there was watching us all the time—more than one using binoculars.

They didn't watch us *all* the time, of course. They must not have seen those times when I came home in the wee hours of the morning. Which would explain the surprisingly warm greeting I got on one of those occasions. I was returning home so late—or so early, depending on your perspective—that the neighborhood café was already open. I decided to stop for milk and fresh bread before heading home to bed. People were already inside drinking coffee, and when I greeted the owner, everybody there seemed to recognize me as one of the three new girls on the block. The owner made a big fuss over me and showered me with praise—praise that was totally undeserved. "Those other students sleep in all day," complained the owner. "Thank God I see here at least one student who is up early and serious about going to classes." (The owner apparently equated my having lipstick on with being ready for class.)

By the time I had departed for university, my parents were living primarily on a pension; my sharing an apartment was a good way for me to save on expenses. Unfortunately, freedom proved a bit heady at first, and I quickly picked up some bad and expensive habits: French cigarettes, fashion magazines, and, worst of all, some of the fashions I saw in those magazines. I can remember the horrified expressions on my parents' faces when I stepped off the plane on my first trip home, for Christmas. I was wearing a slit maxidress, boots with platform heels, and a hat. My makeup was extensive and my nails were long—I hadn't trimmed them since I left home—and painted bright red. It was another "stroke" for my father and another quarrel at home with my mother. "What will our neighbors think?" she said. "Do I care about their opinion?" I retorted. Though I was now a university student and, to my mind, a full-fledged grown-up, my father had not become any more permissive. When I was invited to a highly respectable party in honor of a member of Parliament, my father insisted that I be home by midnight, practically afternoon by Greek social standards. And when I missed getting home by that deadline, I was met by the all-too-familiar wintry-rough-sea eyes.

School proved stormy too that first year. I quickly ran out of spending money, as did my roommates. So we began assigning one person the responsibility of saving money each week so that we could put food on the table. We ate collectively, often with an extended group of friends. Sometimes there would be a dozen people eating out of the same pot. When it was my turn to cook, I remember thinking that I should have paid more attention when my mother was giving lessons. One time I made a giant pot of spaghetti and accidentally dumped it into the kitchen sink. Fortunately, I had cleaned the sink that day. Even more fortunate, nobody was around to witness me shoving the pasta back in the pot. Mercifully, my mother sent relief packages by ferry each month. Actually "packages" doesn't do justice to the scale of her relief efforts; they were giant cartons filled to the brim with meatballs, dolmas, cheeses, and other staples of Greek cuisine.

If only my mother could have rescued us as easily from our academic problems. At year's end, I was prepared to discuss Wilhelm Reich and to defend the various political positions of student demonstrators, but I wasn't remotely ready for the finals in my law courses. The most revealing and embarrassing episode involved my commercial-law class. Before the exam, I spied a very attractive, well-dressed man, no more than forty years old, watching from the side of the packed auditorium. I uttered an appreciative "wow" to one of my friends and asked if she knew "the hot guy." "That's our professor, Lampros Kotsiris," she informed me. The class was held from eight to ten in the morning so I had never attended. Years later, when I had become well known in Greece, that professor—still very handsome—paid me a courtesy call. I confessed my classroom sins and we had a good laugh together.

That first year I wound up failing half my exams and had to spend the entire summer studying to retake them so that I could proceed with my degree studies. I would become a far more diligent student and, also important, far more astute at navigating academics at the university. When I faced classroom difficulties, I would go see the professors outside of class to ask, perhaps even to beg, for a second chance or for some extra work to boost my grades. I was intelligent, earnest, and eager. I was also aware that my charms worked well on male professors (and some female professors as well). Some might consider the use of one's charms to be less than charming behavior. But in actuality it was a real-life lesson in working the system, a lesson that proved invaluable later when I had to navigate far more treacherous political terrain.

After my first year, I decided I would fare better living alone. My roommates were lovely people, but they each had a boyfriend, and the logistics became too complicated in the apartment we shared. As soon as Thalia and Stella graduated, they returned to Crete and married those same sweethearts—to lead a life that, at least in my view, wasn't all that dissimilar to their parents'. Today, they are living happily in Heraklion. But I had grander dreams. I wanted to open my wings and fly.

I lived alone for the final three years of university. I won't pretend that, after my initial stumbling, I became a model student. But I did learn from my mistakes. I had been so eager for my first taste of real freedom, so busy trying to demonstrate what an independent spirit I was, that I had neglected to take responsibility for my life. I came to understand that flying requires pulling your wings in as much as it does spreading them out. There was probably no surer sign of my growing maturity than my decision in my last semester to invite my mother to move in with me while I prepared for final exams.

After my sister went off to the university in Athens, life had become somewhat trying for my mother. She was quite depressed to find herself an empty nester. So she was thrilled to discover that there were a whole lot of young people in Thessaloniki who needed her care in the worst way. A big group of law students studied together for exams. We would gather in the late afternoon and wouldn't close our books until the sun was coming up. My mother became "the gang's mother," cooking two meals a day for all of us. (As it turned out, she would also play this role now and again in the years ahead.)

And in many ways, because of her help, I became the first woman in our family to graduate from a university.

Chapter 6

THE GOLDEN HORSE

EVER SINCE THE DAYS of the Daskalakis-Fazakis family vacation where I attempted to frolic barefoot in the streets of Athens, I always knew I wanted to live in Greece's capital city. To me, Athens has always been much more than one of the world's oldest cities and the seat of the government. It was (and is) a cosmopolitan international city in which I knew I wanted to make my future.

As you've already seen, helping to determine the future of my country had been my goal since girlhood, and Athens, the seat of the national government, was the place where I could achieve that goal. Had I arrived in Athens at age eighteen for my law studies, the big city might have swallowed me up. But I had learned some valuable lessons about discipline and responsibility studying in Thessaloniki, and now I felt much better equipped to take Athens on. I arrived with at least the outline of a career plan as well as some notion of where I hoped my ambitions would lead. The first challenge was to establish myself as a lawyer, familiarizing myself with the city—its bureaucratic networks and its political landscape. Once I had attained some proficiency and success as an attorney, I would start to be on the lookout for political opportunities. I believed that my future would lie not in a courtroom but in public service. I wanted to solve problems on a larger scale than one case at a time.

As I mentioned earlier, my father was retired and living on a pension. So, when I moved to Athens, I felt that I couldn't ask him for financial support. It was time for me to take complete responsibility for my own life. To save money I moved in with Eleni, who was still studying at the university. Without a job and without a source of income, I was forced to sell all the gold chains and other jewelry I had received as gifts through the years, mostly from my parents and my godmother. All those gifts had great sentimental value, but you can't eat sentiment. As I was gathering the jewelry to take to the shop, my sister began to cry. "Why are you crying?" I asked. "I didn't take your jewels." "No," she said, "I am crying because I am so sorry you have to go through this." "It's okay," I reassured her. "I'll find a way out."

But even with a law degree, finding a way out wasn't easy, and certainly not an easy thing to do quickly. In Greece at that time, before you could take the bar exam and hang out your own shingle, you were expected to apprentice at an established law firm. That meant a year or two interning at no salary. Many of the nation's law students—especially in Athens—came from affluent families and, with parental support, could afford to work without pay without experiencing any hardship. For me, the jewelry would make that path possible, but it was, at best, a short-term solution.

I decided to approach a renowned Athens lawyer by the name of Nontas Zafiropoulos about an internship. Though Zafiropoulos had a very small practice—only about four partners—he boasted many important clients and was exceedingly well connected among the Athenian power elite. And he had a hard-earned reputation as a winner in court. But absent any connections, the question was how to gain an audience with him. Throughout my life, I have found that persistence pays off. Sometimes you just have to show up and keep on showing up until you wear down the resistance. Show up and you wind up making acquaintances that have the potential to become alliances. It's amazing how often people are willing to help you reach your goal if only you can convince them that you deserve a chance. When at long last I got to see Zafiropoulos, he was quite aware of the substantial effort I had made to get in to see him, the kind of effort that could prove a virtue, he said, in a young lawyer. He was also impressed with my background and the can-do, will-do attitude I projected. He agreed to take me on, awarding me one of the coveted internships in his law firm.

The firm of Nontas Zafiropoulos and partners handled a vast range of legal matters, from apartment rentals to criminal cases, from shipping documents to divorce. Over the next year, I did a little of everything. Actually, I did a whole lot of everything. I read documents, wrote documents, ran documents to offices all over the city, appeared in court on routine filings, and performed all the basic duties that filled the days and, too often, the nights of the firm's interns. It didn't take me long to demonstrate that I was faster, more efficient, and more dedicated than the other interns in the office. I proved particularly useful at court and in government offices where lawyers were often stymied by the long delays that resulted from necessitous document searches. The archives were a mess and, in the prehistoric pre-computer era, the process was unwieldy and often unyielding. The bureaucrats there had a reputation for being brusque and willfully obstructive. I made a special point of courting these people who were so often the object of attorneys' wrath. As a result, some folks reputed to be among the toughest were willing to help me out with surprising dispatch. The lawyers at my firm believed I worked miracles. The first rule became: If you need it in a hurry, send Gianna. The second rule was: If you need it done well, use Gianna.

I had quickly become our law office's "golden horse," the intern they rode to a considerable profit. But while my efforts—the hard work and long hours—were recognized and garnered considerable praise from the partners, there was never a suggestion that I would be compensated financially any time soon. The system was clearly exploitive and, given my workload and the financial pressure I was under, my resentment was becoming increasingly acute. Finally, after nearly a year, I requested a personal meeting with Zafiropoulos. I prepared to plead my case with the same thoroughness I used when I headed to court. "Look, I'm very happy here and know that I am lucky to have this position," I told him. "I also know that you are under no obligation to pay me. But my father can't send me any more money, so I can't survive like this much longer. I know you are aware of how much work I've done for you, how many cases I've helped with. And I know how much money you have earned off those cases."

As I paused to catch my breath, I noticed he was actually blushing. He had five children and perhaps he understood—maybe even felt guilty about—my struggle. If so, he never said. What he did was far better than a verbal pat on the back. He immediately paid me three months' back wages and ordered all his associates to compensate me for any future work. The salary was not huge, but it covered my living expenses. Even though I celebrated a great personal victory, I hadn't as yet done anything to change the system.

My modest compensation proved to be even more essential than I had anticipated, because I was about to make a naive decision. I accepted a marriage proposal from a man I had been dating, a handsome divorcee with two children who appeared to be affluent. He had a good job and excellent prospects for the future—or so he told me. I thought I was getting a hardworking husband who was a doer, a man I could respect and whose opinions I would trust. But he preferred playing backgammon to working hard. He was far from a doer. Later, after I won elective office, tensions between us would escalate as I realized that he hoped to capitalize on my new position to secure business opportunities. That was hardly unusual behavior in Greek politics, but not acceptable to me.

I don't have too many regrets about that unhappy marriage, if only because I have from it one of the greatest blessings of my life, my daughter, Carolina, born in 1983.

I continued practicing law to pay the bills. At the same time, I made my first move to get into politics. As a result of my boss's work with the Athens Bar Association, I had become increasingly involved in civic matters. Some of the people I met urged me to take that involvement to the next level and run for office. I have never been the type of person who saw a problem and liked to sit around and complain about it. I've always believed in taking responsibility and taking action. But when they first approached me, I was constrained by the fact that I had a demanding job and a baby at home.

By the mid-1980s, problems in Athens were far worse than mine. On September 14, 1981, the *Globe and Mail*, a leading Canadian newspaper, warned, "Choking on Growth, Athens Turns into Nightmare." Two years later, on May 12, 1983, the *New York Times* headline confirmed that warning: "Now It's Official: Athens Smog Is Europe's Worst." Athens was a dismal, unbearable place with four million inhabitants: a gray city with gray buildings, a gray atmosphere, and gray people. Pollution smothered the city and nobody on the streets seemed to be smiling. This civic depression, both economic and emotional, represented a critical challenge, and in the absence of an infrastructure and initiatives by the government to address the problems, my friends pressed me once again to take it on. "You have much to offer," they said. "You are smart, you are energetic, and you are tough. You can make things happen."

So, with Carolina at least toddling along, I felt ready to take the political plunge. Part of my motivation was admittedly personal. I was not happy at work; I felt I did a lot of the heavy lifting while the firm's partners shared all the glamour and glory—and almost all the money too. And I was not happy in my marriage. I had reached a kind of dead end in my life.

After being admitted to the Athens bar, I left the law firm of Nontas Zafiropoulos and opened a small law office specializing in criminal law. I preferred criminal law because the stakes were greater and it was all about winning. But most important, being out on my own freed me up to pursue my political ambitions. I had set my sights on becoming a candidate in the 1986 municipal elections. The only problem was that to run for city council I had to convince a political party to include me on its slate.

As you'll recall from the previous chapter, at university I flirted with all ideas, marched with all kinds of people—even extreme leftists— and gave full vent to the natural idealism of youth. But as my political identity evolved, I realized I was the furthest thing from an ideologue. I was, at heart, a pragmatist, anxious to use the power of government to solve problems and eager to work with people of all political stripes who shared the same goals. There was, however, no straddling the center in Greece's fractious political divide. On the left side of the divide was the Socialist Party, PASOK; on the right, New Democracy. As in American politics today, Greece at that time was paralyzed by the polarization of the two dominant parties. Balanced precariously between the left and

the right, the Greek Parliament was unable to take the action necessary
to improve life in Athens and the rest of the country.

By the time I was interested in running for office, PASOK had
held power for about five years and—at least to my mind—had created
nothing but turmoil. They were good at dismantling the foundations of
many Greek institutions but failed to build anything substantive to put
in their place.

I felt I had no choice but to cast my lot with the only viable
opposition, New Democracy. Admittedly, that choice was made more
attractive by the fact that the party seemed poised to return to power.
However, I was hardly a perfect fit with New Democracy; I would
always have a lot of Embaros in me and wasn't inherently comfortable
with the party elites who too often seemed to govern by self-interest,
which coincided with the interests of the wealthy Greek establishment.
I didn't want to be hamstrung by ideological or political considerations.
By Greek political standards, that made me far more of a revolutionary
than a classic conservative.

Before heading to my law office each morning, I would detour to
New Democracy's headquarters intent on making some acquaintances.

At first I would simply stand outside and greet a few people as
they arrived at work. Eventually some folks recognized me and would
stop to chat. My strategy was this: If I met ten people maybe a couple
of them would prove sympathetic when I shared my goals. And all I
required was a few sympathetic people. If I met a secretary willing
to help she might invite me inside. Once inside, I might be introduced to a more important secretary who might usher me into the
inner sanctum. There I might meet an assistant to the party leader.
If he or she liked me I might be ushered along to a more important
assistant . . . and onward and upward. It didn't always happen quickly
or smoothly. But I was always confident that if I kept showing up, I

would, in the end, reach the right people. And if I reached those "right people," they would undoubtedly recognize how much I had to offer the party. At New Democracy, I thought I had an additional advantage. The party leader, Constantinos Mitsotakis, was a Cretan, as were many important people on his political team—and that is a tie that binds. Throughout my adult life, island bonds would prove critical in bolstering many of my most critical initiatives.

Eventually my persistence paid off and—thanks to the ministrations of his trusted assistant Saki Kypraiou—I was invited for a sit-down with Mitsotakis. A forty-year veteran of the Greek political arena, he was a formidable man. He had been first elected to Parliament as a liberal member of the centrist party. But in 1965 he was among a small group of dissidents who broke with that centrist government, leading to the downfall of the government and earning him the eternal enmity of the other political parties. When the junta seized power, Mitsotakis escaped arrest and fled to Turkey before moving on to Paris, where he remained in exile for six years. Upon his return to Greece, he founded a small centrist political party that eventually merged with New Democracy. He had already served as a key Minister in two governments, and in 1985, at the age of sixty-seven, he had his eye on the Prime Minister's office.

Mitsotakis was not a man who suffered fools gladly. And after all the effort I had invested in securing the meeting, my very first move was a gaffe. When I passed him my CV, which I had placed inside a plastic folder, he literally cringed at my offering. "Take it away," he said with as much distaste as if I had handed him a Socialist manifesto. "I don't like plastic folders. It looks like something you bought in a supermarket." He told me I should present my résumé as if it were an important document prepared expressly for that purpose. (It wasn't my only gaffe in trying to build a bridge to the party leader. Three years later, when I wanted to secure my name as a parliamentarian candidate, I was waiting outside his office and said, "I want to wish him a happy birthday." A woman nearby shook her head. "That would be a foolish move. He is turning seventy and is not yet Prime Minister. This is not a happy thing.")

To my surprise, after he chided me about the plastic folder, Mitsotakis quickly became warm and sympathetic. "You are from Crete like me. And very young," he said. "A year younger than my Doraki." (His daughter, Dora Bakoyannis, then his Chief of Staff, would become the first woman elected Mayor of Athens, and she held that position during the Athens 2004 Summer Olympics.)

Mitsotakis regretted, however, that he wasn't in a position to make any promises about the municipal election. "But you are the party leader," I protested. He told me that Miltiadis Evert, the man who would top the New Democracy ticket as its mayoral candidate, had very strong opinions and was very stubborn. He would likely balk at including a candidate whom he felt was forced upon him. Later I would discover that Evert was frequently trying to undermine Mitsotakis, hoping to eventually become party leader himself. (He would attain that goal in 1993.) It would be better, Mitsotakis counseled, if I could win Evert over first, and he promised to speak to him on my behalf. "I will tell him that he is very lucky you came along at a time when we want to include many women to show that we respect them."

This was an attitude I detested—lip service rather than genuine commitment. *Saying* you respect women is hardly the same thing as *respecting* women. I held my tongue, nevertheless, which was a good thing because I have sharp tongue. I departed his office optimistic that I would soon get the call to action. But no call came. So I simply resumed showing up at New Democracy headquarters. I would ask a secretary or a security man when Mitsotakis was expected, and I would make sure he caught a glimpse of me so as to remind him of my aspirations. I pursued him relentlessly, and whatever sympathy I had originally detected appeared to have been replaced by irritation.

Perhaps I simply wore him down. Perhaps, fed up with my stalking him, he just wanted to pass the buck. Whatever his motive, Mitsotakis ultimately kept his promise and set up an appointment for me with the mayoral candidate. Evert was a huge, bulky man whom they called "the bulldozer." He even used that in his campaign slogan: "The bulldozer who comes to clean up and build anew." I handed him my résumé —this time in an attractive folder—and, to my surprise, he seemed enthusiastic about my involvement. I was only a little disappointed when I discovered why. "You are a young, beautiful girl, and this time I will include many women," he said. "We'll show them that we respect women." There was that same b.s. line again. But sensing I was on the verge of a breakthrough, I once again managed to hold my tongue. I will not leave it to others to note the irony that my political career was launched when I managed to hold my tongue not only once, but twice. Some would say that is not something I have done as many times since.

True to the party's pledge, New Democracy did include a record number of women on its ticket and, at just thirty years old, I was among them. I was excited to be making my first foray into politics. I was even more excited when I was assigned to run as a candidate from the important Athens center-city district. My bubble burst, however, when party insiders told me the real deal. While a young woman with no political experience, no money, and no powerful connections would be an excellent symbol of progressive values and change, a young woman lacking political experience, money, and powerful connections had no chance at victory in that high-profile district. I would certainly earn the party's gratitude, respect, and, likely, future favors by running an energetic campaign, but I couldn't possibly win a seat. I was meant to be a sacrificial lamb or, more precisely, a sacrificial woman.

Chapter 7

A TOUCH OF BASIL

ALTHOUGH I WAS YOUNG AND POLITICALLY INEXPERIENCED, I wasn't completely naive. Greece may have seemed to be a two-party democracy to the average voter, but behind the scenes, the parties (more than two dozen of them) were interested in anything but democracy. Greek politics was all about paying dues, doing favors, and waiting one's turn for a taste of political spoils.

I understood that the party didn't really believe in Gianna Daskalaki. Party leaders simply viewed the candidacies of women as an easy way to demonstrate that New Democracy had truly embraced the "new" in its name—that is, despite being politically conservative, the party had progressive views and would, if it assumed power, become an agent of societal change.

But the view of New Democracy's leadership regarding women wasn't remotely progressive. Evert, our mayoral candidate, once offered me foolish and offensive advice that he wouldn't have dared suggest to a man. He wanted me to undergo a makeover, warning me not to wear much makeup or any of my nice clothes or jewelry. Poor people, he insisted, would resent any display of affluence; moreover, he assured me, other women would be jealous of my youthful good looks. "Try to be humble and not show yourself to be so pretty," he urged me. I ignored him and the other party hacks. If I had to be a symbol of anything, I wanted to be a symbol of what I was: a lawyer and an honest, hardworking woman. "I won't play some humble, miserable person with the goal of misleading voters so as to win their trust," I told the party pros. "I will shower each morning, wear makeup and nice, modern clothes and maybe even some little jewels. It doesn't matter what we show them, only what we do afterward."

Obviously, my campaign problem wasn't the "envious poor or jealous women." My campaign issue was that the Athens district is one of the most challenging in Greece. Its voters were educated and informed about the issues and the candidates, while I was a virtual unknown with no public track record. From the day in September 1986 when my name was officially announced on the ticket, I had only about six weeks to make a favorable impression on voters.

It was one thing to buck the party establishment about wearing makeup. It was another to come up with a viable alternative strategy that, in such a short time, could give me a chance to contend. I wasn't even an official member of my own political party yet. I had no powerful connections. I didn't belong to any political family; I didn't have family money and lacked any financial backers. I couldn't afford to flood the district with banners or to pay to get my picture in the newspaper. My face never showed up on TV like other candidates' did so that people who went to the polls might say: "Ah, I recognize her. I will vote for her."

Some rival candidates boasted multiple campaign centers around

the district, staffed by supporters in spiffy uniforms. I had solely one
office, generously provided to me at no rent by a supporter and run by
my friend Lena Zachopoulou. She had recently closed her cosmetics
shop and was looking for something to occupy her time. It was a perfect
fit since I was always so busy out campaigning. I just handed her the
key to the office, told her where it was located, and three days later she
had it up and running. Besides Lena, whom I paid a very modest salary
(she works with me still, twenty-six years later), I depended on a staff
of devoted volunteers. These were mostly ladies I had met from nearby
neighborhoods. I would come in early—before hitting the streets—and
deliver the day's marching orders. In the early days, I would bark, "Call
him and her and him and her"—and, though Lena and the ladies might
not have even known who "him" or "her" was or have had a clue how to
reach that person, they managed to get the job done.

The only thing I knew how to do was to get out on the streets and
introduce myself to people. I asked an actress friend for some tips. She
told me it was important when I arrived at a campaign stop to identify
the people who seemed genuinely interested and to aim my efforts at
them, not to waste time forcing my attentions on those who weren't
engaged. When I talked to voters, it was vital to remain focused on
them—never to be caught scanning the room for others or to appear
impatient to move on.

I quickly learned the art of what they call in America "retail politics."
Each morning I ventured out to the markets, to the cafés, to the taxi
stands—anywhere and everywhere that people congregated. And I
didn't return to the office until it was dark outside. When I talked to
people, I made no big promises. I didn't b.s. them. I simply told them
I believed that I could be useful in Athens, and all I could absolutely
promise was that I would work hard on their behalf to earn their trust.
I listened to everyone, including Communists and Socialists that others

told me were a waste of my time. It wasn't a waste. While I didn't always like what they said, I did get a sense of what the voters were concerned about: smog, a deteriorating infrastructure, and a decline in the quality of life in Athens. And compounding these concerns was a distance between the politicians and the people. Everyone understood the problems, but it seemed to the voters that the politicians were indifferent and more interested in their own careers than in improving life for the Athenian electorate.

At night when I got back to the office, I'd regale my "staff" with tales from my day on the campaign trail. We'd keep a count, estimating how many people I met each day and how that might add up. "If maybe I met a thousand today, how many might vote for me? You think maybe a hundred? Maybe fifty? If I can do that every day, who knows?" Quite honestly, I had no clue. I was a complete novice. One knowledgeable election veteran, however, wasn't nearly as impressed with my efforts as were the ladies in my office. He told me that while I was demonstrating great energy and almost certainly connecting with some voters, effort alone wouldn't enable me to pull off an upset. "You have to reach more people," he said, "and to do that you need some tricks." I didn't really know any tricks. And even if I could think of some, how—lacking money—could I afford to deploy a trick or a gimmick?

I clearly needed professional counsel, so I fell back on the one tried-and-true tactic I knew, the same one I had used to get my law internship as well as to land a spot on the New Democracy ticket. I would show up at the right office, talk my way in to see the right man, and then make my earnest plea. So I made an appointment with Thalis Koutoupis, a top election strategist who had a reputation for being very savvy—he had done campaign work in the United States—and very pricey. The moment I sat down in his office I confessed that I didn't have any money to pay his fee. I was counting on three things: that my honesty might disarm him; that I was already sitting in his office and he had set aside time for me; and that I was young, attractive, and charming. Just as I had hoped, I was able to coax a minimum consultation out of him.

I impressed him enough so that he made a small investment in my future. That investment paid off. Years later, I heard him boast, "I was there in the beginning for Gianna Angelopoulos-Daskalaki when she really needed help."

What he told me was a more sophisticated version of the earlier advice I'd received about using some "tricks." Greece, he said, was way behind the times in campaign strategies. In America, campaigns were all about marketing, finding slogans and messages that were easily digested by the public. The challenge was to penetrate the clutter surrounding elections and to get your message through to voters. That couldn't be accomplished through random one-on-one encounters. I left his office with my brain on fire, mentally juggling some vague notions of how I might meld traditional Greek values with cutting-edge American campaign techniques.

Then it came to me: the basil plant! Basil is essentially the national plant of Greece. It is one of our simplest yet most powerful symbols. In the summertime, every household grows at least one basil plant. The churches put it in the holy water. The ancient Greeks believed basil would open the gates of heaven for a person passing on. The smell of basil is the smell of summer, of the Greek home, and of the holy church. That makes it one very powerful fragrance.

When I told my supporters about my basil idea, they joked: "So what do we do? Send everybody a plant?" We all started laughing hysterically as we imagined dead plants arriving at people's doors. (Basil needs a lot of care; it cannot survive for a day without water.) Wouldn't that be the perfect metaphor for my first campaign?

But when we all stopped laughing, I realized it was the seed of a great idea—literally. We wouldn't send a plant. We would send the seeds instead. Seeds had the added virtue of being just about what our budget could handle. We raced out and bought them by the kilo. We sealed a few seeds in little plastic pouches and stapled the pouches onto campaign mailers, which a fellow Cretan had printed for me at no charge. The flier had room for only the most basic campaign pitch along with—most critically, we realized—a picture of a basil plant. Otherwise, people might have no idea what the seeds were. My message became crystal clear: Basil represents hope and new beginnings, and it is synonymous with a better quality of life. If everyone planted the seeds it would not only mean sweeter-smelling homes but also a sweeter and greener future for Athens.

I mailed the seeds to thousands of Athenians. When we ran out of addresses, we went into stores and shops and began handing them out. Our effort made a huge impression. This was long before the environmental movement had taken hold, particularly in Greece, so it came across as a very fresh idea. The basil resonated with Athenians who were sick of the ugly smog that blanketed our city. Even the media was taken with my simple, fragrant campaign symbol. All of a sudden I had a public identity in the minds of voters and in the press: I was the young female attorney, the young mother, who wanted to make Athens greener. I reached out with a touch of basil. I would run more campaigns and accomplish much for my country, but to many Greeks I will always be remembered as the woman with a touch of basil. Even today, people approach me to tell me about how surprised they were to receive those seeds—and how the basil plants have endured.

Some political pros would later tell me that even *I* might not have recognized what a novelty act I was in the city's political landscape: a slim, elegant woman with a distinctively vibrant personality and the high energy—they described me as a perpetual motion machine—of youth. As my profile rose in the city, even Evert took notice. He suddenly wanted to schedule campaign events at which we both made appearances. Though I could feel the tide turning my way, I never took a day off the campaign trail. Some people counseled me that champions always rested on the last day, that voters had already made up their mind and you didn't want to appear desperate.

But resting has never been one of my talents. On the day of the election, I went out just as early as I always did and made the circuit of all the polling places. I was convinced that if I could just meet a few more voters, it might mean the difference between victory and defeat. It was nighttime when I arrived at the election center in Neos Kosmos and I was still going full steam. A policeman recognized me and, in a polite way, said: "Mrs. Daskalaki, you are not allowed here any more. We are closed. The election is over."

I went back to my campaign headquarters and closeted myself in my office. I wanted to make an honest assessment of my campaign— one that wouldn't be colored by the results. I concluded: "Gianna, you cannot be unhappy or worry about what might have been. You've done absolutely everything humanly possible to get a favorable outcome. So no looking back. No regrets." That has been the way I have confronted challenges all my life. No half measures. Once I decide to go in, I am in all the way. I do everything possible to achieve the desired result and then, whatever that result, I don't waste time on regrets or second-guessing myself. If there were mistakes—and there always are—you make sure you learn the lesson for next time.

When the votes were tallied, I had pulled off the biggest upset in Athens. I had needed about 2,500 votes to capture a seat on the council; I received almost twice that many, with 4,645 votes! Three months later, in January 1987, the young woman who was given no chance to win put on her makeup, donned her loveliest clothes, and went to be sworn in as a member of the Athens city council.

Chapter 8

SCHOOL DAYS

ANY CITY COUNCILOR WHO TRULY WANTED TO MAKE AN IMPACT was facing a herculean challenge. Athens, a city of 4.5 million, was broken into some forty discrete municipalities, each with a Mayor and a city council. The number of city council members was proportional to the individual municipality's population compared to the population of greater Athens. Central Athens had the largest population, with about one million people and forty-one city council members.

Politics in Athens was a microcosm of federal Greek politics. The city was a maze of jurisdictions. While the Ministry of Agriculture controlled one park, a different ministry controlled the park a few blocks away. Most of the forty municipalities refused to cooperate with one another, creating even more bizarre bureaucratic nightmares. For example, a particular highway forms the boundary between two municipalities. One municipality is responsible for one-half of the highway and one municipality is responsible for the other half. Yet the federal Ministry of Public Works is responsible for the upkeep of the median. Who paves the street? Who maintains the streetlights? This patchwork of responsibility allows Greek politicians to participate in their favorite exercise, finger-pointing. Nothing is ever anyone's fault because there are so many other people and political organizations to blame. Little did I know, then, that this arena was preparing me for becoming the head of the Athens 2004 Summer Olympic Games organizing committee, when I had to deal with more than fifty Mayors to prepare the necessary conditions in Athens and throughout Greece.

It didn't take me long to discover that change and the public interest were not foremost in the minds of my colleagues. They appeared to cast every vote based on one thing only: how that issue affected their future political prospects.

While New Democracy had won the election and Evert had been installed as Mayor, none of the power trickled down to me. I had no real influence in the party and wasn't in any position to effect the changes that had motivated my candidacy in the first place. The party still wanted to showcase its women—and me because of my strong campaign performance—but the emphasis remained on "show." Thus, even though I was assigned a highly visible position as Secretary of the Board of the central Athens city council, organizing meetings and keeping official notes, I viewed my role as little more than window dressing.

Still, I have always believed that to do something right, you have to devote yourself entirely to that undertaking, so I threw myself wholeheartedly into my position and its responsibilities. I essentially gave up my daytime law practice and, with it, the potential for significant earnings, but I managed to get by. While "secretary" may not have been a power position, the job demanded—given the ceaseless array of committee meetings—long and tedious hours. That was hardest on my daughter because I was often at work from morning until night. Carolina, who was not yet four years old and in preschool, was so precocious that we called her "the wild child." Sometimes when she got home from school, she'd climb on a chair to reach the phone and dial my office number, which she had memorized. "I want to speak to my mom," she'd demand. And when I got on the phone, she'd berate me with a litany of complaints and then start crying. "I'm the only one whose mommy doesn't pick her up at the bus to take her home," I can recall her saying. "I always get grandma or the girl from the house."

After a succession of these unhappy calls, I decided I needed to sit down face-to-face with Carolina to discuss our mutual problems and somehow work out a truce. It isn't easy to explain life's complexities to a small child. I started off by telling her that while we could always talk things over, I wouldn't put up with her grumpy faces and grumpy noises because my life wasn't that easy either. Someday, I said, she would understand that we make choices that may be hard on us but are good for other people. I told her that we are sometimes called upon to make personal sacrifices for the greater good of the community. "Do you remember," I asked her, "that day when we went to the playground and everything was a mess? Do you remember how the equipment was broken and the park looked like it had been abandoned? And it was dangerous for children? Well, somebody has to fix problems like that. That's why I ran for city council, and that's why the people voted for me."

I told her that I couldn't be there at the bus every day to pick her up. But I promised her that twice a week I would come home and have lunch with her. What makes a child happy is when its mother is happy. Stressed, unhappy, no-smiles mothers will end up with stressed, unhappy, no-smiles children.

And I promised Carolina that I would occasionally bring her along when I worked late at the office or had meetings out in the community. She thought about this for a few seconds and asked: "You will do a new park? You will do a new playground?" "I'll try," I said. We had our compromise. I would eventually discover that it was far easier to strike a compromise deal with a three-and-a-half-year-old "wild child" than with most of my colleagues.

I remember bringing Carolina to work one evening when I had to supervise a meeting. She couldn't have been four feet tall yet, and she looked adorable lugging this white teddy bear—not surprisingly named Teddy—that was almost as big as she was. Some of the people in the office enjoyed her being there, offering Carolina drawing materials and even joining her in silly songs. The Mayor, however, heard singing and came out of his office looking very unhappy. "What is this, kindergarten?" he demanded. His longtime assistant Phoni said, "Mrs. Daskalaki *has* to bring her daughter because she *has* to work late."

I was certainly a genuine example of a working mother trying very hard to balance parental responsibilities with a demanding job. After my negotiations with Carolina, I did my best to honor our deal. And though I didn't always make it home for lunch and she wound up having to sit through more meetings than she ever imagined, Carolina never again complained about my work. One evening as I was going out I heard her voice from her bedroom. I cracked opened the door and peeked inside. Carolina, who would never play with dolls, had lined up all her stuffed animals—there must have been at least thirty— and she was lecturing them. "I don't want any grumpy faces," she said. "If you want something just tell me. If you want to go for a swim or a walk in the forest you tell me. But no grumpy faces!"

———

I am not, by nature, a patient person. But I performed all my assigned tasks on the council dutifully, worked long hours, and, I believed, demonstrated my commitment to the council as well as to my political party. After some months, I went to the Mayor and asked him to consider giving me some major responsibility that would allow me to make good on my commitment to the city. You know the old saying "Be careful what you wish for. You just may get it." That is exactly what happened. I was assigned responsibility for the city schools, a thankless task and, many believed, a hopeless problem that nobody else wanted to tackle. After all, who in his right mind wanted to listen to the never-ending complaints of parents, however warranted? Who in his right mind wanted to spend countless hours, days, and weeks fighting with the various ministries that held the purse strings over money the state insisted it didn't have?

But I have always been willing to take on the hardest jobs and the biggest challenges—the jobs that should have been labeled "mission impossible." At the time, the city's schools were in total chaos. My electoral district alone had 224 school facilities, and many of those buildings were in dangerous disrepair, and vital equipment and supplies were missing. There was no money for such basic utilities as electricity, telephones, heating oil, or, sometimes, even water. There was no food service or medical support. Some schools had become havens for drug users: Schoolyards were littered with syringes so there was no safe place for the children to play outside. Sometimes you would even find syringes in classroom desks. One school had even been constructed on top of a gas station. The schools were so overcrowded that the kids attended in shifts, alternating between morning and afternoon classes. I had been required to do the same in high school in Heraklion, so I knew how adversely it affected a child's ability to focus on learning. And the irregular hours drove parents crazy. The bottom line—and sad truth—was that our schools were no longer places where boys and girls could go to learn.

I don't pretend to be a miracle worker, but what I did might have seemed like a miracle to some parents. I simply started by showing up. I visited every single school, and I talked to parents at every school, church, and neighborhood meeting. I was out each night until ten or eleven o'clock. I wanted to show people that somebody cared and that the council felt a responsibility for the plight of our Athenian schoolchildren.

Amid this mess, two thousand Athenian boys and girls were offered an excellent summer program on a lovely campus near Agios Andreas on the Attic peninsula. It was a small town with nothing more than a cinema and a few supermarkets—and, of course, the shining Aegean Sea. So many parents wanted to send their children to this free summer program that participants were chosen by lottery. I wanted to show people that I was a new kind of politician, that I didn't just make pronouncements. I was willing to get out there on the front line. I volunteered to go to the camp and help supervise the kids. Sometimes that meant helping the nurses clean lice out of the children's hair. The nurses preferred to send these children home to their parents, but I insisted: "The families do not have the money to send their children on vacations. We can take care of this ourselves."

I took Carolina along that summer because I didn't have a nanny at the time. I was the *only* city councilor to volunteer.

I knew there were limits to what I could achieve in the schools. Consequently, I never made promises I couldn't keep. I told people the truth, even when it was the bitter truth. "Sorry," I would say, "I think we can get this much money, but no more." But I also knew that if we were to accomplish anything substantial, the parents had to believe in me and embrace my efforts. At first, they just wanted to thank me for being there. But I needed more than thanks. I needed them to join me. We began to organize a coalition of parents, teachers, and others who recognized that the situation in our schools was tragic—tragic for our children and, ultimately, for Athens. Then we had to convince the Mayor and other city councilors what was at stake for them. If the future of our children wasn't enough to move them, then we had to demonstrate that we represented a significant number of votes. To the chagrin of my party colleagues, I also began to court all the city councilors, including those in other parties that usually opposed any New Democracy initiative. I called it a moral imperative to act. And I promised that if we did act in concert, I would not try to claim the laurels for saving our schools.

Slowly, just as a stone thrown into a pond creates concentric circles that ripple outward, we began to make some headway. It had been easy for the government to ignore the schools when nobody was challenging them publicly. But it is never good politics to be against schoolchildren. The Socialist government's Ministry of Education promised us more money for the schools and, surprisingly, delivered rather quickly. In the past, all schools had been given identical funding regardless of their size or needs or how many classes they housed. We developed new formulas to distribute the money fairly. We could now pre-pay the heat so there was no shortfall in winter. We began to maintain the schools year-round so they wouldn't deteriorate from neglect during the summer. We built pedestrian walks around schools, added some greenery, and bought new playground equipment so that we were actually beginning to serve education's mind–body ideal.

After that first infusion of money, we had to fight tooth and nail for every drachma. When we determined that 500 million drachmas were required for adequate school maintenance, the ministry offered us 40 million. "Take it," the Minister of Education advised me, reminding me of the value of a bird in hand. Instead, I recommended that we refuse that amount and ratchet up the pressure. The government upped its offer to 60 million. We again refused. It was easy to refuse 100 million because it was clear we were winning this battle. Ultimately, we received 330 million drachmas—not all we had asked for, but more than eight times the initial offer. That brought a lot of change, and parents and teachers were once again able to take pride in their schools.

I wound up learning as much as any of the schoolchildren did. The city of Athens was a big university for me, and I was getting a graduate degree in political realities. I learned that solutions don't come from faith or visions or big slogans or even big mouths, though those can sometimes help the cause. Political problems are best solved by pursuing three steps: first, by gathering knowledge so that you know what you need to do; second, by forging alliances, if not with other politicians then with the voters; and third, by taking decisive action. That approach would serve me well in the future.

But I learned another lesson too. A far more painful one. The Mayor had underestimated me. He never thought such a refined and sophisticated young woman was going to get her hands dirty fighting for and working on behalf of the schools—sometimes literally scrubbing them myself. And he certainly never imagined that I would have any kind of major success, let alone help to reverse the education system's decline. Instead of celebrating the success as a New Democracy triumph, therefore, the Mayor worried that I was too independent and becoming way too visible in my work to reform the school system. So Evert created a new position, the Chancellor for the City's Schools, which left me as the council liaison to those schools but effectively stripped me of executive power over them.

The work for the schools was certainly my proudest accomplishment during my three years on the Athens city council. But there was another smaller success that, as a Cretan, gave me special satisfaction. It involved the island of Gavdos, situated in the Mediterranean just below Crete and thus the country's southernmost island. It is small, only about thirteen square miles, and back then the number of its year-round residents didn't reach much higher than sixty. Despite its isolation and tiny population, the island was an ecological gem, with a unique ecosystem—flora and fauna not seen on Crete just a few miles away—and a species of cedar not found anywhere else in Greece.

The island lacked any communications infrastructure. The federal government had abandoned the meager farming economy, and no authority had taken responsibility for the few residents there. I made up my mind that I had to do something to support this island and its people. I flew to the island in a helicopter provided by a TV network and met with the local priest. By virtue of the higher profile I had developed on the city council, I was able to get a newspaper article—complete with pictures—published, detailing the shameful neglect of the residents of Gavdos.

This article galvanized a whole lot of people into action. The Greek navy began making regular stops there. The city of Athens, the Greek Tourism Ministry, and even the European Commission offered help. Today Gavdos has a thriving tourism industry. Each year, approximately three thousand campers visit the island to enjoy its unspoiled natural beauty.

Some people wondered why I got involved with Gavdos in the first place, given that it didn't fall under the jurisdiction of the city. Truthfully, I was using a small problem to attack a far bigger problem. There has long been a malaise that affects my country. It is a bad case of laissez-faire. People are ready with the excuse "It's always been done this way" as grounds for not making the necessary changes. If you want to know the magic words that *really* set me off—to change me into some kind of cross between a tiger and a tornado—try telling me "We *can't* do that" or "We *can't* change that."

For me, Gavdos was a laboratory experiment in leadership and public policy, and, ultimately, it proved a very successful one. I had demonstrated that we could solve a small problem. We could move the bureaucracy and inspire people to take responsibility for their future. With that same commitment, we could succeed when we addressed the huge challenges confronting our country. Regardless of how things had always been done in the past, we Greeks were capable of orchestrating positive change for the future. I hoped to inspire others who wanted to give back to their community, to act. Change comes only when people seize responsibility and take action. Ultimately, the Gavdos initiative demonstrated that I wasn't your typical Greek politician committed to preserving the status quo. I was—and I remain—an innovator and a problem solver.

Chapter 9

PARLIAMENTARY STEPS

DURING MY THREE YEARS ON THE CITY COUNCIL, my constituents—so many of whom had lost hope—were inspired to discover that change was indeed possible, even in a system that appears to be immutable, if you only join forces and take a stand. To them I may have been a hard-charging, hardheaded woman, but I was *their* hard-charging, hardheaded woman! I felt proud of what we accomplished together in the schools and that I had earned both their respect and their affection.

I would never claim to have evoked the same sentiments among my colleagues, however. It sometimes seemed as if they regarded me as a political virus that had invaded their tidy and comfortable body politic. I didn't play by the same rules they did. I didn't feel constrained by hidebound notions. I consorted with folks they considered the enemy. And I eschewed backroom deals, preferring public candor instead. The jealousy and resentment that the Mayor once foresaw as a potential problem for me with voters emerged instead as a problem with my fellow politicians. They resented my popularity and tried to bring me down with malicious gossip.

Believe me, I heard the stage whispers. "She ran for office to escape a bad marriage." True, my marriage was troubled. But exactly what sin had I committed? It wasn't as if I had abandoned my family to pursue a higher office. A number of my male colleagues wouldn't have been subjected to similar public scrutiny of their marriage or their motives. But that kind of attack was never aimed at men; it was reserved for women, particularly those who defied political convention and refused to go along to get along. For women, it was always an uphill climb to succeed, especially if they were ambitious about their professional careers.

Another insult I heard far too often was that I was a narcissist who had run for city council simply to become famous. How unfair. So many other politicians had an easy path to office. They were wealthy and connected to the party by family ties or were already TV personalities well known to voters. They took their renown for granted. I ran to fulfill a dearly held dream of public service, and I made sacrifices, both personal and financial, to do it. If I had become popular it was only because I did my job well. The recognition came at a high price, and personal attacks—orchestrated by people who foresaw that I would become a threat to them in the future—were responsible for a large part of that price.

One person who wasn't enamored of me and didn't bother to hide it was the daughter of Constantinos Mitsotakis, Dora Bakoyannis. As his chief of staff and office gatekeeper, Dora had tried and failed to block me from reaching her father when I made my first foray into politics. She clearly viewed that as a failure she didn't intend to repeat. She was furious that I had come to New Democracy with no party ties or credentials, viewing my outsider status as a major political sin. "Who is this

Daskalaki and what does she want? She thinks she should be elected just because she is beautiful," she'd sneer to her mother without any concern for who might be listening. I personally overheard her describe me as "audacious and brazen." In fairness, Dora had good reason to worry about me. She recognized that New Democracy, however enlightened it might have claimed to be, could only tolerate a few women in prominent roles. Any success I might achieve would cast me as a rival and a potential threat to Dora's own political ambitions.

After those three years as a tireless advocate for the schools, after finding new and creative solutions for the system's problems, I was ready to take the next step—indeed the next leap—and run for Parliament. Greece is a "Presidential Parliamentary Republic." The Greek state has a President and a Prime Minister. The legislative branch consists of one house of government, the Parliament. The Greek Parliament has three hundred members, each of whom is elected for a four-year term.

I believed I had earned a spot on the New Democracy ticket for the 1989 elections. Despite any lingering resentments, party leader Mitsotakis appeared to embrace my ambitions. He praised my energy and my dedication and promised that I would be included on the party's parliamentary ticket when the next elections came around.

When elections were called for June, I readied my campaign. One morning in May, on the day when New Democracy would reveal its ticket, Mitsotakis beckoned me to his office for what I assumed would be his formal blessing. My election team was waiting back in my office and I was prepared to hit the ground running. The only thing I wasn't prepared for was the news delivered by the party boss. "You know, Gianna, I so wanted to include you," Mitsotakis began. "But I faced a lot of pressure. There are people who are your elders who have been waiting far longer for this chance."

If he was the least bit ashamed of how he had misled me, I didn't detect it. I was so stunned, hurt, and angry over his betrayal—and humiliated by his choosing the very last possible second to do it—that, for perhaps the first time in my life, I couldn't even speak. I just sat there staring at him, tears running down my cheeks. It hadn't occurred to me that I would need to wear waterproof mascara. He was obviously discomfited by my crying and tried to find some comforting words. "You are so young, Gianna. I promise I will find another time to include you."

I put on my sunglasses and left without saying a word. When I got back to my campaign headquarters, I sat alone in my office and cried for another half hour. Then I composed myself, redid my makeup, and summoned my campaign team. Everyone had heard the news on the radio and was as upset as I was, perhaps even more. But I had already made what would prove to be the most critical decision of my political career.

I wasn't going to let the party cut me out of its future. I wouldn't give my enemies the satisfaction. I would take Mitsotakis's promise for the future at face value—even though I no longer trusted him, I had no real choice—and treat this episode as a mere bump in the road. Instead of withdrawing in bitterness, I used all of the money I had saved for my campaign to send all three hundred thousand voters on my mailing list a letter expressing my enthusiastic support for New Democracy.

I was convinced that I could reverse this situation and turn it into an advantage. There was one minor flaw in my plan, though. I needed my letter to go out immediately and I was emotionally spent. I feared that I wouldn't have the composure to craft an upbeat and conciliatory letter without exposing my underlying anger and bitterness. So I asked my most trusted confidant, Lefteris Kousoulis, to write the letter without reflecting my true feelings. He got it pitch perfect: I accepted the decision; I stood by the party; I would work hard for the ticket; and I hoped my day would come. The letter concluded on an optimistic note. "I am convinced that in our common effort for a better Greece—a Greece we all deserve—we will meet again."

And we would.

At the time, however, my team was appalled by my decision. "Have you gone crazy?" they asked. "Are you going to thank them after the miserable way they treated you?" And then I got to hear a lot of "the bastards this" and "the bastards that." I let them vent, much as I had taken the time to cry. "I can't pretend this is good," I told them. "But if I don't want them to destroy me, I have to make this work for me." I had made my decision: I never take "no" for an answer—not from the party leaders and not from my own team either.

Faced with a Gordian knot, I had conceived a masterstroke to cut it. I sent out the letter and went to work as a low-level volunteer in party headquarters. Everybody had their eyes on me as I worked long hours performing the most menial tasks in an ugly campaign office with horrible furniture, writing routine reports about the party platform, going to help build crowds for rallies. I was the fifth wheel. It wasn't easy to watch the other candidates running where I should have been. But I kept reminding myself that if I didn't give my very best effort on their behalf, I would wind up the biggest loser in this election—regardless of the actual results. "Gianna, you have no other option," I kept telling myself. "You may be bleeding, but you are not dead. You must do this if you want to survive."

My plan worked to perfection—better, frankly, than I could have ever imagined. Many party people who had dismissed me as brash, egotistical, and self-promoting now realized they had been unfair to me. That was when I won the "heart" of the party and its voters. I had demonstrated to them that I had integrity, that I could be selfless, and that I was someone who actually had the greater interests of the party at heart.

Thanks to new rules imposed by the Socialist government, the June

1989 election results proved to be a mess. Though New Democracy won the most seats by a comfortable margin, Mitsotakis nonetheless fell short of what he needed to form a government and was again denied his dream of becoming Prime Minister. Instead, Parliament accepted a coalition government with an interim Prime Minister, and new elections were scheduled for November.

In September, shortly before New Democracy's ticket would be announced, the terrorist group Revolutionary Organization 17 November assassinated Dora Bakoyannis's husband, Pavlos, a journalist who had won election to Parliament in the previous election. (Three years earlier, the same group had killed my future husband's uncle, Dimitris Angelopoulos, one of the nation's leading industrialists.) This devastating tragedy opened the road for Dora to run for Parliament, and she won her husband's seat.

As I left Dora's husband's funeral in Karpenissi, in central Greece, I sensed that my fate had changed. I looked out the window of the car and saw seven continuous rainbows. I could never have imagined that both his widow and I would enter Parliament two months later and take the oath of office together.

Be that as it may, when a call beckoned me to Mitsotakis's parliamentary office two full days before the November ticket was to be announced, I thought maybe somebody was playing a joke—as on *Candid Camera*—on me. The call, though, was genuine. I was understandably nervous as I drove to meet with Mitsotakis once again. I wasn't sure I could control myself if he were to betray me a second time.

This time, however, betrayal was not in the air. From the moment I walked into his office at ten o'clock that night, Mitsotakis was warm and even a little apologetic. "Gianna," he confessed, "I felt bad that I did not include you last time. But I really appreciated how you acted afterward and how you worked for the party. This time you will be included."

Then came his political prognosis and only then did I get a sense of déjà vu. While the parliamentary district in which I would be running was the same one in Athens I had served on the city council, the stakes were higher and the standards more demanding. The criteria were much stricter. These were national elections, not district, not local.

Moreover, I would be running against some of the most prominent politicians—"legends" was the term the party leader used—in Athens. It would be impossible for me to pull off another election upset. However, he was confident that this time around New Democracy would win with a sufficient majority to form a new government. He promised that there would be a place for me. In other words, I could expect to lose the election yet be rewarded with a government job.

But I had never wanted a handout and wasn't looking for safe harbor in some bureaucracy. I wanted to perform on the country's biggest political stage. From the moment I was included on the ticket, I ran like an athlete at the peak of her game. I went nonstop for forty-five days. I campaigned everywhere and talked to everyone. People would warn me: "Don't go there. It's all Communists," or "Stay away from there. It's all Socialists." I ignored all such advice. I would tell those voters: "Okay, I know you support another party. But hear me out because, for all our differences, we share the same problems." I would take a similar approach during Athens's campaign for the 2004 Summer Olympics, engaging all of the International Olympic Committee's voting delegates, including those who were committed to rival cities.

I didn't come up with any gimmick quite as clever as the basil seeds, but I did have a few novel campaign ideas. My pamphlet featured a list of what I viewed as the critical responsibilities of government. It bore my signature, signed on a blackboard. This was my way of showing that these weren't just empty phrases; I pledged myself wholeheartedly to every word written there. I asked voters "to sign with me" if they shared these beliefs. I literally had them sign a document, hoping that would create a genuine bond between us.

I also created a stir by passing out a pamphlet that saluted all the women who had served in the Greek Parliament regardless of their party affiliations. The list included Mrs. Eleni Scoura, who, in 1953, became the first woman elected to the Greek Parliament. Mrs. Scoura was a tremendous inspiration to me, which I shared with her when—to her surprise—I visited her in the hospital before the election.

The list on my pamphlet also included the name of Melina Mercouri, one of Greece's national treasures. An internationally known actress whose performance in *Never on Sunday* won her the best actress award at the 1960 Cannes Film Festival and a nomination for best actress at the Academy Awards, she was a vocal opponent of the military junta that ruled Greece into the mid-1970s. She was first elected to Parliament in 1977 and became the first female Minister of Culture for Greece in 1981. Among her many other accomplishments was the movement Melina spearheaded to reclaim the sculptures that once graced the Parthenon but are held in the British Museum.

My only regret in publishing this pamphlet was that there were so few women to mention.

Greek politics in 1989 was even more polarized and bitter than American politics is today. The leading parties portrayed each other as intractable and the opposition politicians as mortal enemies. And sadly, both sides insisted they were right. I maintained that there was middle ground. And unless we faced our common problems together—with open minds across party lines—we would never find any solutions. It was a simple, perhaps idealistic notion, but voters seemed eager to embrace it as the fresh thinking of youth.

Again my hard work paid off. I won the seat in Parliament with a total of 28,625 votes. The following year I was reelected with almost 36,000 votes. I'm not sure New Democracy ever grasped why I was successful at the polls; they seemed to dismiss my good fortune as a fluke or an aberration. But I understood why voters responded to me. They were contemptuous of the nation's politics but didn't lump me in with all the conventional politicians. I respected them enough to tell them the truth about what needed to get done and how challenging it would be to do it. I didn't make promises I couldn't keep. Constituents took me at my word. And between voters and elected officials, trust was the rarest bond of all.

I had dreamed of becoming a member of the Hellenic Parliament. But even after I won my first election, I didn't believe that my dream had come true until I walked up the red carpet into the Parliament building. Shivers shot up my spine as I realized that I was walking the same path that Greek legislators had walked since the Parliament's founding in 1843.

With my right hand raised, I repeated the vow, "*In the name of the Holy Trinity I swear to be faithful to my Country and the Democratic State, to obey the Constitution and its laws, and to consciously fulfil my duties.*"

More shivers were to come later in the evening when I met another female member of Parliament, the woman whose picture had graced my campaign flier: Melina Mercouri. She was one of only a few individuals who were known throughout Greece by her first name. And as it turned out, as I became a public figure, I would begin to be identified by my first name, Gianna—a symbol of the closeness and comfort people felt with me. But it was the thrill of a lifetime when the seventy-year-old Melina embraced me warmly. "You are so beautiful," she said, clasping my hands. "You can do whatever you want in life. Decide and just do it. Don't ever listen to all those men bastards around you!"

Chapter 10

TURKISH DELIGHTS

I ARRIVED IN PARLIAMENT eager to continue the work I had begun on the Athens city council. I wanted to improve education and the quality of life for all Greeks. One thing I was not interested in was acquiring privileges and other perks of office that seemed to fascinate many of my fellow Parliamentarians.

It took only a few weeks after winning a seat in Parliament before the glow of my victory turned into a slow burn. I arrived one day to find the whole place abuzz with excitement. I learned that the Angelopoulos family, one of Greece's most prominent, was hosting a special ceremony in Istanbul to honor the Greek Orthodox Church. The ceremony was to be held at the Church of St. George in Fanar, for more than four centuries the seat of the Ecumenical Patriarch of Constantinople, the spiritual leader of all Greek Orthodox Christians. Burned many times over the centuries, the Church of St. George today is modest in size, in accordance with Islamic laws governing the construction of churches in what was once the capital of the Ottoman Empire. But the interior of the church is a magnificent space with majestic colonnades and rich ebony pews.

The Angelopoulos family had offered an all-expenses-paid trip to all the members of the Hellenic Parliament. All of them, that is, except me.

I knew of the Angelopoulos family's reputation from what I had read in the press. In the 1920s, the family decided to leave their impoverished home in the mountainous Arcadia area of the central Peloponnese to try their luck in Athens. Starting with nothing but a strong work ethic, they built a small operation to manufacture metals and steel wire. After their steel plant was destroyed in World War II, they rebuilt it. Their steel business underwent successive phases of modernization and expansion, playing a major role in the reconstruction of postwar Greece. The family interests diversified into operations in Switzerland, the United Kingdom, and elsewhere, as well as into shipping.

The dean of the family was the late Theodore Angelopoulos. His four sons, Angelos, Yiannis, Panagiotis, and Dimitris, followed divergent paths. Angelos, who was not involved with the family business, was an economist with an international presence. He had been a supporter early on of an alliance government in postwar Greece that included leftist members, and he took responsibility for the portfolio of social services. Yiannis passed away at an early age. Panagiotis (my husband's father) worked in the family enterprise. The "brain" of the family was Dimitris, a brilliant businessman who became my husband's mentor. As I mentioned earlier, tragically Dimitris was assassinated in 1986 by the terrorist group Revolutionary Organization 17 November.

In addition to being a successful industrialist, Panagiotis Angelopoulos was a devoted supporter of the Greek Orthodox Church. He had funded a three-year renovation of the Church of St. George as well as the reconstruction of the Ecumenical Patriarchate's main building, which had burned down in 1941.

Panagiotis Angelopoulos would also be celebrating his eightieth birthday that weekend, and the entire Greek government and Parliament were invited to attend the ceremony where he was to be honored with the title grand logothete, the highest honor bestowed by the Patriarchate of the Greek Orthodox Church. Today, his son—my husband— holds that same honor.

Thus, the ceremony honoring Panagiotis Angelopoulos was a major social and spiritual event, and the most prominent Greek businessmen, politicians, and spiritual leaders would be vying for the opportunity to be counted among the select few to witness the ceremony at the Church of St. George.

Although I was by no means a member of the Greek elite, I was nevertheless a member of Parliament, and if the Angelopoulos family had invited all of the other members to Istanbul for the ceremony, it was only fair that I receive an invitation as well. I had no idea whether the failure to invite me had been an oversight or a deliberate snub. All I knew was that it was unacceptable and I did not intend to let the insult stand. I would not be excluded from my rightful place at what would be a major event. But while I had always favored direct action, no obvious remedy occurred to me. I didn't know anyone in the Angelopoulos family, didn't even count among my friends anyone who knew the Angelopoulos family.

I instructed my assistant, Lena, to call the Athens headquarters of the steel company owned by the family and ask to speak to the manager there. Lena just stared at me and said, "Are you crazy?" I told her I wasn't crazy and that I wanted her to inform the manager of the plant that Mrs. Daskalaki had not yet received her invitation and that she wondered if it was on its way. Lena made the call but couldn't even get the manager on the phone. I told her to try again later, but still no luck. At my insistence, she kept phoning; finally, the next day, she reached the manager. She explained the situation exactly as I had asked her to and he explained that he was not a member of the Angelopoulos family. He underscored that he had no involvement with the events in Constantinople and therefore nothing at all to do with the invitations.

I told Lena that we should try approaching the problem from another direction: I would call the Patriarchate in Istanbul and explain my situation to them. I reached a very cordial Bishop Meliton who was delighted to hear from a member of the Greek Parliament. He said he hoped that I would be coming to the celebration. That was exactly the problem, I told him. I hadn't received an invitation. "How could this have happened?" he said, sounding genuinely surprised. He said he had no influence over who would receive an invitation, but if I chose to come, he would personally arrange for me to be admitted to the church for the ceremony.

Naturally, that meant I would have to pay my own way, something I really couldn't afford. Moreover, I hated the idea of being a second-class guest who had to sneak into the church through a side door. I wanted my invitation to come from the Angelopoulos family, and I wanted to walk in the front door like all of the other guests. But I decided that, regardless, I would attend, and that meant I would accept the Bishop's help because I deserved to be there. Afterward, I would confront the Angelopoulos family and tell them to their faces how ashamed they should be to have invited everybody except me.

If I could, however, I preferred to avoid such dramatics. So I told Lena to call the manager of the steel plant one more time to beseech his help. For some reason, this time he was sympathetic and willing to lend some assistance. He repeated that he had nothing to do with the matter, but that the Angelopoulos family happened to be there at that moment, working on the plans for the festivities, and he would inform them of the error.

To my surprise, he apparently did just that. I only know Theodore Angelopoulos's version of the events, which he shared with me later. The family was meeting to deal with the immense logistical problems of the weekend, including the headache of transporting so many members of the Greek Parliament, prominent judges, and a host of other powerful politicians to Istanbul. The manager of the factory appeared and said he didn't know what to do, but he had been receiving repeated calls from a Mrs. Daskalaki, distressed that she hadn't been invited. "Who is Daskalaki?" asked Panagiotis Angelopoulos. His son replied, "You know, the beautiful lady who was elected to Parliament?" And the elder gentleman said: "Ah, yes, but we can't invite her now. It's too late anyway." Theodore disagreed, suggesting it was wrong to discriminate against any member of Parliament. His father considered the matter for a few seconds and acquiesced. "Okay, invite her."

So on the Tuesday before the big weekend, Lena came into my office beaming. "I received a call and you're invited," she said, relishing what was in many ways her triumph. But a call was not good enough for me. I needed to see the invitation in writing. I needed to hold the plane tickets in my hand. It has always been and will always be that way for me. Don't tell me what will happen. Show me the documents. (When my older son, Panagiotis, was accepted to Harvard, he came to me saying, "Mom, Harvard accepted me." He probably wasn't surprised when I insisted, "Show me the letter.") The very next afternoon, I had the invitation in hand along with a letter explaining the etiquette of the occasion. Proper dress was required and suddenly I had another problem. The short skirts I owned would clearly not be appropriate. I would have to invest some money I couldn't really afford in a more formal wardrobe.

The whole affair was a mad scramble for me. But by the time I arrived at the airport to depart for Istanbul, I was just one of many politicians milling about the waiting room. I had asked a friend what to wear, and she had told me to wear something black and white during the church ceremony. Years later, when we talked to our children about how we met, Theodore insisted that I was wearing a miniskirt in the church and I showed him photos proving the opposite! I spied the elder Mr. Angelopoulos leaning against a counter as a steady stream of politicians paid their respects to him. I went over to introduce myself. How could I ever have imagined that I was meeting my future father-in-law? Or that one day my eldest son would be named after him? I said, "You don't know me Mr. Angelopoulos—"

"Oh, I think I do," he interrupted me.

I continued politely: "I want you to know how sorry I am that I was so insistent about the invitation. I wanted so much to be there and to admire your work."

"It's okay. You enjoy yourself." He understood exactly what I was saying—that I knew I was rude, but now I was very grateful—and I think he liked hearing this semi-apology from me.

And then I spotted a clean-shaven man who was wearing glasses and a conservatively tailored suit. What really conveyed his importance was that even though he appeared reserved, a lot of people were coming over to greet him. That was my first impression of Theodore. When next I looked up, he was standing right in front of me. He introduced himself as Theodore Angelopoulos—"I'm the son"—and asked if I wanted an espresso or some other refreshment. He explained that he had been present when they reviewed my request for an invitation. I told him I had already thanked his father, and I thanked him as well. "Okay," he said, though he had yet to smile, even once. "Now that you are here, enjoy yourself."

To be honest, I took him for something of an aloof industrialist. I even felt that he might be mocking me about the invitation. "Typical rich person," I thought, "who looks down on average people." All the same, I said to myself, "Okay, Gianna, you fought to be here, and now that you made it, take their advice and enjoy yourself." And that was my not very romantic first meeting with my future husband.

He would tell me later that it wasn't actually our first meeting. He had bumped into me coming up the stairs at party headquarters on the way to meet party leaders on the night of the New Democracy election victory. He introduced himself and congratulated me. "I'm Angelopoulos," he had apparently said, as if I should know exactly who he was. That night was pretty much a blur to me. Besides, he lived in Switzerland and wasn't all that visible in Greece. Although I didn't recall meeting him, I pretended I did. It seemed like the diplomatic way.

When we arrived in Istanbul, I saw Theodore again, this time with an attractive blonde in a striking red dress. She reminded me of the old movie star Lana Turner. It turned out she was a pharmacist from Zurich and, far more important, Theodore's girlfriend. I didn't have much time to think about her before being caught up in the swirl of events. We were whisked off to the Hilton Hotel where we were staying and, later, taken by bus to a fancy Turkish restaurant overlooking the Bosporus for dinner.

The restaurant was set up with long banquet tables. A short man I didn't know greeted me warmly and said he was absolutely delighted to see me there. He turned out to be the manager of the steel company, Vangelis Vavvas, the man whom Lena and I had pestered about the invitation and who proved to be our ally. He told me that in order to make amends for not sending the invitation early enough, Theodore Angelopoulos had requested that I be seated at his table. "Early enough," I thought, suddenly annoyed with this perfectly nice man who had, after all, done me such a favor. They would never have invited me at all if I hadn't insisted. But I wisely kept my thoughts to myself.

I had thought Theodore might be dining in a private room, but the manager pointed me to one of the many tables, where I saw Theodore— at this point I thought of him as that unpleasant man I had met at the airport—seated with the blonde I had spotted earlier. Our dinner group comprised some friends of Theodore, including his architect, the manager of the steel company, and the same Bishop I had called for help. "You did it," he said approvingly.

As the dinner progressed—we enjoyed doner kebabs, taramosalata, and other exquisitely prepared Turkish specialties—I began to see a very different side of Theodore. Perhaps it had simply been an awkward situation at the airport, because now he seemed genuinely solicitous of me, anxious that I should enjoy myself. But the dinner was even more awkward than the scene at the airport had been because he and his girlfriend both talked to me. She told me, in English, that she was a pharmacist and could bring me cosmetics next time she visited Greece with Theodore; he, on the other hand, was speaking Greek, which I could tell she didn't understand.

Through the evening it became pretty clear, though I hoped not to everyone else at the table, that Theodore was flirting with me. I was a little flattered, but I certainly didn't take it seriously. I wasn't thrilled when he called attention to me by announcing that something was very wrong: My wine glass was empty. He chided the Bishop seated next to me for not taking sufficient care of their special guest. "Mrs. Daskalaki is one of the newest members of Parliament," he said, teasing me, though gently. "Be sure to keep her wine glass filled."

The Bishop was wearing his traditional long black robe. When he stood up to pour me another glass of white wine, he stepped on his robe and lost his balance, spilling the contents of the bottle of wine all over my new dress. Everybody—Theodore, his friends, his girlfriend, the Bishop—was suddenly falling all over me with white napkins—like a scene out of a movie farce—to try and sop up the wine. I couldn't stop laughing. Eventually, when things calmed down, one man said: "Mrs. Daskalaki, this is good luck. Money is coming!"

And it is true that when we spill wine in Greece, we say, "*Gouri, gouri*" (Money is coming). Sometimes we even intentionally spill a few drops. So, with everybody assuring me that a fortune was coming my way, one man piped up, "Maybe this year you will become a Minister." All I could think of was that I had barely rated an invitation to this party, and now I was ascending the political ladder very rapidly.

The chatter was very lively—the accidental spill had given Theodore an excuse to be even more solicitous of me—when a platter of fruit arrived for dessert. I was feeling the wine a bit, if largely through my dress, and I joked: "Only fruit for dessert? No Turkish delights?" Theodore was clearly delighted with my jest. In Greek, he urged me to return with him to his hotel where, he assured me, he had the very best Turkish delights in his room. I was slightly taken aback, wondering, "Who does this guy think he is?" So I said ironically, "You mean I should come to your room for Turkish delights?" No, he said, he would be happy to bring them down to me in the lobby. I smiled and treated the Turkish delights banter as a joke.

When the dinner was over, I was putting on my coat to head back to my bus when I sensed someone hovering behind me. It was Theodore, asking if I would join him on his bus. "Your bus, my bus, what's the difference?" I asked. "Aren't they both going to the same place?" Theodore, who seemed to be a much warmer and more genuine person than I had originally thought, replied, "Just give me the pleasure of your company." When I sat down on his bus, he sat next to me, and I could see that one of his associates was seated next to the girlfriend.

It wasn't a long ride, but Theodore had lots of questions. He asked about my election campaign, about my family, and about how my family felt about my career decisions. "My family has nothing to do with that," I told him. "I decide how I lead my life." When we arrived at the hotel where all of the guests were staying, he made good on his promise and sent somebody to his room for the Turkish delights. All of a sudden I was talking and laughing with a small group that included Evert, the Mayor of Athens, several members of the Supreme Court, including its chief judge, and Theodore of course.

As much as I was enjoying myself, I thought it would be appropriately discreet on my part to make an early exit from our happy gathering. Theodore insisted on one final bit of gallantry, escorting me to the elevator to say good night. He would later tell me that his girlfriend was furious over his behavior that evening. Theodore had been annoyed. "Why the big fuss?" he had asked her. "I was just being polite." One should never underestimate a woman's intuition in such matters. Sometimes we can smell fire even when there is no smoke.

Chapter 11

UN COUP DE FOUDRE

ON SUNDAY MORNING, everybody had to get up early to head over to the church for what we knew would be a long ceremony. I had just enough time to have a cup of coffee before getting on one of the last two buses to depart. When we arrived, the Church of St. George was already overflowing with guests inside and was thronged with eager onlookers and a TV crew outside. Tzannis Tzannetakis, who in the past had served a brief stint as Prime Minister in an interim government and was standing with me at the entrance, took one look at the mob scene and gave up. "We can't get through," he said. "I will just stay outside."

But after fighting so hard to get invited, I wasn't going to miss out. My constituents were going to see that I was important enough to be an insider.

So I just kept inching forward, saying "excuse me, excuse me" until I had pushed my way into the church. Eventually I managed to reach an excellent standing position from which to view events. I wound up directly opposite the Angelopoulos clan, including, naturally, Theodore. To my discomfort, he appeared to be staring at me as I took my place. When the ceremony began, I tried not to look over at him. But every so often I would take a peek across the church and every single time he seemed to be looking right back at me.

It turned out I took a lot of peeks because, as I expected, it was a very long ceremony. The church was hot and crowded and the air was thick with the scent of incense. After more than three hours on my feet, with no food in my stomach, I began to feel woozy. I was afraid that my desire to be seen by my constituents might be more than fulfilled if I were to faint and be carried out of the church. I summoned what remained of my strength and pushed back a few places to where I found some government Ministers' wives who were sympathetic. They got an elderly member of Parliament to relinquish his seat to me and, in a church miracle, found me some drinking water too. By the time the ceremony ended half an hour later, I had regained my equilibrium.

When I was leaving the church, I encountered a prominent ambassador, Christos Machairitsas, who asked what had happened to me during the ceremony. I told him the truth, namely, that I had felt light-headed and feared I was going to faint. "Mrs. Daskalaki," he said, "if I were you and Mr. Angelopoulos had been staring at me in such an intense fashion, I would have fainted too." So it wasn't my imagination. And apparently it had been quite obvious to anyone who had been paying attention.

Ambassador Machairitsas was headed to a VIP reception hosted by the Angelopoulos family and invited me to accompany him. When we got there, Theodore approached me and he too inquired what had happened to me in the church. I explained briefly, but then tried to engage him in slightly more formal conversation, which I thought more appropriate for the occasion. I thanked him and his family again for creating something so special and meaningful to the Greek people. "I feel very honored as a Greek to be here," I said. He started laughing and replied, "And I wanted to thank you for all those hours you stood opposite me, giving me somewhere to look." "Oh my," I thought.

The next morning I had an early departure back to Athens because I wanted to prepare for a meeting at Parliament that evening. (I took great pride in never missing a meeting. Even when I lost my voice—as I did a few times—I would attend and pass notes.) A few other government officials were there when I arrived in the hotel lobby. Just as we were about to depart, Theodore showed up, thanked us all for coming, and wished us a safe trip. On the way to the airport, one government Minister said: "That Angelopoulos is truly fantastic. He got up early just to bid us good-bye." Theodore would later confide that the sole reason he had roused himself early was because he wanted to see me one more time.

A few days later I wrote to the elder Mr. Angelopoulos, thanking him for the extraordinary weekend. When Theodore learned of my note, he called me at my office. At first, when I was told it was Mr. Angelopoulos on the phone, I thought my office was playing a joke. But indeed it was Theodore, telling me that they had received my gracious letter. "That's the least I could do to thank you for your hospitality," I replied. And then because sometimes I don't know when to stop and shut up, I added, "I wish I could do something more to reciprocate." He assured me that I could. "Invite me to lunch," he said. Oops. I explained that I was very busy in my new position, but he wasn't listening to any excuses. He would be in Athens just two more days, so he proposed lunch the very next day. I believe I was shaking my head "no," but what came out of my mouth was, "Okay."

Honestly, it didn't feel okay at all. It wasn't that I never dined alone with men. But the occasion was always business, something required by my job—never a purely social encounter. Even though my relationship with my husband at that point was difficult, I was still a married woman and I respected my marriage. And Theodore was involved with the woman I had seen in Istanbul. Besides, we had nothing at all in common except a shared weekend. What was I going to say to him? Yet I was stuck. I would have looked even more foolish if I had changed my mind and canceled our lunch.

Nothing happened the next day to relieve my anxiety. I had a meeting that morning with nurses at a major hospital. Theodore had made the reservation at a fancy French restaurant, Abreuvoir, in the chic Kolonaki area, a cab ride's distance from the hospital. That day there was a general strike in Athens—not an uncommon occurrence—so when I emerged from the hospital, traffic was at a standstill. I always wore high heels, even when I was campaigning. My father destroyed his feet in the war, and I like to say that I destroyed mine in stilettos. However, I had no choice but to hoof it. I sprinted the last five hundred yards so that I arrived only fifteen minutes late.

Theodore was standing at the door—I thought maybe he was getting ready to leave—and it was clear that he was quite cross. I think he wanted to show me that he was no pushover, not someone who could be taken for granted. When I caught my breath, I apologized profusely, explained the problem, and tried to calm him down. I was quite anxious when we were seated, so it took me a while to realize that we were the only diners in the restaurant. Theodore must have booked the entire restaurant—he won't admit it to this day—so that we could be alone. That only made me more nervous, a conspicuous reminder that not only did we not belong together, we did not live in the same world. He proceeded to order lunch—*une salade Cote d'Azur, un filet Café de Paris*, and *pommes frites*—without even asking me what I wanted.

I had agreed to this lunch so I figured I'd try to make the best of it. To melt the ice, I started talking about my daughter and brought out pictures to show him. He relaxed a little—the wine helped us both—and he talked some about his life and his work. And slowly, over a very long lunch, we began to talk quite easily and openly. As he had in Istanbul, he asked a lot of questions about my job and my family, and, surprisingly, I found him to be an excellent listener. I began unburdening myself about my marriage, revealing that it was unhappy and that I could not count on my husband for support. I told Theodore I didn't know what to do about it or, indeed, if I was going to do anything at all, because my greatest responsibility was to provide for my daughter.

The conversation was flowing so comfortably and had become so intimate that I found myself becoming nervous again. I told him that this engagement was uncomfortable for me and that I hadn't a clue why we were lunching together in the first place. "Because I wanted to see you," he replied calmly, then added, "and I want to see you again."

"Why?" I persisted.

"Because I want to."

"But don't you understand my situation?"

"Yes, I do." He was persistent, though not intimidating. His voice was surprisingly soft and his tone was gentle. And he seemed so certain of himself and what he wanted. As I have learned through the years, when Theodore is certain, it is very hard to tell him, "No, I won't do that." It's pretty much the equivalent of telling me, "No, you can't do that." It's no deterrent at all.

After we exited the restaurant and were chattering away on the street, we almost bumped into a woman who was the wife of his former brother-in-law. "This is exactly what I didn't want," he said after she left. But I was less focused on the awkward encounter than on a revelation that hadn't come out at lunch. "You have an ex-wife?" I asked. "Of course I have an ex-wife," he replied. Then I asked him if the boys who were standing next to him in the church in Istanbul were his sons.

"Those boys are my nephews," he said. "I don't have any children, and I don't think I ever will."

As we were nearing the corner where we would go our separate ways, he asked, with some urgency in his voice: "Do you think it will be possible to see you again? I want to see you. Do you want to see me?" And while I struggled to find the right words, I knew I couldn't refuse him. Nevertheless, all I managed was a feeble response that I didn't really know what I wanted, but that our time together had been nice. Then I panicked again and started repeating how complicated it all was. He just kind of hushed me and said, "It's okay—one step at a time." And then, as we were standing in the middle of the street, he leaned over and kissed me.

"I will invite you to my house when I return from Switzerland next week."

"I can't possibly come to your house," I protested.

"I can't come to your office and you are clearly nervous about being out in public. So where might you suggest? The least you can do is let me offer you a cup of coffee at my home. No matter where we meet, we will find a way."

"A way for what?"

"A way for you to decide if you want to see me. Probably you won't want to see me again. Or maybe I won't want to see you again."

It wasn't the most promising note on which to part. But neither of those things happened. Our relationship proved to be a *coup de foudre*. I was completely smitten with Theodore. He was strong and solid, yet also understanding and supportive. He started coming to Athens weekly, which had people in his office wondering since he normally came only about once a month. Remarkably, we managed to keep our relationship out of the public eye. On the few occasions we dined out, it was in undistinguished restaurants where we were unlikely to meet anyone we knew. As an added precaution, I wore big glasses as a disguise. Only his house staff and, eventually, my most trusted associate, Lena, knew of our relationship, and they all knew to keep silent.

My work in Parliament continued. On one day in 1990 when Theodore and I had planned to meet, my party sent me quite unexpectedly to Crete to deliver a speech on education policy. This was in the days before mobile phones and I had no way to let Theodore know that I would miss our date. I couldn't call his office because I couldn't identify myself to whoever answered the phone. I decided I would send Lena to his office with an apologetic note and flowers, which she concealed in a big handbag.

Security was very tight at the Angelopoulos offices because his family had been targeted by terrorists in the past. But Lena has always been a force of nature, and somehow, despite refusing to identify herself, she talked her way into the building and up to the floor where Theodore's office was located. Security was less receptive there and wouldn't let Lena proceed, but she caused enough of a commotion to bring Theodore out of his office. Mind you, at this point, he and Lena had never met. All Theodore saw was this attractive woman insisting she had to see him urgently.

"What do you want?" he asked politely.

"I can only tell you that in private," she replied.

He insisted that she tell him there and then, but still she refused. Exasperated and perceiving no threat in this elegantly dressed woman, he gave in and waved her into his office. He was standing behind his desk when he saw her reach into her handbag; he instantly recoiled, thinking, "Could she possibly be reaching for a gun?"

When she pulled out a bouquet of flowers and an envelope with my handwriting, he relaxed. His face lit up, and he invited Lena to sit down and have a coffee. She politely declined. Mission impossible had become mission accomplished.

Even though I kept our relationship secret from almost everyone, I couldn't help but tell my mother that I was dating someone without mentioning his name. She was thrilled at the news and at the happiness that my new relationship had brought me. A few days later, she gave me some *halva*, her favorite dessert, to give to my new beau.

I'm not sure how long we would have been able to maintain our secret. Theodore was beginning to chafe at the restrictive nature of our relationship. A few times he even insisted on driving me to political events, figuring that in a suit he could pass for my chauffeur! There were always bigger-name politicians in attendance; had Theodore been spotted, everyone would have assumed he was there to hear one of them. Nobody could have imagined he was coming to see a little-known freshman member of Parliament. One time I was going around kissing all the people in campaign fashion when Theodore demanded that I kiss him too. "Since you're keeping me a secret, then at least kiss me like you kiss everybody else here," he said. "If you don't I'll tell the world our secret." So I kissed him—exactly like I kissed everybody else.

I didn't like sneaking around any more than Theodore did. We had been together just a few months and already I was exhausted from my double life. I was getting home either very late or very early. One night Carolina asked: "Why is Mommy away? Are there beds in Parliament?"

I had many good cries over the tangled mess my life had become. Sometimes a good cry clears everything out of your system—and sometimes it clears everything up too. That's what happened for me. I decided I couldn't wallow in self-pity any longer. Instead, I would do what came far more naturally. I would take action. I was very much in love with Theodore. My brief time with him had made clear to me which of the two relationships I valued most. I told Theodore that before we could proceed further with our lives together, I had to resolve my marital situation. He asked if I needed any help. "No," I said, "I will deal with this alone."

Chapter 12

SECOND CHANCES

I HAD GOTTEN INTO MY MARITAL MESS ALL BY MYSELF, and I thought it was only fair—both the right thing and the brave thing—that I end it all by myself. There were also practical considerations. Discretion was of utmost importance. Elections would be held again in April, the third national election in less than a year, and I had to run again to hold my seat. It obviously wouldn't help my campaign if my name started appearing in the gossip columns rather than in the news pages. Moreover, beyond any potential for scandal, I didn't want Theodore thrust into my political life.

In the spring of 1990, after seven years of a contentious marriage, I decided to confront my husband. The conversation with him proved to be much like the marriage; it didn't go well at all. I didn't mince words. "Our paths are different," I said. "This marriage is over." He didn't

mince words either. He was furious and combative. He threatened that
he would never grant me a divorce, and he warned that if I pursued one,
he would humiliate me publicly. As unsettling as his threats were, they
didn't deter me. "Do as you like," I said. I left the room, took Carolina
by the hand, grabbed only my passport and identity card, and left home
for good. Other than the clothes on my back, I left behind everything I
owned. I just wanted to get out of that house.

It didn't take me long to realize that trying to handle my extraction
from this marital mess alone might have been the honorable path, but
it was a foolish one. Since my husband seemed as miserable as I was
in the marriage, I had hoped we could dissolve it amicably. Once he
threatened me, however, it was clear I needed some help. My parents
happened to be coming to visit, so I asked a friend to pick them up at
the airport. I didn't have enough money to secure accommodations for
them, so I asked Theodore if he could arrange a hotel room for them
as well as Carolina and me. And the next day I called a high-powered
lawyer, Alexandros Lykourezos, whom I had met when, as a law student,
I went to see him perform in court. I didn't expect him to remember
me, but I was pretty sure he would recognize my name. When I phoned,
however, my name didn't get me past his secretary, who informed me
that he was busy and didn't have any appointments available. I hung up,
went directly to his office, and confronted her. "If he knows I asked to
see him and you didn't allow me," I told her, "he will be very cross." This
time, with me standing right in front of her, she agreed to speak to him.
And he agreed to speak to me.

I had no idea how much he normally charged to handle a divorce. I
told him money wasn't an issue because I had none. When he laughed
at my predicament, I took that as a good sign. There was no reason he
should do me this favor, but I suggested that, having gone through a

divorce himself, he knew how painful it was to be stuck in a bad relationship. "I'm trapped," I said. "And he threatens me. Please help me." And Lykourezos did, a gentleman helping a woman in distress.

Despite that good news, Theodore was not optimistic. His own divorce had been an ordeal and had taken more than four years to complete. But my lawyer was very good and very tough, and the fact that we did not have many assets to fight over proved to be an advantage. It also helped that I was making no demands on my husband and was willing to leave all material possessions behind. In the end, despite my ex-husband's anger and bluster, I got my divorce in just twenty-nine days, which must be some kind of Greek national record. What is not known publicly is that—despite the ugliness surrounding our divorce—I would later help my ex-husband financially. Credit goes to Theodore for that idea. He believed it was important to try and maintain a civilized relationship with my former husband, if only for Carolina's sake.

Almost overnight, a life that had been riddled with turmoil and despair was transformed into a calm and remarkably sunny existence. I was happily divorced and had moved, with my parents and Carolina, into a small but lovely apartment near the presidential palace in central Athens. And I had easily won the 1990 reelection in April, garnering 25 percent more votes than in my first run. New Democracy had won big as well. And I was even happy to see Constantinos Mitsotakis, a man who had both mentored and betrayed me, finally assume the office of Prime Minister. We had made our peace and, if further proof of that were required, he would become the godfather to my second son, Dimitris. (The ceremony in which Mitsotakis became godfather, Dimitris's baptism, was unique in that it was personally conducted, for the first time, by His All Holiness Bartholomew, the Ecumenical Patriarch of the Greek Orthodox Church.) And most important, I had introduced Carolina to Theodore and the two of them had clicked immediately.

Her favorite of all her stuffed animals was the huge white bear named Teddy, and to her Theodore was just another big "Teddy." For a man who had no children, Theodore was remarkably kind and patient with my little six-year-old.

We took the next big step as a couple when I agreed to visit Theodore's home in Zurich. He had insisted that making this visit was important, so I arranged to take two days off from Parliament. Given that I pretty much worked all the time, this was a big deal for me. After Theodore picked me up in Zurich, we drove into the city and entered the garage of a building that didn't look like it could be a home. Had I been asked to guess where we were headed, I would still be guessing today. The correct answer turned out to be a bank, and I found myself—with no clue why—sitting in the office of the bank's CEO while he and Theodore conversed in German. I couldn't follow much of it, but I understood when the banker asked Theodore, "Are you sure about this?" Theodore assured him he was, and the banker presented me with some papers to sign. Theodore explained that he felt responsible for both me and my daughter. Who knew what the future would hold for us as a couple, he wondered. He told me he had a history of minor heart problems. I could find myself all alone with my daughter. "I don't think I will ever have children," he said. "And it will make me very happy to know that you and Carolina will always be secure." He wanted to ensure that no matter what happened between us, Carolina and I would be well taken care of.

Nothing he said, however, could have prepared me for what came next. The documents the bank CEO presented to me revealed that Theodore's gesture was an amount that, at that time, made me dizzy.

Theodore's extraordinary generosity was the first of many things I experienced during a brief trip that was beyond my wildest dreams. After our bank visit, we went to Theodore's home. It was three floors (with an underground swimming pool), and each floor was, essentially, a separate apartment. The top floor was his bachelor pad: light and airy, with lots of marble and beautiful antique furniture. It was the home of somebody with excellent taste and the money to exercise it. But what really took my breath away was the art displayed on the walls. I was staring at paintings the likes of which I had seen only in books or museums. At least that's what I assumed I was looking at. There was one painting of two female dancers that I couldn't take my eyes off. I was pretty sure I knew the artist. But I was already dizzied by the extraordinary events of the day, so I didn't quite trust myself. The last thing I wanted was to appear uneducated and uncultured. I inquired tentatively, "Is that what I think it is?" I expected Theodore to launch into an expansive discourse on his artwork. Instead, he simply said, "Yes." End of the day's art lesson!

I didn't pursue the matter. But that night, after he went to sleep, I found a magnifying glass in his study and sneaked out to examine the paintings. Below the two dancers was the very signature I had expected: Degas. There was also a Renoir, a Picasso, and two Pierre Bonnards. I remember thinking I really was a world away from Crete.

My next surprise came early the next morning. Very early! It was just 6:00 AM when I was awoken, having sensed a shadow in my room. It was Theodore, who apparently found it perfectly normal to rise at that hour. I have always worked long hours, but I hate it when I have to start really early in the morning since I am always careful to look my best. (This would become a problem for me when I ran the Athens 2004 Olympic effort and had to meet regularly at 7:00 AM with the International Olympic Coordination Commission.) Seeing Theodore appear so cheery at six o'clock in the morning, I buried my head in the pillow so he wouldn't hear me groan and thought, "My God, it will be a nightmare if I stay with this man."

The day didn't turn out to be anybody's idea of a nightmare, however. *Au contraire*. By the time I was both awake and presentable, Theodore was ready to present me with what he called "our options."

"What do you think if we spend the day in Zurich and later have dinner at the Kronenhalle restaurant and enjoy its magnificent art collection?"

"Or?" I asked playfully.

"Or, we could take the car and drive about an hour outside Zurich to visit a very picturesque medieval town, Schaffhausen, where there is a lovely little hotel with a three-star restaurant."

"Or?" I said, continuing to tease him.

"Or," he paused, "there is another option, but I should check the forecast first." After a quick phone call, he turned back to me. "The forecast is very good for Switzerland and Italy. We could take a private jet to Genoa where my yacht is docked and from there sail to Portofino."

"That third option," I said. "That one sounds okay."

It was okay indeed! Very, very okay. The roughly one-hundred-foot yacht (it seemed to me more like three hundred feet!) had an Italian crew, and while they sailed, Theodore gave me the tour. In the VIP guest bedroom, I admired the sheets on the bed. Theodore said, "Elizabeth Taylor liked them too." Apparently I was not the first date to sail on the *Alfa* with Theodore.

I had packed light for my Zurich trip—it may have been the only time I ever traveled with Theodore and just one suitcase—and had brought just my two best parliamentary suits. They were fine for work, but hardly appropriate for boating and touring along the Italian Riviera. It wasn't as if I had cruise wear lying around. Even Theodore, who was hardly fashion conscious, always wearing one of his one hundred identical suits, recognized that I looked a little ridiculous standing on the docks of Portofino in heels and a business suit. He gestured, "Come."

And so I entered one of the true fashion temples, the Hermes store, for the first—but not the last—time in my life. Theodore bought me a few things to wear, a pair of flats, and a tracksuit that was both casual and stylish and which I have to this day.

It has been that way my whole life with Theodore: always surprises, both big and small. He loves complex arrangements with a little deception thrown in. Like a magician, he performs for an audience, enjoying my reaction as much as I enjoy the surprise. I remember one birthday in London, for example, when he gave me Tiffany boxes with gifts hidden under other gifts. Only after pretending how thrilled I was to receive a mobile phone and then a simple clock did I discover the Harry Winston ring along with a beautiful set of earrings. Theodore makes everything more fun than it already is. Twenty years on and I have never been bored with him.

Athens 2004 opening ceremony (top) *and closing ceremony* (bottom)

Yiannis Papadakis, my mother's father

First dancing lesson

My maternal grandparents, Rodanthe Mpitzaraki and Yiannis Papadakis, circa 1919

My mother, Marika Papadaki (being held by her babysitter), *and her two older siblings before their father passed away*

My paternal grandmother sent this photo to her husband, who was working in the United States, to show him how their children had grown. My father, Frixos, is on the left.

Frixos Daskalakis (seated)

Aunt Ioanna,
Frixos's sister

My parents' wedding day, in January 1955. Joining the happy couple are (from left to right) *Aunt Ioanna*; *Grandmother Parthenia*; *Radamanthes*, my father's best man; and my cousin *Lena*.

On their honeymoon, my father took his young bride to visit the Parthenon.

Rebellious Gianna, leading her parents

My first birthday, with Grandmother Rodanthe

My first boyfriend, Nikos. Sorry, Theodore!

Aunt Ioanna, me, and my mother. My mother and I share the same fashion sense: polka-dotted dresses.

In our garden in Embaros

My paternal family in the courtyard of the Embaros homestead: (back row, from left to right) Aunt Ioanna, my father, my mother; *(front row, from left to right)* my grandmother, me, and my grandfather

My father (far right) *worked to promote exports from Crete. Here, he is inspecting chopped fruit at a citrus factory.*

Here, chunky Gianna and her chunky younger sister, Eleni, stand on the Acropolis in contrast to the caryatids, the most beautiful women in the ancient world.

In a school parade, I march at the head of the line in honor of my good grades.

The boisterous Gianna on a high school excursion with Thalia (back row, second from left) *and Stella* (front row, center). *In college, we were known as the "Three Graces."*

The metamorphosis is under way. Dreaming about the escape.

Young lawyer Gianna, "the golden horse"

Marching in solidarity with a lawyers' strike with my sister, Eleni (far right)

Campaigning everywhere—even the meat market—here with Miltiadis Evert, Mayor to be (center, in dark suit)

The secret ingredient to my campaign: basil seeds

Handing out basil seeds on a shoestring campaign for Athens city council

Schooltime. Working to improve the Athens school system.

Carolina, Teddy, and me

Briefing the beneficiaries

Gavdos

With a priest in Gavdos

Taking the oath of office for my first term in the Hellenic Parliament

Melina Mercouri ... "Don't ever listen to all those men bastards around you!"

Addressing the Hellenic Parliament

Constantinos Mitsotakis, leader of the New Democracy party, with his female MPs

Entering my fate. Walking into the Church of St. George, Fanar, Istanbul—after having hijacked (almost) the invitation.

The first picture together (and apart) with my future husband, Theodore. In the back row stand Theodore and his father and mother.

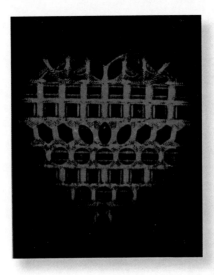

I gave my heart to Theodore
(Andy Warhol, from our collection).

Ready for my wedding on July 26, 1990,
in the Claude Montana suit I converted
into my "wedding gown"

Presiding over the wedding was Papa
Vassilis, who almost denied us the
authorization to get married because
Theodore didn't have the proper
documents.

A new family:
(from left
to right) my
sister, my father,
Theodore, me,
my mother, our
best man, my
father-in-law,
my mother-in-
law. Standing
behind them are
Theodore's brother,
and his family.

Twenty-one-year-old Theodore serving in the Greek navy

Theodore as a young businessman with his Uncle Dimitris, his mentor

The Angelopoulos Dynasty: (front row, from left to right) *Uncle Yiannis, Uncle Dimitris, Uncle Angelos, and Panagiotis (Theodore's father);* (back row, from left to right) *Constantinos (Theodore's brother), Dimitris (Angelos's son), and Theodore*

Theodore was very moved by the christening of our first son, Panagiotis. I was the encouraging mother.

For the first time as Patriarch, Bartholomew performs a baptism: our son Dimitris's in the Church of St. George, Fanar, Istanbul.

*Leaving the Hirslanden hospital
in Zurich with Dimitris on
my left arm, Panagiotis on my
right arm, and Carolina happy
to have two soldiers under
her command. Theodore was
wondering how on earth he had
acquired such a large family in
less than two years.*

*Forceful love
expressed by
Panagiotis for
Dimitris. Grandma
Marika looks on.*

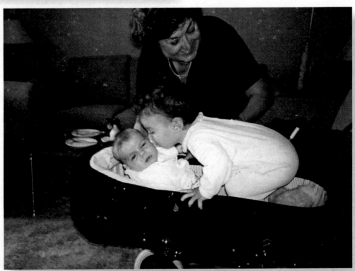

*Two grandmothers,
a young couple,
and their heirs
dressed in
traditional Greek
tsolias costumes*

Christening one of our ships . . .

And another . . .

And another . . .

And a yacht for a change!

Sailing, competing . . .

and winning.

Carrying the weight of the family

The first trip to the "Big Apple" for Pan and Dim

Happy cruising on our yacht around Mykonos

First day in London, first day in the Greek school

Housewarming reception in the Old Rectory, Chelsea, London

Drawing room in the Old Rectory set for a luncheon

The gazebo in the garden prepared for another luncheon

Chapter 13

NO GAIN WITHOUT PAIN

THOUGH WE HAD STROLLED THROUGH THE STREETS of Portofino together, Theodore and I continued to be very discreet when we were out in Athens. Both of us were well known and neither of us was eager to find our lives discussed or, worse, dismembered in the gossip columns. And it seemed like only a matter of time. I had confessed my secret to Lena only after another staffer had told her that something strange was going on. The young woman had heard me in my office—it was late and I thought everyone had gone home—singing a passionate love song called "I Dare" (the title in Greek is "Tolmó," performed by Marinella) about giving up everything for just one moment with the one you adore.

Women in public life have to get used to a lot of unsavory speculation about their private lives. And once I was divorced, it was inevitable that nasty gossip about me began to circulate. Fortunately, none of it

involved Theodore. When he called my office, he always used the name
Mr. Nikos, one of the most common names in Greece. He expected me
to know instantly that he was the "Nikos" that was calling. One day in
July 1990 "Mr. Nikos" called, expressing a need to talk to me as soon
as possible. I was participating in a parliamentary commission meeting
on employment, so Lena dispatched an office volunteer to deliver the
message. I found a pay phone and called Theodore, who said, with
surprising urgency in his voice, "I have to see you." I told him I had a
long day of work ahead, but he insisted, "Find a way."

This was extremely unusual. I had never heard Theodore sound
quite so insistent—at least not with me. But when you find someone
like him—a gift from God (which is what his name means in Greek)—
you do as he says and find a way. A couple of hours later, I excused
myself and hurried to my apartment. Theodore was there playing with
Carolina. When I arrived, he told her that we needed to be alone. "Do
you want to kiss my mom?" Carolina asked. "I want to watch."

"I'll kiss your mom in front of you, but this is something serious,"
he told her.

This talk out of the blue about "something serious" made me
uneasy, but Theodore got to the point quickly. "I want to marry you
next Thursday, July 26, 1990!"

I didn't swoon. Instead, I said, "Are you crazy?"

"I am crazy," he agreed. "But experience has taught me that sometimes
if you wait for the timing to be perfect it's a mistake. Sometimes you wait
to see if the match is perfect, and by the time you decide to get married,
it's about time to get separated. I'm fed up keeping our relationship a
secret. We're free and I want to marry you. So before I change my mind,
please tell me whether you will marry me next Thursday. If so, I have to
leave right away because I have to go inform my parents that I intend to
marry you. Either they will approve of our marriage or they won't. On

my way back, I'll come to meet your parents. Either they will approve of our marriage or they won't. I don't care. Either way, you and I will marry."

I was so overwhelmed by his sudden proposal that I could only think about practical considerations. "I am honored by your proposal, and I would happily marry you, but we can't possibly take care of everything in a week's time." That should reveal how shaken I was by his surprise. Never before had I admitted I couldn't do the impossible.

Theodore was having none of it. "You are a lawyer. You are a member of Parliament. Don't tell me you can't find a way to plan a wedding!" And so we agreed to be married one week from that day at the Agia Varvara church near his parents' home, in Chalandri.

Since he was leaving almost immediately—he was going home to Zurich, then flying to the United States, where his parents were traveling, and then returning to Athens for the wedding—it occurred to me that I had better measure his finger for a wedding ring. He had brought some sweets from Zurich for Carolina, and I took the ribbon off the package and wrapped it around his ring finger. (The ring turned out to be way too big. It dangled on Theodore's finger during the wedding ceremony.) Then he was gone. And I was engaged.

After Theodore left, I went to tell my parents the good news. My mother burst into tears. It's her way. She cries through the greatest catastrophes and the greatest joys. This was without doubt one of the latter. My father was not in good health—he had suffered a few strokes in recent years—but his mind remained sharp. He scolded his wife for such histrionics. "Don't you dare cry for our daughter. This is the very best thing that could happen to her." Then he turned to me and said: "Gianna, I'm so proud of you for so many things. And I am especially proud that now you will be part of this great family."

Later my mother told me that she knew things would turn out this way because she had been praying to God!

The next day I went to the office and told Lena the news. "Thank God I'm sitting," she said. I only told Lena and one other close friend, Tania, of our plans. The two of them took care of pretty much everything from the rings to the flowers. I didn't have all that much to do.

I didn't want anyone to find out about the marriage, so I went to a fashionable store to buy a suit instead of a wedding gown. They recognized me right away. I told them I was looking for something light for summer but also suitable for special occasions.

"For the Parliament?" they asked.

"No, not exactly."

"For a funeral?"

"Not at all."

Slightly mystified, they recommended a Claude Montana suit in fine white linen—with a short skirt, of course. It was perfect for me, but it had buttons that were too plain.

"I love the suit," I told them, "but do you have buttons that are more suitable for evening wear?"

They found the perfect buttons, and that was how I created my "wedding gown."

My only other responsibility was to arrange the newspaper announcement that was a legal requirement for the marriage. I placed it discreetly in a provincial newspaper a good distance from central Athens.

When Theodore called me three days before our scheduled wedding date to ask how everything was proceeding, I could honestly say things were going remarkably well. All we needed was for him to be sure to bring his certificate of divorce so that we could get the marriage license. He said he would arrive in Athens the next day, Tuesday, with the papers, and we'd take care of everything. That Tuesday evening happened to be the date of the most prestigious political reception at the presidential palace in celebration of democracy. It was the first time

8

I had been invited to this annual event and I felt some pangs of disappointment to have to miss it.

Theodore likewise wasn't in the best of moods when he arrived. He had had a tense week. In Zurich, he had to impress upon his former girlfriend that their relationship was truly finished. (Apparently she had kept their breakup a secret because later, when news leaked out that Theodore Angelopoulos was married, people began calling to congratulate her!)

Then Theodore caught up with his parents, who weren't exactly thrilled when he told them the news. I hadn't expected them to approve, given the hasty marriage, the ambitious woman he was marrying, the interjection of politics into a family that considered itself nonpolitical, and the fact that I was recently divorced and had a daughter.

Theodore had been surprised that they didn't seem entirely shocked by the disclosure of our relationship. The explanation proved again what a small world our big world is. His parents had been traveling with the American Archbishop of the Greek Orthodox Church, Iakovos. About a month earlier, I had accompanied Theodore to Boston where he underwent a medical examination. The doctor's very next patient was Archbishop Iakovos. Apparently the doctor couldn't resist sharing the "Greek" news about the woman from Parliament who, just moments earlier, had been there with Theodore Angelopoulos. The Archbishop was regarded as a consummate politician—some Greeks called him CIAkovos—because of his intelligence-gathering skill, and he, in turn, must have dished to Theodore's parents. Regardless of their initial distress, I considered it an honor to become a member of the Angelopoulos family, and I was intent on proving myself worthy. When Theodore left his parents in the United States, he told them the wedding would take place that week with or without them. I considered it a good sign when they chose to come and celebrate with us.

The next step was procedural, the one that required us to make certain promises as to our intentions as well to provide our certificates of divorce. I chose a priest (Papa Vassilis) that my mother knew to handle the paperwork, and when he saw the two of us together—he knew me personally and Theodore because of his family's preeminence in the church—he was clearly thrilled. He said he considered it a special privilege to assist us with this formality. So we proceeded through the assorted details—"Yes, our children will have the name Angelopoulos"— until the moment came when he needed to see the divorce certificates. I gave him mine, waiting for Theodore to show his.

Theodore dug into his briefcase and, after much rummaging, pulled out a pink piece of paper and laid it triumphantly in front of us. Theodore wasn't wearing his glasses, but I could see all too clearly what was written on top of the document in huge letters: THIS IS ONLY A COPY. IT IS NOT VALID FOR MARRIAGE.

The priest apologized as he pointed out the problem to Theodore and told him that he needed the original document. The priest also suggested it wouldn't be such a big deal to delay the wedding just a few days beyond the twenty-sixth to get our papers in order. Now Theodore, who had just gone through a trying week with his ex-girlfriend and his parents, got a little steamed. The priest apologized again but explained that there was nothing he could do without the proper papers. "Look," Theodore said, "I'm going to marry Gianna in two days. Either you want it to happen here or you don't. If you don't we will go to Las Vegas and get married there."

"My son, not to Las Vegas," the priest demurred with as much genuine horror as if he had been told Satan would be the best man.

"Yes," Theodore repeated. "I'll marry her in Las Vegas and everyone will know that a member of Parliament and the son of Panagiotis Angelopoulos couldn't get married in the Greek Orthodox Church because you didn't allow it." The priest was murmuring an apology and saying, "But my son . . ." when Theodore stormed out.

He was so angry that he didn't say a word. And I kept quiet too because I didn't want to irritate him further. I was scared that I might say, "Are you so stupid that you couldn't bring the proper document?" When we arrived at his house, he shut himself in his study. After about ten minutes, he burst out of the room; it was a different Theodore, though, wearing a big smile on his face. "I called my lawyer," he said.

His cousin Nikos Tritsimpidas had handled his divorce, so Theodore inquired if he had any idea what had happened to the divorce papers. The answer both amazed and amused him. "You don't remember, Theodore?" Nikos said. "You told me, 'Lock it in a safe and don't give it to me. I don't ever want to get remarried.'" Theodore laughed and told Nikos that he had had a change of mind and a change of heart. Now he wanted that precious paper in his hands.

We thought we had dealt with the last of our wedding problems, but there proved to be one final snag. While Theodore was in the United States, his mother had asked if she could do anything to help. He took that as an encouraging gesture, so he asked if she would contact the priest who would conduct the ceremony (Papa Christos) and make sure everything was set at the church. When he informed me of this, I sat silently. He read my silence correctly. "You think this may not be such a good idea?" he asked. I didn't say a word. "Maybe you're right. I know the priest. I'll call him." But after several futile attempts to reach him, Theodore was told the priest was away on vacation. "He can't be on holiday," Theodore objected, "because I'm sure my mother told him that I'm getting married in two days."

It took a few hours, but we discovered that the priest was in a small village somewhere in the middle of Greece. Theodore obtained a phone number for the local coffee shop and the proprietor there located the priest. After a time, Theodore was put in touch with the priest. "Why are you still on holiday?" Theodore asked.

"Why not?" the priest replied.

"Didn't my mother call you and tell you that I was getting married the day after tomorrow?" The priest obviously had no idea.

Theodore asked him to come home—"take a taxi"—that very night. "Please, I need you to be there."

"Certainly, my son," he replied. "I'm sorry that your mother couldn't find me." The priest had one last question. "Do you have all the necessary documents?"

"Don't worry, I will have them," Theodore promised. "Trust me!"

The next day we met the parents. I wanted to bring a small gift to his mother, so I raced out to buy some confectioneries on a pretty plate. Theodore had warned me that his mother considered the color green unlucky and a bad omen. Of course, every plate seemed to have green on it somewhere, and it wound up taking longer than expected to stave off the bad luck. I had met his father on the trip to Constantinople, but that was a far cry from meeting him as Theodore's bride-to-be. Both his parents were polite, and there was no mention of the "confusion" over the priest. After that, I took Theodore to meet my parents. My mother once again just started crying and kept crying. As you might expect, both of my parents were enormously proud of their new son-in-law.

The day after all the introductions we were married in a simple church ceremony. It was a very small wedding. Our parents were there along with Theodore's brother and my sister. (Carolina was away at summer camp.) I had invited my confidantes and wedding planners, Lena and Tania. His family had only one guest, a businessman named—ironically, but perhaps predictably?—Nikos. Nikos Soutos. I wanted both of my parents to walk me down the aisle, something pretty much unheard of in Greece at that time. After all, they both had raised me and both deserved this special moment. My mother was crying, naturally. My father was beaming. So was Theodore. He looked so incredibly happy.

At one point in the ceremony, as is the custom in the Greek Orthodox Church, we stood next to one another and our best man stood behind us holding two *stefania* (the Greek word *stefani* means wreath or chaplet) connected by a ribbon. He placed those on our heads, then lifted them off and crossed them above our heads three times, each time setting them back on our heads. Luckily the garlands did not fall off, which would have been a sign of very bad luck.

After the ceremony, we went back to Theodore's house. I overheard his father on the phone telling family and friends, "Theodore is now married to Gianna Daskalaki and we are all happy." We called Carolina to give her the good news. For our honeymoon, Theodore and I flew to the south of France, where a new yacht named *Alfa-Alfa* that he had just had built—always with the surprises—was waiting. We took a long, leisurely sail and eventually wound up in the Greek islands, where Carolina joined us. Theodore is not really a holiday person, so this time was truly special. It remains the longest time we have ever spent together on a vacation. I wanted it to last forever. I knew I was coming back to an unfamiliar life, and that was a little frightening. But I was returning home with an extraordinary man who, in my thirty-fifth year, had opened me up to a love and a life that was wholly new. I felt I had been given a second chance—a very special chance—and I didn't intend to fail at it.

It was sometimes hard for me to fathom the changes in my life that had occurred over such a short time. Was it really just a few months earlier that I had been desperately calling a stranger in a steel factory hoping to secure an invitation to an Angelopoulos family affair? Now I was a member of that family. And that family was about to grow by one more. Theodore had been so certain he would never have children that he told me: "It's okay. I will have Carolina as my own." Now I had the pleasure of telling Theodore the joyful news that I was pregnant. The following year I would give birth to a son, Panagiotis, named in honor of Theodore's father.

There was no question that after our child was born I would move to Zurich. It was not just that Theodore's business interests were centered there. Our marriage had created quite a splash in Athens, which can be a very small city. Our courtship had been spent in virtual hiding. Now, although we could go out anywhere, we were recognized everywhere. We were under intense media scrutiny and became the objects of curiosity for everyday Athenians. The media would always have its sport with me, but most of the Athenians we encountered were generous with their good wishes. Yet it was all a bit suffocating. We wanted to start our new life and our new family with some degree of privacy. Switzerland, by its nature, pretty much assured that. In Zurich, we would be just another affluent businessman and his family.

Despite my eagerness to embrace my new life, I felt a sense of sorrow and I knew I had to deal with it quickly. It had been such an extraordinary privilege to serve in Parliament, to be entrusted by voters with their most vital needs. While apparently nobody in my party would object if I kept my seat while living abroad, I knew I wouldn't be doing justice to my constituents. I had no choice but to resign.

Party leaders who had so often been irritated by my independence—I could remember their faces when I stood up in Parliament and questioned why so many government officials required black limousines at their service—were dismayed by my decision. They tried to convince me to retain the seat, saying I could fly in occasionally for important meetings or votes. "Nothing was given to you," the speaker of the Parliament told me. "You succeeded by yourself. You can't now abandon something you tried so hard to attain."

But how could I possibly speak to people about their needs when most of the time I would be in my lovely mansion in Switzerland, far from Parliament and far from Greece? Did the party leaders really believe that I could claim to represent working people from a distance and given my changed circumstances? Did they actually think I could jet or yacht in a couple of times a month for votes and then go home having done my duty? That didn't fit with the serious notions of public service I had nurtured during my life. It would be dishonest, a fraud on the voters whom I had promised just two things: I would tell them the truth, and they would be the beneficiaries of my total dedication. And the truth was that I could no longer give them my total dedication. If I felt guilty—and I did—it was not for forsaking my dream, but their dreams.

There was a rumor that because the Angelopoulos family was politically nonpartisan and, with its wide-ranging interests, needed to work with politicians on both sides of the aisle, my father-in-law had encouraged my parliamentary exodus. That's not true. Never happened. In fact, Theodore was quite disappointed with my decision. He was very proud of the position I held and enjoyed seeing me in the limelight.

Neither Theodore nor party leaders could change my mind. Because the decision was so wrenching and emotional for me, I wasn't sure I would get the words exactly right. Once again I called on my trusted friend Lefteris Kousoulis, the man who had written my letter of support to New Democracy that had propelled me into Parliament. Now he would write my letter of resignation, dated September 5, 1990, effectively book-ending my parliamentary career.

Ironically, my resignation paved the way for Nontas Zafiropoulos, the lawyer for whom I had worked fresh out of college, to win my former seat in Parliament. I went from being his golden horse in the law firm to his golden chariot in politics.

Years later, even after I had accomplished a great deal for Athens with the 2004 Summer Olympics, people would tell me of their disappointment over my quitting, because they had believed in me. They didn't really understand when I explained that I had quit out of respect for the office and for them. That decision—both right and necessary—still pains me. But that has been the story of my life. Nothing has been attained without some pain. People see me today and they think that it has been easy for me, that I merely grabbed opportunities or had doors opened for me. There is no truth in that. Nothing came easy to me. And every opportunity I received demanded that I sacrifice something I truly loved.

Chapter 14

GENERATION NEXT

IN JUNE 1991, we celebrated the baptism of our son Panagiotis at our home in Athens, with Archbishop Iakovos conducting the ceremony. Our immediate families, our closest friends, and anyone who was important in Greece at that time were there. Theodore's parents, Panagiotis and Eleni, were the godparents. It was a joyous occasion, one of the happiest days of my life. I was thrilled that my father was there to see his grandson all dressed up in the white silk christening outfit that Theodore himself had worn at his baptism.

It would be the last time I saw my father. I am so lucky to have that day as a final memory. While I was pregnant, his health had continued to decline. On July 25, while Theodore and I were in Italy celebrating our first wedding anniversary, my father, Frixos Daskalakis—a tower of strength, a man of enduring principle, and an inspiration to me throughout my life—passed away.

What a turn of fate. After my father and the rest of my family gathered for the joyous event of Panagiotis's christening, our family gathered again, this time in Crete, mourning at my father's funeral. I cried, and I cried hard. I couldn't help it. My life had turned in an unexpected direction. I had begun to live a new life, a life of love and high expectations, a life so unlike the life I had led before. And my heart broke because my father was not there to share my happiness. Our happiness.

In September, more than a year after our marriage and my resignation from Parliament, we made the move to Zurich. For me, everything felt new—a growing family, a big home, a new city, a new language, and a life that centered around the demands of my husband's business.

I dwelled mostly on my own challenges. But what a shock it must have been for Theodore too, even if it was a happy one. A year before, Theodore had been a confirmed bachelor, certain that he would never marry again or have children. Now his quiet home had been overrun by a wife, two children (and another one on the way), nannies, teachers, dogs, and all the other trappings and accoutrements of a household of considerable means.

I expected I would be kept busy with household duties, which would certainly delight my mother. But Theodore was already well taken care of by a Portuguese couple, a butler, a maid, a chef, and a chauffeur. So, as a housewife, I was pretty much out of a job. Theodore liked it that way, at least while I was pregnant. He would have preferred it if I just lay in bed. He was overly protective, worried about the baby every time I made the slightest move, lifted anything, or bent to pick something up.

The combination of the final months of pregnancy and my first Swiss winter meant I was usually confined to our home. Theodore and I had a lot of time to talk. He confided in me about his earlier marriage. He and his wife had been unable to have children and had gone through extensive tests without finding any medical explanation for the problem. He told her they didn't need a child who looked like them, and they had discussed adopting children. Theodore suggested orphans from Asia or Africa—and as many as she wanted (and this was before Angelina Jolie). They would love any child whom they brought into their lives. The plan didn't work out and Theodore said "end of marriage." So it was natural he regarded our children as treasures and the very best kind—unexpected treasures.

Despite all the demands of work and of a home that was now bustling with life, I was amazed how our lives proceeded in orderly fashion, kind of like a Swiss clock. Okay, sometimes it may have been a bit of a cuckoo clock. The night Dimitris was born was certainly one of those occasions.

Theodore's bachelor home, with its three separate floors, hadn't been designed for the lives of a married couple with three children and a large staff. Consequently, while I was pregnant with my third child, we moved into the Dolder Grand Hotel nearby so that our home could be transformed into something a little more family friendly. It was quite late on the wintry night of February 16, 1992, when I announced to Theodore that our baby was coming that very night and that he had better call the doctor.

"You're going to call a doctor at this hour?" Theodore asked, his years in Switzerland having apparently yielded an overly developed sense of orderliness and propriety.

"I should tell the baby to wait until it's working hours in Switzerland?" I replied. "And if the baby won't wait, will you promise to stay here with me and deliver the baby? Give me a break." So I called the doctor myself and obviously woke him up. I could tell he was every bit as annoyed as Theodore had anticipated he would be.

"Are you sure?" the doctor asked in a sleepy voice. When I told him I was, he said he would meet us at the hospital.

Theodore still couldn't get over how I had bothered the doctor at that hour. Exasperated, I told him: "I don't give a damn. I want a healthy baby."

So we grabbed the suitcase that was already packed and ready and headed off: Theodore, my mother, and the nanny (who was really a nanny-in-waiting), and I all piling into our Range Rover. It was snowing heavily, but we proceeded to the hospital without incident— and without any further discussion of inconveniencing the doctor. He arrived shortly after us, clearly annoyed. And he was even more annoyed when he examined me and determined that the baby wasn't coming imminently. "It's not time yet," he pronounced. "You are not ready." We began arguing. I told him I had given birth twice and knew when my baby was coming. And he insisted that he had delivered a lot more than two babies and that my baby wasn't coming soon. "Go back to the hotel and go to sleep," he ordered, "and when the baby is ready, I am sure he or she will call us." When I suggested that it would be easier if I remained at the hospital, he practically barked, "Go home!"

It was after midnight when the four of us piled back into the Range Rover and returned to the hotel. When we got there, the concierge asked, "Mrs. Angelopoulos, what happened?"

I was still mad at the doctor, so I took it out on this poor man. "Does it look like anything happened?" I snapped.

Theodore tried to calm me, assuring me that the gentleman was only conveying his concern. "With a silly question?" I said. "I left with a belly and returned one hour later with the same belly. What possibly could have happened?" Then I told Theodore I needed a scotch. He was so stunned by my request—I neither smoked nor drank alcohol while I was pregnant—that all he could do was inform me that the bar was closed. I told him to get it opened. A hotel employee eventually fetched me a scotch and I downed it in one big gulp.

We returned to our rooms, put on the TV, and sat around for a while until Theodore said he needed to go to bed. I went too, but I couldn't sleep. At about four thirty in the morning, I shouted, "Theodore," and when he lifted his tired face to me, I told him, "It's time."

"Time like last time?"

"No, time like it is now." I called the doctor once more but there was no answer. He had apparently taken his phone off the hook.

So, once again, Theodore, my mother, the nanny, and I all piled into the Range Rover and drove back to the hospital through the snow. When I got there, I told the nurse to wake the doctor because the baby was on its way. After a quick examination, she agreed that the baby was coming—and coming very fast. When the doctor arrived, looking no happier than the first time, Theodore explained that he wanted to be in the delivery room. "In Greece, at the last minute they locked me outside and I never forgave the doctor," he said. Having already butted heads with me that night, the doctor didn't want any more trouble. He assured Theodore there would be no problem.

And for once the doctor was right. Indeed there were no problems at all—except for one. While I was doing my breathing exercises, Theodore and the doctor were chatting away like they were at a cocktail party, going on about cars and watches and the stock market. The whole night had been conspiring to make me crazy, and I was telling myself, "Now don't go boot the doctor out of the delivery room, because you need him there." Having had enough of their mindless chatter I barked, "I am so bored with the two of you."

The doctor said, smiling, "Then give birth right away."

I'd really had it with this doctor and told him I was leaving the room to take a walk. When I tried to get up, the baby must have taken it as some kind of signal because it was on the way.

I have this extraordinary image etched in my mind from right after

Dimitris's birth. It wasn't yet seven o'clock, and through the huge windows of the delivery room I could see the snow coming down as the light was just coming up in the sky. Against that shimmering backdrop, I first looked at my beautiful son who is named after Theodore's revered Uncle Dimitris. Then the nurse took the baby and handed him to Theodore so he could wash him. I could see how Theodore panicked, imploring with his eyes, "Gianna, Gianna."

"Theodore," I told him, "I can't help you now."

All mothers and fathers know that whatever the ordeal in bringing a child into the world, giving birth turns out to be the easiest part with kids.

Just like any other mother, I had my share of headaches and missteps in raising all of my children. Some of them were unforgettable.

For instance, I remember one time when our nanny and my mother were feeding Dimitris. He was sitting in his high chair. His nanny grabbed a bottle of clear liquid, thinking it was water, filled the sippy cup, and handed it to him. Dimitris sucked on the cup and exploded into tears as if he were being tortured, and he turned red. When I ran into the kitchen, I realized that the nanny had filled the sippy cup with my mother's homemade raki (the alcoholic beverage I described in chapter 1). "I sure am a great mother," I said to myself, laughing as I took the cup away from Dimitris. "I'm training my baby boy to drink raki!"

On another occasion, Panagiotis grabbed an ice cube and put it into his mouth. Theodore, who was drinking his scotch, thought Panagiotis was choking. Panicked, he got up, picked up our son, and ran downstairs shouting, "Gianna, Gianna, help me!"

Or the time Carolina grabbed a fruit-flavored hard candy wrapped in cellophane and ate the whole thing—cellophane and all!

Despite those inevitable mishaps, of all the things Theodore and I have accomplished in our lives, I'm proudest of how we raised three wonderful and remarkably well-adjusted children. Our kids are intellectually curious and have dreams and ambitions of their own. They have been privileged, but aren't spoiled, and none of them would consider sitting around and living off family wealth. Though we obviously could afford it, they have never asked for expensive gifts, have never tried to show off, and have never bragged about our business or our money. Never. They have always been down to earth. Because of their parents' lives, our children met many famous and wealthy people. But they understood that it was never right to drop names or gossip with their friends. In our family, the dinner table was a bastion of privacy. Theodore and I talked freely around our children, confident that, even from a very early age, they grasped the concept of discretion.

Nevertheless, Theodore and I worried about the effect of their growing up in a strange world of wealth and power, where everyone they knew lived in a megahouse and was surrounded by nannies, tutors, butlers, and chefs. Growing up in that world—our world in Zurich—the children weren't exposed to what we thought of as "real people." Real people were those we ourselves had encountered every day of our lives growing up in Greece. As you've read, I grew up in modest circumstances and attended public schools. At a young age, Theodore began working in his family's steel plant. Before he mastered business and a host of languages, his father required him to work alongside the men who were doing the toughest jobs and the heaviest lifting. Theodore learned all of their names and about their lives and families. He showed them the same respect that they showed his family. We shared that critical belief in the dignity of labor. My father had taught me how important it was to respect people who worked hard no matter what their job.

Our children are polite and respectful to everyone who works for us, whether a top executive or lawyer in the shipping company, or the person who cleans our home. Both boys took hard-hat jobs at a shipyard in Holland, where one of our companies builds yachts. They were treated the same as the other workers, which was the way they preferred it. We told our children repeatedly that they shouldn't expect to graduate college and come to work in the family business—not in the exalted position of boss's son or daughter nor as a hard-hat either. After they went out in the world and had careers of their own, then if they wanted to join the family business, we would see.

Theodore has always been very sweet and affectionate with our children. They find it easy to talk to him. I am a bit tougher and more demanding, the one who assumes the role of the enforcer, but in no way am I the mother who always says "*No!*", "*Don't!*", "*Be careful!*", and so on. But when the time comes that I do say "*No!*" everybody understands that I mean it. I never cared what other parents allowed their children to do or to own. But I was often willing to negotiate with my kids about things that truly mattered to them. If Carolina agreed to be home from a party at 1:00 AM and was two minutes late, the next time there was no deal. I know it sounds a lot like the way my father raised me, an arrangement with which I wasn't enamored as a young girl. But I have come around to see certain matters his way. My children learned at an early age how important it was to honor promises and to respect a deal, principles that have provided a good foundation for their lives.

I had to be away from home quite frequently while they were growing up because of business or Olympic-related trips. I confess I have felt guilty like every working mother does. When I was home, I always tried to connect with them at dinner, even if I had to return to work afterward. Sometimes you can learn a great deal just by watching their faces closely because faces betray a lot of feelings. If the children had already eaten dinner I would ask them to sit with me while I ate. I was very honest with my kids. I encouraged them when they were doing well. But I was not one of those mothers who believed that everything they did was automatically swell. If they misbehaved or underperformed I let them know it. I offered criticism but tried to temper it with advice on how they might have fared better. I didn't always try to protect them from hard truths or to assure them that all in life would be sweetness and light. Our family has two mottos: "Life is not always fair" and "Others may, but you must not take anything for granted."

I told my children that just because they behaved correctly and met their obligations, they shouldn't expect that their efforts would always be appreciated. I encouraged my children to set high standards for themselves, not because they would be rewarded but because that was the right way to live. I told them that if all was proceeding well they should never assume it would remain that way. Life can be treacherous. If things are going badly, however, that doesn't have to be forever either. They had the power to seize control of their lives and to change course.

It's easy to have principles but not always so easy to put them into practice. Our desire for our children to lead "normal" lives was tempered by all-too-real security concerns, concerns that, with the painful memory of the assassination of Theodore's uncle, would always resonate within the family. Nevertheless, when we started sending our children to summer camps, they went without any security people, which many urged us to provide. I felt it was important for our daughter and sons to have a genuine camp experience: to learn to cook their own food, to organize their tents, to swim in cold water, to climb mountains, and—most important—to make new friends. How could they be expected to enjoy any semblance of normality with armed men trailing their every move?

Later, after we returned to Greece, the government urged us to accept extra security. We agreed, and when the boys went to school, they had security guards assigned to them. They hated it. One day I found Panagiotis back at home without his guard. He had sneaked out of school and walked home alone, and he angrily declared he was up to the challenge of eluding his security on a daily basis.

Carolina has a strong personality. (I wonder where she got that!) Divorce is never easy for a child, yet she never complained. I explained to her that her father's feelings about me should not shape her feelings about him. That she should be patient and form her own judgments. While she and Theodore are very close—she calls him "Dad"— Carolina, to her credit, has kept a balance. But she was brought up by Theodore and me. From the beginning, she was always my daughter and Theodore's daughter. And to his credit he was and is her confidant.

And, believe it or not, from a very young age, Carolina was my trusted confidant. I had agreed to introduce her to Theodore on just one condition. She couldn't tell anybody about him. Even though she was just six and a half years old at the time, she did as she was told. She can keep a secret like nobody else. And she's pretty good at digging up secrets too. When I was pregnant with Dimitris, I took her along on one of my routine visits to the doctor. I didn't know—and didn't want to know—what gender my baby was. Somehow when Carolina was alone with the doctor for just a few minutes, she pried the secret out of him, promising him she would never reveal it. When Dimitris was born, Carolina was away on a school ski trip. We called her with the news and she shouted to her friends: "It's a boy. I knew it! I knew it!" And in truth, she had known.

When she was young, it was as if I had three boys. Carolina never liked to be dressed in fancy clothes or to play with dolls. We once bought her a navy-blue dress with an organdy collar and party shoes to match, for example. I made her wear the outfit to her birthday party and she didn't try to conceal how miserable she was. There is a wonderful picture that captured her feelings; her eyes reminded me of my father's—that angry gray green of a wintry rough sea. I knew she would have preferred to shed the outfit for shorts, a T-shirt, and sneakers.

We wanted our children to be secure in our love, but it was just as important that they loved and valued each other. With the boys and Carolina, that was easy. She, being so much older, was like a goddess to them. In their eyes, Carolina knew absolutely everything about life and she was terrific at all sports to boot, from skating to skiing to soccer. All the characteristics she demonstrated as a young girl served her well as a student at the American University of Paris and, later, as a young woman beginning a career in banking—not in a family business. Carolina has always amazed me with the way she deals with whatever life flings in her path. She has great strength, integrity, and discretion, and she works very hard, persevering without complaint. (You'll read in chapter 24 how I drew upon her abilities during the Athens 2004 Summer Games.) She's a real tough cookie!

Panagiotis is very well read and well educated and, like his paternal grandfather, is open-minded. As Pan has grown up, Theodore has observed more than once, "I think he has something from you." But where I was pragmatic, Pan is far more of an intellectual, with a lively mind and a diversity of interests, combined with strong convictions. He has surprised and astonished me with the speed with which he learns, and the speed with which he has matured. He cares about our family's history, and about the lives that other people live. I remember how surprised I was to learn that without discussing it with me, he had been camping in Crete, exploring villages and places even I hadn't been. In 2012 Pan graduated from Harvard, where he studied economics and history. In his senior year, he wrote an essay on economics and the global financial crisis for the *Harvard Political Review* that, despite my law degree and my business experience, I had to read twice to grasp! Dimitris, whom the family affectionately calls Dim, is a "killer," and I mean that in the very best way. He is realistic, tough, practical, analytical, and focused on his law studies. He is very wise for his age. When we deal with a serious issue, for example, Dim amazes us by totally identifying the situation, clarifying the problem, and calmly pointing us to the solution we are seeking. Like a Doric column, his arguments and presentations stand strong without unnecessary adornment. I see him as someone who is more likely to work inside power structures to make change than to agitate from the outside, though he has not hesitated to be publicly active on behalf of the causes he cares about. He also graduated in 2012, as a pre-law student, from the London School of Economics. That same summer he traveled to Uganda to help build houses for orphans. He will probably practice law for a while, at least to get his feet wet, much as I did.

In truth I really don't know what any of our children will wind up doing professionally, or where their lives will ultimately take them.

I have always liked the imagery of Turkish poet Nâzim Hikmet that pictures parenting as "a bow and arrow." The parents are the bow and they launch their children, the arrows. The arrows land—often far away—and each will be his or her own person. Don't think because you invested so much love, time, energy, or money in them that you in any way own your children. Don't think they will be like you or that they will think like you. I have been very blessed in life and have achieved a great deal. But my children have turned out spectacularly and are by far my greatest pride.

Chapter 15

BACK TO UNIVERSITY

THEODORE HAS ALWAYS HAD A STRONG SENSE OF DUTY when it comes to ensuring the futures of his wife and children. In his mind, this required far more than cutting a check. The extended Angelopoulos family was involved together in so many businesses and other ventures with so many potential financial repercussions that he worried. "What if something happens to me? Who will watch out for my family's interests?" He didn't want us to be totally dependent on anyone else, not even his father and certainly not the lawyers and accountants who worked with him. It didn't take him long to decide that the solution was close at hand. If he were gone, he decided, I should be the one in charge or at least the one responsible for making the critical decisions affecting our family.

Obviously I hadn't brought any business experience or financial expertise to our marriage. But Theodore admired my intelligence, my boldness, and my willingness to take action when it was required. He knew what an absolute tiger I could be in pursuit of what I believed was my right or the right path. (He once told me that, after all his years in Switzerland, he was delighted that we could have marital spats in Greek. He swore best in his native tongue, and he appreciated that I was a worthy combatant who could dish it out as well as take it.) He resolved to school me and involve me in his businesses so that if I had to act sometime in the future—when a tigress was needed to protect the family—I would understand the issues and know the right answers.

Essentially, it was back to university for me, except there were no formal lectures. Theodore simply began talking to me about his management approach.

The lessons ran the gamut from his mundane daily tasks to the strengths and weaknesses of key employees to how to read balance sheets and accounting ledgers. He particularly wanted to familiarize me with the shipping businesses, which are his strongest suit. His father and uncles had pioneered the family's steel business, but shipping had been Theodore's baby. He was ushering me into a new world, one with its own language that was completely foreign to me. At first I had difficulty keeping track of the names of the various types of ships—bulk carriers, tankers, aframaxes, suezmaxes, VLCCs, handymaxes—and the numerous shipyards as well as the financial aspects of the business. But I soon caught on.

In addition to delivering his steady discourse on all matters business, Theodore would come home from the office and dump piles of documents on the table for me to read. He absorbed these materials like a computer, but I didn't even know where to start reading. They covered matters like wet markets and dry markets that I couldn't yet define let alone understand. There were complex analyses of international trends in shipping and product demand. I had no recourse but to jump in because that's the way I've always tackled big challenges. Theodore wasn't always patient with me and sometimes got frustrated by my inability to master the materials as quickly as he had hoped. I understood his feelings. Patience had never been one of my strong suits either. In hindsight, his assessment of my struggle to grasp the complex material was much more generous. He would say that he marveled at how I soaked up information like a sponge.

On top of the business curriculum, there were language lessons: I was starting German as well as trying to improve my English. I had already studied French at my school in Heraklion.

Unlike during my first academic sojourn, this university—as long as Theodore remained Dean of students—wouldn't tolerate my skipping classes. And the Dean couldn't be charmed into giving me a better grade than I deserved. This was business, and the thing I learned most quickly from Theodore was that business was serious business.

I would compare the learning curve, at least for me, to attending a play by Shakespeare or Sophocles. At first the words and the rhythms of the language sound strange and it's hard to fathom their meaning. And then, at some magical moment, it all clicks and begins to make sense. So it was for me with the language and practices of business. One day it began to click and Theodore's world opened up to me. It was clear that my husband was developing more confidence in me. I began going to the office regularly and staying there for several hours or longer. And I attended business meetings. Not all of his lawyers, accountants, and other executives were happy when I began showing up. Nor were all the family members thrilled to have me on board.

I no doubt contributed some to this tension. I hadn't yet learned how to make a quiet entrance. Nobody would ever have said of me, "I didn't even know she was here." My voice, my laugh, and my sharp tongue—I always made my presence known. But whatever the employees or family members thought, Theodore's was the only opinion that counted. And while he may have been a tough taskmaster, he privately encouraged me and urged me on. "There are so many things you have to be aware of. You have to know the rules of the game. You have to know the information and the data. You have to have some plans, some courses of action mapped out. That's the way it works."

I began to grasp his meaning. The dynamics of business are somewhat like a game or sport. First you have to learn the rules. Then you have to play enough so that you improve. I learned some discretion. I learned that sometimes you could hold back your opinion to better effect. Like every challenge I have taken on in my life, I engaged it totally. I wanted to be an asset for the business, but not as a clone of Theodore ready to step into his shoes. Rather, I sought to complement him as a consultant and, later, as I learned more and more about his business and his world, as his partner and most trusted ally. I wanted to show Theodore that not only could he trust me in his arena but also that, ultimately, he would be foolish to trust anyone else.

It was a tremendous challenge, especially because so much went against my natural style. I had always instinctively gone forward and now I was learning to hold back. At times, especially early in the game, I stumbled. Sometimes my impatience showed. I remember one meeting in Theodore's office that was being conducted in English. I was tired of sitting there just listening and was anxious to show off my improved command of the language. So I said something I thought was reasonable or, at the very least, innocuous. Theodore was visibly unimpressed. Afterward, he scolded me: "Are you still a politician? Do you think you are in Parliament or running for an election? Talk about things you know. If you don't know don't talk. People won't underestimate you if you stay quiet. But you are in danger of having them laugh at you if you say stupid things." I was quite upset and protested that what I had said wasn't stupid at all. "Maybe not, but you were talking about things that the people there knew you don't know about yet."

Within a few years, I did know about most relevant matters and, more important, felt no need to show off my knowledge in meetings because Theodore knew I knew. He liked the way I analyzed things, a helpful by-product of my legal experience. And he liked my fighting spirit, how I never wanted to give up on a good idea. If he said, "We just can't do it," he could count on me demanding: "Why not? Tell me why not." Even from my husband, even from this brilliant businessman, I wasn't willing to take no for an answer. If he had a good idea, I was willing to push—and push him if necessary—to make it happen.

Working alongside Theodore only made my admiration for him grow. He is a straight shooter in a world where so many people throw curves. Theodore is such an honorable businessman and so respected by those with whom he conducts business that he can seal multimillion-dollar deals without a signature. Just his word—"Let's do the deal"—in any of the five languages (Greek, English, French, German, Italian) that he speaks—is sufficient.

I remember one time he agreed to purchase six ships for $32 million each, but he hadn't yet signed any contracts. Very soon thereafter we had an opportunity to buy the same vessels from another seller at $28 million each. "Talk to your lawyers," I urged Theodore. "You haven't signed any contract."

"My word is my contract," he replied. I kept arguing that it had just been a phone conversation. And I pointed out, as if he didn't know it, that the $24 million we would save was an awful lot of money. Finally, he just stopped me in my tracks by repeating his decision loudly and clearly so that we would never again have this kind of discussion: "I gave my word."

I was continually struck by the differences between the world of politics and the world of business. Many Greek politicians only talk. They never take action. They rarely make decisions. They don't reach goals. No one knows whose interest they are working for. Is it their own or someone else's? As we say in Greece, "They only keep stirring the pot."

Business, on the other hand, is all about goals, action, decisions. You identify your goals, you take action, and you make decisions. Business appealed to me because, at least on the surface, it was straightforward. We needed ships, we negotiated until we reached an agreement, we signed a deal, we paid the money, and the ships were delivered. It was a logical and coherent process to follow in solving a problem. It wasn't always as simple as all that. It could be arduous, involve complex negotiations, and produce its share of surprises and treacheries. But there wasn't the constant b.s. that plagues politics and government. When I would take charge of the Greek Olympic Games efforts, first the bidding competition and later the Athens organizing committee, my experience in both these worlds, politics and business, would prove invaluable.

My education wasn't confined to meetings, documents, language teachers, and Theodore's tutorials. The world was my university now. We traveled extensively around the globe and met, socialized with, and entertained prominent businessmen, powerful politicians, and royalty. I noticed that the bigger the name or the greater the person's responsibilities, the sooner we would hear back from the individual with a report on our meeting, a proposal, a solution, or just an immediate note thanking us for the hospitality or the pleasure of our company. The social notes always included some specifics about the occasion, if only a mention of some lovely item I wore or some delectable food we shared. It was an invaluable lesson that, beyond good manners, demonstrated how to connect with people and make a favorable impression. Simple courtesies can go a long way to bolstering a relationship—and not just a business relationship.

I taught my kids from an early age to send thank-you notes, birthday cards, and holiday greetings to their family and friends. I told them that a handwritten message was much more valuable than any expensive gift. The important thing was to communicate their love, respect, and gratitude in a meaningful way. To this day, I value the cards, the simple drawings, and the collages my kids sent me as my most treasured collection of art (and, believe me, we have a world-class art collection). Maybe we have all inherited my father's insistence on the personal touch, even when we are touching thousands of people.

In the fall of 1993, after just three years in power, New Democracy lost in the Greek national elections, marking the beginning of more than a decade of Socialist rule. At that time, my life was focused more on Switzerland and, indeed, the world than on Greece and its politics.

But there is an old saying, which I've heard in many other countries as well: "When one door closes, another one opens."

And that proved to be the case in my life. The next year my interest in leadership and public service would lead me to forge a new and thrilling connection that has endured to this day. Theodore's family had a longstanding friendship with a physician named Ahmed Mohiuddin, who lived in Boston and who had close ties with Harvard University. He was aware that both the John F. Kennedy School of Government and the Harvard School of Public Health were serious about becoming more international in their programs and outreach. On one of my visits to Boston, he arranged introductions for me with top university leaders and senior staff. This is how I met my trusted friend Holly Sargent.

And though I had no idea what might come of it, I was thrilled simply to engage some of the best minds at one of the preeminent universities in the world. I apparently made an impression too. My résumé—political, legal, and government experience, along with my involvement in global business ventures—was perfectly aligned with Harvard's new ambitions. The Kennedy School was forming a new Dean's Council, and I was asked to join as vice chair. Beyond advising the Dean, my responsibilities included serving as an ambassador for various international projects as well as representing the Dean at certain events.

My first formal duty was to represent the Dean at a dinner in Boston welcoming thirty newly elected members of the Russian Duma. It was the first time the Kennedy School had conducted its renowned executive leadership program for representatives from the Russian National Assembly. I was meticulous in my preparation, from my smashing Yves Saint Laurent outfit to the carefully crafted speech. I hope the outfit was a hit because the speech was a disaster. The dinner was on the Boston waterfront, and my brief remarks were drowned out by a cacophony of ferry whistles and foghorns.

My new relationship with the Kennedy School gave me regular opportunities to engage faculty in discussions of the issues in my homeland. Moreover, during my frequent travels, I established close bonds with Greeks abroad. I was struck by how my fellow Greeks had become so prominent and successful—but only after they left Greece and settled in the United States, Australia, the United Kingdom, or other countries.

The paradox was obvious: Why do we Greeks fail at home—trailing far behind other Western nations in productivity and creativity—while Greeks abroad flourish and become leaders in so many fields, from politics to business to arts? In 1995, with the assistance of renowned foreign-policy expert and the school's former Dean Graham Allison, that question evolved into to a major symposium—"The Greek Paradox"—at the Kennedy School. I had the privilege of welcoming to Harvard an extraordinary cast of academics, politicians, and journalists, including, among others, the President of Greece, Constantine Stephanopoulos; former Massachusetts Governor Michael Dukakis, a

Greek-American who had lost the presidential race to George H.W. Bush in 1988; John Kenneth Galbraith, distinguished economist and former American Ambassador; and Monteagle Stearns, former American Ambassador to Greece.

In 1997 we published *The Greek Paradox: Promise vs. Performance*, a book that included fifteen essays from the distinguished scholars and leaders who had participated in the symposium.

If there was one theme that threaded its way through all the contributions, it was this: Greece could no longer afford to shirk its responsibility to address the fundamental structural and social problems that constrained its growth, threatened its economy, and curtailed the success of its citizens.

If *The Greek Paradox* had been a prophecy, the Delphic oracle would have been proud. More than a decade before the world even began to take notice of Greece's problems, our book laid them out coherently and presaged the tragic circumstances that all of us have witnessed in recent years.

The contributors wrote that Greece had to transform its civil service. Greece had to streamline its bloated state-owned companies. Greece had to make sure that all Greek students learned salable skills. Greece had to eliminate tax evasion. And Greece had to decentralize the government.

Furthermore, the essayists urged and warned Greece to take action and "step up to the challenges and opportunities or face grave results."

As symposium participant Vasilios Tsingos observed, however, the Greek leadership would have to change in order to drive these reforms. "The domestic and foreign challenges facing Greece in the 1990s require innovative problem solving and a 'can do' attitude to replace the deep-seated cynicism and inertia infecting Greek society today . . . The lack of vision and forward-looking leadership in Greece has become apparent as Greek political structures in the 1990s have proven ineffective, even incompetent. The public has lost confidence in the state's ability to handle the country's problems."

The Greek Paradox opened with this dedication: "This volume is dedicated to the leaders and citizens of Greece. May they seize the significant opportunities before them and inspire the spirit of democracy around the world not only by their history but by their performance." It was a clarion call, one that went unheeded. And for that, Greece today pays a terrible price.

Chapter 16

LONDON CALLING

LOOKING BACK AT YOUR LIFE AND YOUR FAMILY HISTORY, you can see how certain threads weave their way from one generation to the next. Some are easy to spot, like the one that connected all the reading that my paternal grandfather did at night during his four years working at a steel mill in America with all the reading my father did during the four years he spent as a prisoner of war in Germany. That love of reading was a legacy I inherited, one that I have treasured and have, in turn, passed on to my children.

Not all the connective tissue of life is so obvious, however. Only after several years in Zurich did Theodore and I decide to move our family to London. It may be hard to recognize how our moving to London was in any way similar to my father's insistence on our visiting his family homestead in Embaros when I was a young girl. In fact, it's likely that London and Embaros have never been mentioned in the same sentence before. Yet the motives for those actions were not dissimilar. My father's was an urgent desire for his children to have their lives rooted in what he saw as "real life." Ours was to leave a city that, though easy and comfortable, was too homogenous and quiet. While a well-organized society can be a virtue, it can also create a rather sterile atmosphere. With our children getting older, we wanted to give them the opportunity to lead lives in a more diverse environment—a little more "real" in my father's parlance—and expand their horizons beyond what Switzerland offered.

We had talked about returning home to Greece, but it was not the right time for that move. Most of my husband's business interests were abroad—some in England—and the future of his business was increasingly international. The move also boosted his independence, putting a little more distance between him and his family. I was excited about my new involvement with Harvard, and that connection was easier to maintain from London. And the city did offer all of us the opportunity to connect to a large Greek population. These may not have been the real Cretans of Embaros or the real Greeks of Crete, but at least they were real Greeks who shared and valued our culture.

And this is how it happened. In February 1995, Theodore went to London on business and I accompanied him to look for a home. I had called the best agencies and told them what I was looking for: a distinctive home of the highest quality. But I didn't really know London and couldn't offer much guidance beyond that. "Surprise me," I told them. And they sure did. The first house I looked at was one of two homes in the Holland Park section—the real estate agent told me they were virtually identical—owned by a self-made British billionaire. He happened to be there when I arrived and couldn't have been more gracious and welcoming. And the house couldn't have been a bigger mess. Shoes were piled on coffee tables, clothes were scattered all over the place.

The indoor swimming pool smelled like a sewer. I quickly excused myself and called Theodore to make sure he didn't show up to take a look. "You would be shocked," I told him.

I wouldn't be surprised if this shock treatment was a deliberate tactic used by the real estate agents to make a prospective buyer more receptive to almost anything that followed. Indeed, as soon as I had escaped that house, the agent began talking about another one—a really special home in Chelsea—though it might not be to our taste and quite likely was too expensive. Naturally, I was intrigued. The home turned out to be the Chelsea Rectory, a historic nineteenth-century building where many Londoners, including Charles Dickens, had been married. A recent renovation had transformed it into what many regarded as the most spectacular home in London. While the outside had been maintained in strict accordance with historic preservation laws, massive additions to the original building had increased the living space to thirty thousand square feet, with ten bedrooms and a giant ballroom.

It also boasted a black granite swimming pool that—when you were underwater—let you peer into the gymnasium. (And when you were working out in the gymnasium, you could look into the swimming pool.) Perhaps most enticing of all, at least to me, was that when you entered the front door, you were gazing out on a magnificent garden. It was huge, a full two acres, and filled with cherry trees. Most magnificent of all was the magnolia tree right in the middle of the garden. (We had magnolias in our garden in Athens too, and I suddenly felt very much at home.) Later, when we hosted Prince Charles for dinner, he would tell me that it was the second largest private garden in London; only the garden of Buckingham Palace was more extensive. The way the garden flowed into the home, the connection between inside and outside, felt very Greek to me.

When I called Theodore, I couldn't contain my excitement. He immediately urged me to rein in my emotions. I was looking at the home as art and Theodore was preoccupied with the art of the deal. "Don't ask the price," he cautioned me. "Believe me, it will come out in good time. And don't show that you are so impressed. Be cool." For more than twenty years now, I have heard him repeat that advice, but it has not proved particularly helpful. Theodore does cool much better than me. I tend to run hot.

The next day we were treated to real London weather: raining cats and dogs. I worried that when Theodore saw the house in the rain it wouldn't make the same grand impression on him. But as far as anyone could tell, it made no particular impression on him whatsoever. When he looked at the exquisite swimming pool, he asked a question about the generator. And that's pretty much what he did throughout the house, discussing piping and wires and asking a lot of male-type engineering questions. I couldn't tell if he had even noticed the magnolia tree. He didn't betray any feelings, didn't provide the least hint—not even with a wink or a discreet gesture to me—of how he felt about the house. And when we were finished with the tour, he said to me in something of a stage whisper: "It's okay, but you're right. It's too big for us and it will probably be too expensive."

The next day, without even telling me, he began to negotiate despite those obstacles. And later that day, he surprised me by saying we had to go and see the house again.

I was confused. "Why are we going back?"

"I think maybe that's the ideal place for us, for you and the kids. If we can afford it, then it's okay."

And that's how we bought the magnificent home we would continue to call the Old Rectory.

We wanted to move in right before the kids started school in September. But before we could do that, we required some alterations that would turn the house into a home that was more suited to our family.

Essentially, we wanted it a little more "us," which meant more Greek touches. Theodore directed me to Jon Bannenberg, whom he knew through his shipbuilding business. Bannenberg was an Aussie who had become the most famous and innovative yacht designer of the twentieth century. Theodore warned me that he was very talented but also very opinionated and very strict about his work. His office was right in Chelsea and he had a reputation for being creative and stylish without sacrificing functionality and practicality. "Right now it's a British house," I explained, "and we are a Greek family with our own culture and traditions. We want our home to reflect our identity."

He was clearly thrilled about the prospect of working on such a historic building in his backyard and wanted to go see the Old Rectory immediately. But first I had to clarify two important matters. Regarding all financial issues he would deal directly with Theodore. And, we needed to be in the house by the end of August.

"August, next year?!" he responded.

"No," I said, "August *this* year. I want my family to have dinner there on the last night of August, and the next day my children will start school."

He looked aghast and began shaking his head. "You can't be serious." But it doesn't take smart people very long to figure out when I am serious. And after we looked at the Old Rectory, Jon, who is a genuine eccentric, couldn't resist the challenge. He took the deal—complete with our "impossible" six-month deadline.

On August 31, 1995, we moved in and had our family dinner in the big dining room—Jon had even arranged a butler and a chef for us. The next day the boys began their studies at a Greek school, Hellenic College, which was located nearby in Knightsbridge and had been founded by ex-King Constantine of Greece. Constantine had ascended to the throne in 1964 at the age of twenty-three, and three years later he fled

Greece after leading a failed counter-coup against the military junta. In 1974, when the junta fell, Greeks voted against restoring the monarchy and, ever since, Constantine had lived in exile in London.

Theodore believed that the English language would be central to our children's futures, but I insisted our boys attend the Greek school. I was confident that their English skills would flourish just by virtue of living in London and wasn't the least surprised when the children quickly began speaking English among themselves. But despite "Greek only" dinners at home, the boys were deficient in our native tongue. "I am a lawyer and I was a member of Parliament and you are from one of the most distinguished families in Greece," I told Theodore. "Yet our boys speak a kind of broken Greek. I cannot accept that they do not speak the language excellently." (Carolina, having spent her first eight years in Greece, didn't have the same educational deficits and so happily attended an American school.) We would also hire professors from Greece to live in and tutor the children in Greek language, history, and culture.

I cherish the memory of the first time I went to see the boys perform in a school play. It was about the war against the Turks, and my sons—Panagiotis was five years old, Dimitris just four—played soldiers, dressed in our national costume complete with the short white skirts. When they started dancing, I did a very good imitation of my own mother. I just started crying and couldn't stop. If I had ever doubted my decision to put them in a Greek school, in that moment I knew for certain that it had been the right one.

I was very excited that very first morning in our new home as our children prepared for school. But it didn't turn out to be the biggest excitement of that morning at the Old Rectory. We had hired two British nannies, and they had their own little kitchenette near the children's bedrooms. As we were readying the boys for school, Theodore and I heard sirens that were apparently coming from the local fire station. Theodore was glad that Chelsea had its own firehouse and that we lived close by, just in case we needed assistance. While we were chatting away, totally unconcerned, the sirens grew louder—*closer* and *louder*. At last, we went to the window to see what was going on. Our security people were racing to the front gates to open them up for the fire brigade. The boys could hardly contain their glee since—at their age—nothing was more thrilling than fire trucks.

It turned out one of the nannies had left her slice of bread in the toaster and the burnt toast had triggered the fire alarm, which fortunately was connected directly to the fire station. We were embarrassed and apologetic. We later sent sandwiches and cookies to the firehouse as an expression of gratitude from the new neighbors. Unfortunately, it would not be the last time we had to apologize to these firemen. Very soon afterward, my mother visited. Because she is devout, she wanted to bless our home by lighting incense throughout the house, as they do in Greek Orthodox churches. That set off the fire alarm and sent the fire trucks racing to our home. Once again it was sandwiches and cookies at the Chelsea firehouse.

But none of these incidents produced fireworks at the Old Rectory to rival those that would be set off by a single telephone call to me from Greece in early 1996. The call—one that was totally unexpected and from a man I'd never heard of—changed my life. It would lead to an opportunity for me to fulfill my childhood dream a second time: to do something truly great for my country.

Chapter 17

SLEEPING WITH THE ENEMY

I WASN'T HOME THE AFTERNOON THE PHONE CALL CAME. My secretary, Sannah, told me it was from Athens, but neither of us recognized the name of the caller—Andreas Fouras. Today we would have Googled the name and quickly learned most of what we needed to know. But back then my way of securing such information was to make several calls to close associates in Greece to inquire about the gentleman. According to them, he was no gentleman. "A typical Socialist" said one, reflecting the eternal enmity between political parties in Greece. Beyond the harsh partisan assessment, I learned that Fouras had recently been named Deputy Minister of Culture—in charge of sports—in the new government of Prime Minister Costas Simitis.

Simitis had just succeeded the veteran left-leaning Socialist Andreas Papandreou, who had resigned due to ill health and would die just five months later. Ever since the restoration of democracy more than two decades earlier, Papandreou had been the face of socialism in Greece. He headed the Pan Hellenic Socialist Movement from 1974 until his death and had served as Prime Minister three times, holding that office for more than a decade. His family has been the most prominent in Greek politics over the last half century. Papandreou's father, Georgios, served three short terms as Prime Minister, the first just after World War II and the last ending in 1965, when he was driven from office by the turbulent events leading up to the '67 coup. Papandreou's son, George, became Prime Minister in 2009. He too was forced to resign after a troubled two-year tenure when, amid the frenzy of the debt crisis, he wavered on implementing the austerity program demanded before Greece would receive further European aid and reach an accord with its debt-holders.

None of this background provided a glimmer of a clue as to why Mr. Fouras would be calling me. Though I had been willing to talk to and work with the opposition during my political career, it was always surprising—in the Greek political universe—to hear from the "enemy." Because Simitis wasn't the polarizing figure his predecessor was, I didn't hesitate to return his Minister's call.

The message from Athens proved to be another surprise. "Mrs. Angelopoulos," Fouras said with considerable pomposity, "the Prime Minister proposes that you join the Athens bid committee."

"What bid committee?" I asked, which must have been a rather deflating response.

"The bid committee for the 2004 Olympic Games," he replied.

Until that moment, I was only vaguely aware that Athens had been contemplating a bid for the 2004 Summer Games. But like most Greeks, I knew a great deal about Greece's Olympic history—ancient, modern, and, quite important, recent. I learned of the ancient Olympics at my father's side in Olympia. The Games date back to the eighth century BC

and were held every four years—an Olympiad in the Greek timetable—
on the plains of Olympia as a tribute to Zeus and other ancient Greek
gods. The competition pitted men from rival city-states. Only free men
who spoke Greek were allowed to compete, and the men raced naked.
Winners were crowned with an olive tree wreath called a *kotinos* and
were hailed as conquering heroes upon their return home.

The first Olympics featured just one race, closest in distance to
today's 200 meters. The first Olympic champion was a cook named
Coroebus from Elis, the region that included Olympia. Subsequently,
other events—running, throwing, jumping, riding, chariot racing, and
various forms of combat—were added and the festival was expanded
from one to five days. Religious activities were incorporated into the
celebration, and Greek arts were prominently displayed. The Olympics
were so revered that temporary truces were established between warring
city-states so that the competition wouldn't be jeopardized and athletes
and spectators could travel safely to and from Olympia. The Olympics
were held for more than a thousand years—until the year 394 AD when
Theodosius the Great declared Christianity the official religion of the
Roman Empire and banned the Games as a pagan cult.

Some fifteen hundred years later, a young French aristocrat,
deploring the lack of athletic training for young Frenchmen (especially
in comparison to their English, German, and American counterparts),
began advocating the advancement of sports in his country. Baron
Pierre de Coubertin did not find a very receptive audience in France,
but he had already embraced a bigger idea. He began to call for an
international competition modeled on the ancient Olympics. Beyond
the intrinsic value of athletic excellence for young men, he believed
an Olympic revival could have broader societal ramifications by
bolstering an understanding across many cultures.

Thus in 1894 he hosted an international congress at the Sorbonne in Paris where his Olympic vision carried the day. The first modern Olympics would be held in Athens two years later, in April 1896, when King George I of Greece opened the Olympics before eighty thousand people in the newly restored Panathinaiko Stadium. Thanks to the largesse of Greek businessman, philanthropist, and Olympic booster George Averoff, the stadium had been rebuilt in the splendor of white marble. The crowds there were the largest ever to have witnessed a sporting event. While the numbers are inexact, more than two hundred male athletes—no women were allowed to compete—from more than a dozen countries contested events in nine sports, including such new Olympic entries as cycling, swimming, shooting, gymnastics, and tennis. Spyridon Louis, who came from Maroussi, just outside Athens, and earned his living helping his father sell water in the city, thrilled his countrymen by winning the marathon. All winners received an olive branch and a silver medal. Runners-up were given copper medals; third place wasn't yet considered a medal-worthy result.

The Games were a stirring success and some consideration was given to making Athens the permanent site for the Olympics. But the 1900 Olympic Games had already been promised to Paris, and the idea of an Olympic rotation was put into place. (Incidentally, women would compete there for the first time.) Over the next century, the Summer Games would be competed in twenty cities—Paris, London, and Los Angeles each staged two—on four continents without returning to Greece.

For the 1996 Centennial Games, much of the world and all of Greece had expected that the Olympics would once again be staged in their birthplace. In September 1990, when the International Olympic Committee (IOC) gathered in Tokyo to award that centennial honor, Athenians filled Constitution Square to celebrate the anticipated victory. On the fifth and final ballot, Athens lost by a decisive vote—51 to 35—to Atlanta, a second- or even third-tier American city in the eyes of those Greeks who had actually heard of it. The outrage in Greece was fierce, the Greek people's sense of betrayal overwhelming.

Unfortunately, that has too often been the Greek response to disappointment. It can't possibly be our fault, so somebody must have betrayed us. When I eventually got involved in the Greek Olympic movement, I realized what an uphill battle we faced around the world. We had to overcome this image of arrogant Greeks battling among ourselves, of meddling politicians with self-serving agendas undermining each other, of a government with no strategy claiming what it believed was Greece's due—and then pointing fingers at others when things didn't go our way.

The Greek Olympic campaign to host the 1996 Games had essentially demanded the Games as the nation's birthright, an inevitable dictate of history. In disagreeing, the IOC demonstrated its limited interest in old legacies. New legacies—airports, highways, trains, and stadiums built specially for Olympics—as well as new economic synergies trumped old legacies and left Greece empty-handed.

The 1990 vote showed that many IOC delegates regarded Greece as a backwater, that is, a third-world European nation that lacked the infrastructure, the government efficiencies, the economic clout, the technological know-how, and the capacity for innovation to host a successful Olympics on the cusp of the twenty-first century. And perhaps most important of all, they had seen no evidence among either the Greek leaders or the Greek people of the discipline and teamwork that an Olympic effort demanded.

So, when Fouras, the Minister of Culture for Sports, informed me that Athens—still bruised and battered after its centennial defeat—was going to risk disappointment again, I was rather taken aback. The host city for the 2004 Summer Olympics would be decided in September 1997, just eighteen months ahead; if Athens hadn't yet launched its campaign in earnest, Greece could be headed for another humiliating failure.

Fouras insisted that things would be different this time. Greece was investing in a major overhaul of its infrastructure. Work on a new airport, new highways, new subways, and new stadiums had already begun. An Olympics would be "the jewel on the crown," he promised, providing an international showcase for a new Athens and a new Greece. When I wondered what I could contribute to this effort from abroad, Fouras said that I shouldn't worry. I wouldn't be required to do much work, certainly no heavy lifting.

I understood perfectly. The bidding process would be a massive undertaking, requiring exceptional managerial and political skill. The bidding process is very complex: Each city submits a bid file with responses to questions ranging from the budget to the athletes and media villages; from the climate to the sports program; from the sports venues to the cultural program; from the torch relay to the volunteers; from the preparation of the public to the consensus of the political parties; from security to visa considerations; from the sponsorship program to the broadcasters' requirements; from the transport program to the new infrastructure required; and many more.

Most significant of all is that the national and local governments *guarantee* all of the above—and more—for the successful hosting of the Olympic Games.

After the bid file has been submitted, the Evaluation Commission of the IOC visits each candidate city and checks to see if all the proposals in the bid file are viable.

The Evaluation Commission reviews every aspect of each city's candidacy, and publishes a report.

Then the Selection College of the IOC chooses a short list of the final candidate cities. IOC members, representatives from the international sports federations, sponsors, broadcasters, and others visit each city. Each of the bidding cities then makes its final presentation to the

IOC session, and all of the IOC members vote to decide which will be the host city of the Games of the Olympiad.

When I was asked to join the bidding process, it was just like when New Democracy tapped me to run for office. I was meant to serve as a symbol, the face—a young international businesswoman—of a more modern Greece. They didn't expect me to build a powerful organization. Telling me I wouldn't have to work was exactly the wrong approach. I never agreed to serve on a committee unless I commanded real control and bore true responsibility. And then I never minded doing all of the heavy lifting necessary to achieve a goal.

But I didn't need to explain all this to a Deputy Minister, so I politely declined his offer and figured that would be the last I heard from Athens about its Olympic bid. A few days later, though, Theodore and I received an invitation from Prime Minister Simitis to a reception in Athens honoring First Lady Hillary Clinton. We had been privileged once to attend a White House dinner hosted by the Clintons. I had been seated at the President's table and had been dazzled by his knowledge of issues. (I would come to appreciate it even more when, years later, I got to work with him on the Clinton Global Initiative.) I left vowing to work even harder on my own preparations in business or for any other matter I might face. Theodore had been at the First Lady's table and was impressed with her commanding aura and confidence. At the same time, he found her approachable, capable of refreshing candor, and possessing a willingness to acknowledge mistakes. Obviously, we were delighted to be included in extending to Mrs. Clinton an Athens welcome.

We got to have a brief, private conversation with the First Lady beforehand at the Intercontinental Hotel. The scheduled reception followed at the Maximos Mansion, the building in which the Prime Minister works and holds certain ceremonial functions. We figured the meeting with Mrs. Clinton to be the highlight of our trip, as we expected the reception to be your standard boring cluster of VIPs. And it was rather boring—until the Prime Minister cornered me, that is. Simitis told me how disappointed he was that I had turned down his Deputy Minister of Sports. He was convinced that because of my wide-ranging experience—in politics, in business, and in the world at large—I would have been an invaluable addition to the Athens team. "We have very big plans this time," the Prime Minister assured me. "Mrs. Ange-lopoulos, this is a golden opportunity for Greece."

After my talk with his Sports Minister, I had called friends in Athens, most notably Petros Efthimiou, a renowned journalist who would later be Minister of Education during our Olympic preparations, to see how seriously they viewed the government's Olympic ambitions. Through Petros I talked to Kostas Laliotis, a prominent figure within the Social-ist government and Minister of Public Works and the Environment.

My friends believed that the government was committed to the massive building program, one that was desperately needed regardless of Athens's Olympic fate.

"I respect that, but I don't like to be held responsible when somebody else actually makes the decisions," I told the Prime Minister, explaining my reluctance. "So thank you very much for the honor, but again I must say 'no.'"

As Theodore and I readied to leave the reception, Prime Minister Simitis again intercepted me and asked, "Would you change your mind if you were to head the bid committee as President rather than just serving as one of the many committee members?"

"But don't you already have a President?" I asked, knowing full well that the sitting President was a local businessman with close ties to the Mayor of Athens.

"I will change that," Simitis promised. "Leave it to me."

I stood there aghast. I glanced at Theodore, who, as always, was prepared to deal. Theodore told the Prime Minister, "I will back Gianna's decision and actively support her if she takes the job."

Theodore's support was critical since the respect he commanded internationally had the potential of being one of our committee's greatest assets.

For a few moments the world around me went blank, and I was totally lost in my own thoughts. I envisioned a new Greece, a novel Greece. Images were flashing through my brain. I saw a beautiful new infrastructure that Greece would proudly show off to its citizens and its visitors. I saw hardworking, disciplined Greeks with smiles on their faces. I saw a country that would once again be admired around the world. What a dream it was. And to imagine that I would have the responsibility to lead this, that I might deliver this to Greece. What an extraordinary honor. What pride I felt.

When I snapped out of my reverie, I didn't hesitate. Clutching Theodore's hand tightly, I looked the Prime Minister in the eye and told him: "Okay. As herculean as this challenge will be, I accept." He immediately beckoned the Mayor of Athens, Dimitris Avramopoulos, and informed him of his offer to me and of my acceptance. The Mayor went pale, an angry shade of pale. But he quickly recovered his poise and invited Theodore and me to join him for dinner.

Dinner was a strange affair at a Polynesian restaurant, with Avramo-poulos spending the entire evening explaining how treacherous the assignment would be and why I should reconsider. Afterward, when Theodore asked my impression, I told him that the Mayor didn't want me in the job because he obviously had the current President and committee in his pocket. "He wants control," I said, "and he's afraid of me." Maybe I should have been more afraid of him. He proved to be your all-too-typical politician who does none of the real work but is quick to take credit for what others accomplish. I would have a similar problem with yet another Mayor of Athens, Dora Bakoyannis, during the 2004 Summer Games. (Yes, the very same daughter of Constantinos Mitsotakis whom you met in chapter 6.) Though politicians would always make my job more oppressive, they underestimated my abilities and my drive, and, ultimately, they failed in their efforts to undermine my success.

The next day Simitis made the appointment official. Neither of us was aware at that moment that we were making history. I was the first woman to lead an Olympic bid committee. While I am proud of that "first," it wasn't nearly as meaningful to me as the lure of patriotism, the chance to serve Greece in a historic quest. I thought back to my letter of resignation from Parliament six years earlier, which included my declaration, "I will find an occasion in the future to again serve my country." I know some people found the notion laughable, certain that I had married my prince and would be content to live out the fairy tale happily ever after in a distant castle. They were sure they had seen the last of me on the Greek public stage. But now I was back and at center stage. And I understood what a huge opportunity this was—both for Greece and for me.

It would take me longer to forge the same level of understanding with the Prime Minister. I was not really sure why he had tapped me. Though we both valued efficient organizations, we had polar opposite personal styles. He was a technocrat—very unemotional—and I wasn't even convinced that he truly wanted the Olympics in Greece. At that time, Greece was in the process of shifting from the drachma to the euro, and Simitis might have thought that a well-conceived Olympic campaign—even a failed one—would promote a new image for the country and help it forge closer relations with the European Union.

Be that as it may, I had to admire his fortitude in choosing me. Greek politics remained a black-and-white (actually a green-and-blue) divide between Socialists and conservatives. And that made me the enemy, deplored by his party as a wealthy capitalist—and, even worse, one who no longer lived in Greece. Simitis took a lot of political flak from his party over the appointment.

We managed to find common ground. We both wanted a bid campaign run by business-oriented professionals, not by the same politicians who had squandered the golden opportunity for the 1996 Olympics. "We were so arrogant last time that the Olympic people were saying, 'Never again, Greece,'" Simitis told me with a pained look on his face. "We cannot go back again and ask for Olympic laurels just because Greece is the birthplace of the Games. We have to form a completely different strategy—a modern one!"

Throughout our campaign, when critics would attack me or attack Simitis because of me, he would respond in the same calm and considered fashion. He'd say, "Mrs. Angelopoulos will be judged by the results of her work."

My gut feeling was that in so saying, Prime Minister Simitis was secretly thinking and preparing for any outcome.

Chapter 18

ATHENS IS IN MOTION

WHEN I WAS NAMED PRESIDENT OF THE BID COMMITTEE IN 1996, we had but sixteen months left before IOC delegates would gather in Lausanne, Switzerland, to announce the city that would be awarded the 2004 Summer Olympic Games. Yet little had been done up to that point to prepare for that moment. Athens was virtually invisible in the Olympic movement. Other countries had been working on their bid for years. Indeed, the IOC had conducted eleven seminars for prospective bidding cities and Athens was the only contender that hadn't appeared at any of them. In Atlanta during the 1996 Centennial Games, other cities that hoped to host the Olympics had set up elaborate informational kiosks to inform and court IOC members and the international press. Ours was assembled at the last minute. It wasn't perfect, but at least we were there. Still, we were playing catch-up.

The first order of business remained getting our own house in order. Before we could sell the world on Athens 2004, our team had to understand that 1997 wasn't going to be a replay of the Centennial Games debacle. Our new "bid concept" memo opened with what was essentially an epitaph for the previous effort: "We realized back in 1990 that our desire and our heritage alone could not guarantee our election to host the Games. In 1990 we thought the Olympic movement owed us the Centennial Games. That was not the case." While our Olympic history and heritage remained important, we recognized that it would only be a footnote in our campaign. If Athens intended to win the 2004 Summer Games, it would have to triumph in the present and on merit.

When I was named President of the bid committee, Rome was the prohibitive favorite for 2004, and its bid campaign already had 150 employees. Athens's campaign had a handful of employees and was being overrun by a typical cast of Greek power brokers—self-promoters, back-stabbers, and do-nothings—who hoped to profit from the association and were prepared solely to bask in the reflected glory should a miraculous outcome occur. All wanted to keep a hand in the process, oblivious to the fact that their interests didn't necessarily coincide with mine, those of the campaign, or even those of one another. I was also saddled with the two Greek members of the IOC, neither of whom was happy to have me on board. The most problematic was Lambis Nikolaou, an inveterate gossip who was always trying to stir up trouble. The other was Nikos Filaretos, who would wear a Stockholm 2004 pin on his jacket lapel during the final meeting of the IOC to decide the host city for the 2004 Summer Games. With allies like that, who needed enemies?

I never expected or even wanted these people to be my friends. I just hoped they'd give me the freedom to do the job for which the Prime Minister had chosen me. Some reliable veterans of Greek politics warned me that I had been misled about the job. "They brought you here to be the scapegoat if Greece loses," insisted Antonis Samaras, who had been Foreign Minister under Constantinos Mitsotakis before breaking with New Democracy to form a new conservative party. (He would later return to the fold and lead New Democracy in the 2012 elections, becoming Prime Minister of a coalition government.)

Fortunately, I was able to put together an incredible team.

Theodore had no official standing with the committee, but he made good on his promise of complete support, becoming, in effect, my consigliere. His assistance proved invaluable to me as well as a stroke of good fortune for Athens. As an international businessman, Theodore wasn't constrained by the provincial thinking that was endemic in Greece. Moreover, he had a gift for cutting through all the political b.s. While the Greek power players persisted in their maneuvering in the wake of my appointment, Theodore suggested that my first move should be to get out of Greece. "You won't learn how to do this from Greeks," he said. "To find a strategy, we need to go to where the pros are." The pros he had in mind were in Lausanne, where the IOC was headquartered; they knew from long experience what a successful bid campaign required.

Theodore immediately contacted ex-King Constantine to seek his help in setting up a meeting with IOC President Juan Antonio Samaranch. Though they were not close friends, Theodore and Constantine had attended the same boarding school, Anavryta Classical Lyceum in Athens, a school founded on the principles of German educator George Hahn and modeled on his most famous schools: Schule Schloss Salem in Germany and Gordonstoun in Scotland. Despite having been in exile for almost three decades, Constantine had remained a controversial figure in Greece, a convenient symbol for the Socialists to deplore whenever it served their agenda. Permitting him any role in our effort risked controversy at home, but we desperately needed a quick leg up in our campaign. As a highly respected figure in the Olympic movement—an Olympic gold medalist in sailing at the Rome 1960 Summer Games and an honorary member of the IOC—Constantine was positioned to accelerate our access to key IOC officials.

In no time we were sitting down in Lausanne with Samaranch, the man who had transformed the Olympics from a prestigious athletic competition into an international economic juggernaut. He wasn't one to waste time on a lot of flowery rhetoric. In clear and concise terms, the IOC President laid out a framework for how we should proceed with the business of our bid. Theodore, more internationally oriented than I was, grasped the implications immediately. He understood that we couldn't be constrained by our country's provincial instincts. We had to hire advisers who had either worked in the IOC or with the IOC and who knew its voters and its processes and how to wage an Olympic campaign. We needed top marketing pros who spoke all three of the official languages—English, French, and the bureaucratese of the IOC—that the process demanded. Though it pained me, I would even tell my trusted associate Lefteris Kousoulis, who had been at my side since my first Athens city council campaign, that unless he could learn English very quickly or was willing to pay for a simultaneous interpreter, he wouldn't be able to play a key role on my team.

All the requirements pointed to hiring outsiders—Americans, Brits, and Swiss—and we needed to get them on board yesterday if not sooner. I hired a number of consultants who came highly recommended. When some didn't work out, I connected with George Stephanopoulos—a friend in the United States whom I had known through his political work with President Clinton. George was the perfect choice. A Greek-American who came from a traditional family (his father is a Greek Orthodox priest), he is a thoroughly modern thinker and a master strategist. Lefteris, whose father was also a Greek Orthodox priest, had come up with the concept "Athens in Motion," and George ran with it, casting our campaign firmly in the present and the future rather than in our gloried past.

Our Olympic legacy would be the physical and emotional transformation of Athens into a modern European capital poised to take on the new millennium. For us, the Olympics were no longer a story of Olympia and the temple of Zeus or the legend of a soldier who ran from Marathon to Athens to bring news of the Greek victory over the Persians. Rather, it was a tale of the new airport, the new trains, the new trams, the new roads, and the new athletic facilities. George proposed that we hire a trio of American media and communications consultants—Mark Steitz, David Dreyer, and Robin Schepper—as point persons for our international campaign. All three of these Clinton-Gore campaign veterans embraced our cause fully and proved to be invaluable teammates.

Before I left Switzerland, Samaranch reminded me of the Greeks' propensity to blame others for their misfortunes. "There are no foreign enemies out there," he said. "You Greeks are your own worst enemy." So while I returned to Greece confident that I was on the right path, I wasn't surprised to find that others in powerful positions weren't quite as sanguine about my first efforts. They were furious that I hadn't first presented my ideas to the committee for approval, a process that almost certainly would have ensured that nothing got done, or, if it did, that it would have been done far too late.

Here's an example—only other Greeks won't be shocked—of the kind of obstacles I confronted at home. We faced a critical mid-August deadline to produce a detailed bid file in which we detailed our plans and sundry projects for the Summer Games. Besides Athens and Rome, eight other cities were organizing bids: Stockholm, Buenos Aires, Rio de Janeiro, Istanbul, Cape Town, Seville, Lille, and St. Petersburg. At that point, Athens wasn't even guaranteed inclusion among the five cities invited to Lausanne for the final IOC vote.

Given that we were already behind schedule, producing a first-rate bid file in just a few months should have been the most daunting of our challenges. But we found experts who somehow managed to render our complex ideas into detailed plans with extraordinary dispatch. The hard part turned out to be securing the deposit that each city was required to submit to the IOC along with the bid file. The ante was only $100,000, petty cash by the standards of our Olympic endeavor. But when I sought the money, nobody in the government—not the Finance Minister, not the Sports Minister, not any Minister—could find any money in their budget for our campaign or was willing to cut us a check! I had been on the job for less than four months and already time was running out on our Olympic dream. How was I going to explain this preposterous failure? "We could afford an Olympics, but not the filing fee." Ultimately, an exasperated Theodore wired the IOC $100,000 from his Swiss bank account to keep our bid alive. It would not be the last time that Theodore and I bailed out Greece by bankrolling its Olympic campaign.

And that was pretty much how it proceeded, with our experts doing their jobs diligently while I begged and scraped for the money necessary to do mine. Because I had no faith in the government effort, I was a total pain in the ass. I double- and triple-checked for accuracy every detail of every document provided to us. And I rode the bureaucrats mercilessly to get the work done on time. The Greeks don't have a word that expresses it quite as well as the Spanish word *mañana*, but that has long been the operating philosophy in Greece. "Okay, we'll do it tomorrow."

And when tomorrow came, there would be endless more tomorrows. Throughout the entire campaign, we would be slowed and stymied by the repeated failures of government Ministers and their bureaucracies to deliver on their commitments to us. They seemed perfectly willing to let the bid campaign fail and then blame it on the committee.

For the entire sixteen months, I just kept telling myself: "Find a way. Be bold. Make decisions yourself and be prepared to fight for them." It was a never-ending war. When I started the job, there hadn't yet been offices set aside for the committee. I was forced to work out of the first floor at the Grand Bretagne Hotel in downtown Athens, which I had booked and paid for myself. It was an impossible situation and I informed Prime Minister Simitis of the problem. He assured me one of his Ministers would take care of it.

Knowing that that meant nothing would be done, I went out on my own and found space at Zappeion, a mid-nineteenth-century building with significant Olympic connections. It was the first building constructed in Greece specifically with the revival of the Olympics in mind and, at the inaugural modern games in 1896, served as the first Olympic village. The fencing competition was also held in its halls. Surprisingly, for all its beauty and historic ties to the Olympics, Zappeion boasted a modern downtown location that abutted forty acres of splendor that used to be the Palace Gardens. In the near future, IOC delegates would be paraded through Zappeion and few were immune to its charms.

Eventually I came to believe that the Prime Minister, at least in his heart, supported my effort. But his low-key style was a problem for me. While he would tell his Ministers to give me whatever I needed, he was unwilling to ruffle any feathers when they disregarded his instructions. His top advisers viewed me as an outsider and, worse, a member of the opposition. I recall one visit to Simitis's office to plead for the funding for Zappeion that he had already authorized. I watched him pick up the phone and call his economic adviser Nikos Christodoulakis to inquire about the delay. I watched Simitis smile and nod his head. When he hung up, he assured me, "Nikos will take care of it."

"Nikos" had no such intention. I was on friendly terms with a journalist who happened to be sitting with Christodoulakis when he received that call. Afterward, while Simitis was smiling and nodding and giving me polite assurances, his economic adviser was venting his displeasure. "I mean this wealthy bitch comes here playing games as if we will really win the [Olympic] Games," he told the journalist. "She comes from the opposition—the people who actually have all the money—and she wants me to spend our money so she can fly around on her private jet, wear her jewels, and have drinks with all these important people. And then in the end, we will lose as well." When the journalist asked about his intentions, Christodoulakis replied, "The Prime Minister will forget and she'll have to go back to him and complain again."

Simitis may not have forgotten, but I'm not sure that he ever believed—until the final weeks—that Greece could win. So he didn't know how much actual capital—both real and political—he should invest in what ultimately could be a losing fight. I was stuck in this ridiculous, even surreal pattern. I would request money, the Prime Minister would assure me it would be forthcoming from a Minister, and the Minister would fail to deliver. I remember asking Simitis on one occasion: "Why don't you just sack him? Or better yet, throw him out the window." Regrettably, I would find myself repeatedly making that same suggestion throughout all the years the Prime Minister and I worked together on the Summer Games. Hearing it then for the first time, Simitis shrugged sort of sheepishly and said, "But Mrs. Angelopoulos, these are my people."

If Athens was to be a viable contender, I simply couldn't wait for the government to get things done. It was Theodore who would say, "Just pay it," or "Hire them." So we were paying rent on our headquarters as well as salaries and consultant fees out of our own pockets. Perhaps that's what the government was counting on, though the Prime Minister always seemed embarrassed and would assure me, "You know, Mrs. Angelopoulos, that we will pay you back." That never happened. After the campaign was over, my final financial report revealed that

Theodore and I had spent five billion drachmas, or about $15 million, of our own money on the campaign.

And that didn't even count the use of our private jet, which we flew whenever time was critical, which was pretty much all of the time. "If we use our jet, we will get places before the Italians do," Theodore would say. At the same time I delivered the final financial report to the auditors, Theodore and I wrote a letter to the Simitis government forgiving its entire debt to us. "We did it for our country," the letter said. And that was the absolute truth.

When I returned to Athens after my first trip to Lausanne, I briefed the Prime Minister thoroughly, including details of the ex-King's assistance, which to me carried no political connotation whatsoever. I could see he was distressed by Constantine's involvement, which flew in the face of a Socialist orthodoxy that offered no room for the ex-King in the affairs of Greece. I assured Simitis that while I was well aware of his government's policy regarding royals, Athens, as an underdog off to a late start, needed to exploit its few advantages. Sometimes, I told him, you have to work with the devil if the devil is on your side. Another appropriate maxim was that politics makes for strange bedfellows, which was pretty obvious given that I was sitting there with the Prime Minister in the first place. "I understand," was all Simitis said. He clearly did not relish confrontations.

The irate call came instead from Sports Minister Fouras. "Who are you to expose our government and Prime Minister to political embarrassment?" he screamed. "Because you have been consorting with the ex-King, you no longer have my confidence."

"I don't give a damn about your confidence," I told him. "Who do you think you are that I depend on your confidence?"

"I am the Minister," he bristled.

"That's right," I said, "and I am the person who is here to do your job, and you are here to assist me. So assist me or go to hell!" It would be that way between the two of us right up until the moment we were all jumping in the air and hugging to celebrate our victory.

From the start, the bid committee was a disaster. All of the members had their own power base that operated independently. Each member hoped to impose his own ideas. The committee's only common interest was in obstructing any steps I took to propel our stalled bid forward. One by one they began to resign in protest over my leadership, a power play orchestrated by the Mayor in hopes of regaining control of the process. Eventually eight of them, or two-thirds of the bid committee, quit. All were prominent members of Greek society.

The committee members' actions proved to be a miscalculation, however. Twice I offered the Prime Minister my resignation. I truly was ready to return to London, where I had the comfort of a wonderful family and a lovely home. In Athens I was often alone and working late hours. A fight loomed every step of the way. The sacrifices asked of me seemed too many, the challenge too daunting. My charge was all but impossible in the face of the relentless obstructionism from the status quo.

But Prime Minister Simitis ignored my offers and set about convincing me that, however cautious he might be by nature, he was truly on my side. "I'll create a new committee," he promised. "Please," I beseeched him, "can it have just three members?" Simitis understood the problems I faced. Another large and recalcitrant committee might cripple our effort. "No, not three. But we can hold it to five members." He also granted me significant executive powers, enabling me to make certain decisions single-handedly. And this time, instead of appointing representatives from all the powerful and vested interests, he chose smart, productive people, including Lucas Papademos, the respected economist and central banker. (In November 2011, he would be appointed Prime Minister, entrusted with the complex negotiations to prevent Greece from defaulting on its debt.) We had started late and wasted precious time on internecine squabbling. But that was beginning to change. For the first time, we—the Prime Minister, the committee, and me—appeared to be on the same page and working together toward the same goal.

The members of the new bid committee were Lucas Papademos, Kostas Liaskas, Yiannis Sgouros, Andreas Potamianos, and me.

The key members of my staff were Marton Simitsek, whom I nicknamed "the General" and whose leadership skills were later rewarded when I named him COO of the Athens Olympic Organizing Committee (ATHOC); Spyros Capralos, a former Greek Olympian in water polo who would also have a post on the ATHOC steering committee; Dionyssis Gangas, an Athens attorney; and Lena Zachopoulou. (You'll remember that she was with me at the very beginning of my political career, when I ran for the Athens city council.)

Our consultant from Switzerland was Jean Michel Gunz, a former IOC employee and my traveling partner whose obsessive attention to detail rivaled my own.

Our strategy team comprised George Stephanopoulos, Lefteris Kousoulis, David Dreyer, Mark Steitz, Robin Schepper, and Michalis Zacharatos.

And of course I must mention Rita Papadopoulou, Nikos Sismanidis, Dimitris Kalopissis, Manolis Papadokonstantakis, Suzanna Apostolopoulou, Angelica Chantzou, and Panagiotis Lattas, who catered for us with such care.

With a team like this, I felt we had a good chance of winning the bid.

Proud to address students at Harvard

With Joseph Nye, then Dean of Harvard's John F. Kennedy School of Government

Meeting with Al Carnesale, Dean of the John F. Kennedy School of Government,
Janet Reno, US Attorney General, and Joseph Nye, Assistant Secretary
of Defense for International Security Affairs

Talking on the phone with my mother on my birthday morning, December 12, 1995.
Joining me are Theodore, Dim, Carolina, and Pan. Behind me
are pictures from my life.

International Olympic Committee (IOC) officials meet with Greece's Prime Minister, Costas Simitis, for the first time in Athens.

Carolina and me at Zappeion, the Olympic village for the first modern Olympics, 1896

Our bid campaign motto was "Athens in motion." In truth, I was in constant motion, from Cancun . . .

. . . to Monaco . . .

. . . to Guam, for Easter 1997.

But my kids spent the holiday with my mom and our Labrador, Sheen, back in London.

Assisting Juan Antonio Samaranch, the President of the IOC, in planting his olive tree in the IOC Members Park in Athens

Marching toward our destiny— September 5, 1997

And the winner is . . . Athens!

Under the watchful eye of Juan Antonio Samaranch, the IOC's President, I sign the documents with the pen Theodore had bought me in Singapore.

And the dream becomes true: I become an ambassador for my country.

Dressed in the Greek flag

In 1998, after the bid effort, my family united for a short holiday in our Athens home.

Together

Things look good at the media center . . . (To my right in the back stands Yiannis Pyrgiotis, an ATHOC board member.)

Starting from scratch! Vasso Papandreou, the Minister of Public Works and the Environment, and I inspect the sports facilities . . . to be.

The Swiss inspector for the IOC (Denis Oswald) with the local Greek inspector (me)

But there are troubled waters at the rowing venue.

Finding my way through the Olympic Village

The President of the Hellenic Republic, Costis Stephanopoulos, visits the future volleyball stadium.

The press had a field day covering my Olympic efforts. It's not a bird. It's not a plane. It's super Gianna! (Note the gamma, the Greek letter for G, on my chest.)

The text was mean; the caricature was great.

Gianna Croft. Mission accomplished.

The Calatrava roof is finally moving.

Just one year before the opening ceremony: "the General," Marton Simitsek (center); the creative director, Dimitris Papaioannou (far right), and his team; Lena Zachopoulou (left); and me

Overseeing one of the many test events

Torchbearer running at the Sydney 2000 Olympic Games, abandoned at the last minute by the minister responsible for the Athens Summer Games

Unveiling the torch in a rock star mood, with
Jacques Rogge, President of the IOC

Carrying the torch

The first international torch relay visits New York City, with Mayor Michael Bloomberg (above) and *Nia Vardalos of* My Big Fat Greek Wedding *(below).*

NBC's Dick Ebersol had this advice for me: "Be careful, Gianna." My reply? "You can say that again!"

Lifting the Olympic torch with Kofi Annan, the seventh Secretary-General of the United Nations

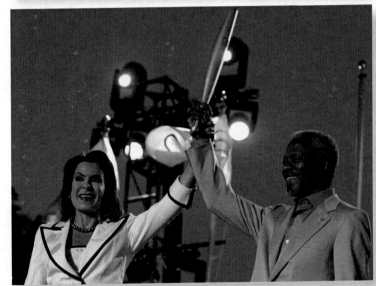

Summer 2004, bearing the torch in front of the palace at Knossos, in Heraklion, Crete

The Greek diaspora honors me in New York City. To my right is Archbishop Iakovos; behind me is George Stephanopoulos's father, Robert, a Greek Orthodox priest; in the second row (far right) is George's mother, Nikki. She was the driving force behind this gathering.

With my trusted friend George Stephanopoulos

Boutros Boutros-Ghali, the sixth Secretary-General of the United Nations

Henry Kissinger

Hillary Clinton

*Vladimir Putin,
the President
of Russia, and
Juan Antonio
Samaranch*

From left: *Juan Antonio Samaranch, me, Queen Sofía and King Juan Carlos of Spain, in Madrid*

Charles, Prince of Wales

Chancellor Gerhard Schröder of Germany

Jacques Chirac, President of the French Republic, graciously receives me at the Élysée Palace. On another visit, he broke protocol to graciously escort me from the Élysée Palace.

Chapter 19

WE COURT THE WORLD

ON MARCH 7, 1997, IN LAUSANNE, exactly six months before the host city would be chosen in the same Swiss city, the IOC announced the technical scores the contenders had received. That meant, most important of all, that the five finalists for the 2004 Summer Olympic Games had been determined. Rome received the highest technical scores, followed by Stockholm. Even though our European rivals led the way, Athens tallied sufficiently high marks to join the final field along with South American rival Buenos Aires and African rival Cape Town.

Each of the four cities with which we were competing presented a formidable challenge, though in diverse ways.

Rome was the consensus favorite. One of the most beloved cities in the world, "The Eternal City" had in 1960 staged one of the most memorable Olympics of the modern era. That impression was undoubtedly bolstered by the fact that they were the first Olympic Games to be broadcast to North America. But even beyond the magnificent backdrop and the pageantry, Rome 1960 was replete with unforgettable performances.

Rome 2004 promised to be no less dazzling. Its technical presentation had been superb and the campaign had big-money backing. Perhaps most important of all, Rome's bid was led by Primo Nebiolo, who, as an IOC member and President of the International Association of Athletics Federations (IAAF), was one of the most powerful and well-connected men in all of international sports. But if Nebiolo was Rome's greatest asset, he also was potentially its greatness weakness. Many in his sporting universe considered him autocratic, and his natural arrogance was exacerbated by Rome's front-runner status. (At times throughout the bidding process, we other contenders got the impression that Rome was laughing at our less ambitious plans and promises. Its campaign team gossiped about our shortcomings and was indiscreet in its public criticism of our efforts. If the IOC President liked to make history, IOC voters historically liked to defy expectations. They have dealt unkindly with front-runners—like Athens in 1990—that appeared to regard the process as less of an election than a coronation.)

Stockholm's plan was impressive, and the Swedes were regarded as the most reliable of the contenders when it came to executing it. Many believed a Stockholm Olympics would produce the least anxiety for the IOC and its partners. Moreover, the Swedish capital hadn't hosted the Games since 1912, almost as long as Athens's hiatus.

Buenos Aires, a long shot because of political unrest and escalating debt there, would also represent a historic decision, as no Olympics had ever been held in South America. And as the only candidate from the Americas, Buenos Aires might carry a solid bloc of voters.

Cape Town was a sentimental favorite given the deep reservoirs of respect and affection for South African President Nelson Mandela. While many in the IOC believed South Africa wasn't ready for such a

massive undertaking, the successful 1995 Rugby World Cup held there
had opened a few eyes. And IOC President Samaranch always had his
eye on making history, which would be the case with the first Olympics
staged on the African continent.

While the technical scoring process was crucial, seldom was there
a knockout. Once the cities passed muster on technical matters, the
competition turned into a classic political campaign. François Carrard,
the IOC Director General, had warned me not to waste time and money
on international media campaigns. "Address the voters, and those are the
IOC delegates." Samaranch echoed his advice, telling me never to lose
sight of the IOC members as individuals who, while sharing a common
cause, differed considerably from one another. There were princes and
business titans among them, but also a teacher from Samoa and a small
businessman from Sudan. We were running in an election with only 107
voters, and each had to be approached as an individual. "You're a smart
person," Samaranch told me. "You will know the way."

Two months after making the final cut, Athens and the four other
finalists made preliminary presentations at an IOC meeting at the Hotel
Ermitage in Monte Carlo. I was scurrying from one task to another
when I almost bumped into Primo Nebiolo. He and his wife were just
coming out of the spa in their bathrobes. I couldn't help thinking that
I was working my butt off and he was relaxing with a soak and a sauna.
He was quite polite, which made me think he didn't consider Athens a
serious threat to Rome. He even invited me to accompany him later that
day to his domain, the IAAF headquarters, above the Hotel de Paris.
When we were returning to the Hotel Ermitage after that tour, I must
have been distracted because I stepped out in the street without looking—right into the path of an oncoming bus. Nebiolo grabbed my hand

and literally yanked me to safety. As I breathlessly tried to thank him, he made light of it. "If I didn't pull you," he said, "everyone would believe I pushed you."

Meanwhile, back in Athens, we had begun to schedule a systematic courtship of the IOC members that would involve hosting them in Greece as well as visiting them in their home cities around the world, while strictly adhering to IOC rules. Between March and August 1997, we welcomed ninety-six IOC members to Greece. When Athens staged the Sixth World Championships in Athletics that summer, sixty-seven IOC members visited, some of them second-timers. Over the course of our campaign, I personally traveled 288,000 miles—a dozen times the circumference of the planet—to generate support for Athens. I made no concession to my personal life. As an example, Theodore and I spent Greek Orthodox Easter on the Pacific island of Guam, presenting our case to the IOC delegates and National Olympic Committee (NOC) members from the region, while our children were home with their grandmother. We also visited and presented our case in Thailand, Cancun, Winnipeg, Iceland, Lausanne (a number of times), Japan, and Korea, among other places.

I was hardly alone in making personal sacrifices. Our adviser Jean Michel Gunz spent so much time flying with me that I honored him with a Cretan name, "Gunzakis." We would always be huddled over a laptop computer as Gunzakis recited our latest assessment of each IOC delegate's preferences. Then we calculated and recalculated our likely vote tally at each stage of the ballot.

When I couldn't make a trip, Theodore usually went in my stead. With some IOC delegates, particularly businessmen, Theodore was a better choice because of others' respect for him around the world. He was really our secret weapon, and he went to extraordinary lengths on behalf of Athens. For example, he once flew to India and Pakistan just to meet IOC members for a couple of hours. Essentially, he put our brochure in a delegate's hands, urged him or her, "Just have a look at us," and was on his way. Another time he flew all the way to Samoa after an IOC delegate there had requested a visit. The man scheduled an elaborate tribal dinner in Theodore's honor, but there was a mix-up over the International Date Line and Theodore wound up arriving a day late. But that was a case when just showing up was more than enough.

There were strict rules limiting how many visits the bid committee could make, and we were sure the Italians were keeping count. But because he held no official position on our bid committee, Theodore could make an extra visit to a critical swing voter. These were in the nature of "courtesy calls" in which he never mentioned the Athens bid or the IOC vote. On ethical matters, I went above and beyond what was required of me personally. Though I may have bristled as a youngster at my father's admonitions, I never forgot what was required of "Caesar's wife." From the beginning of our Olympic involvement, Theodore and I determined that we would conduct no business in Greece for the duration. Nobody would be able to compromise our efforts by pointing to a conflict of interest.

Once the Summer Games were Greece's, Theodore and I received all kinds of proposals, including many offers where we would get a share of the deal without putting up any money. We turned everyone down. The lucky ones simply had their letters returned without a response. But I remember one businessman who had the gall to come to my office and invite me into his enterprise. I threw water in his face and he left looking like a wet kitten in a rainstorm.

Our Athens campaign emphasized the human touch, which was a good fit with our message that our Olympics would be conducted on a human scale. Although that was something of a budgetary necessity, the "human" emphasis resonated with the IOC in that year following the Atlanta 1996 Centennial Games. The southern US capital that had broken so many Greek hearts when it took those games from us was now going to help Athens—however inadvertently—win the 2004 Summer Games.

Back in 1990, Atlanta had sold the IOC on its famed southern hospitality as it bid for the 1996 Summer Games. And the VIPs were certainly wined and dined in warm and gracious fashion during the Centennial Games. But the scene on the streets—and, in particular, on the sidewalks—of Atlanta during the event was the polar opposite. The city's Olympic organizing committee had been greedy and therefore licensed far too many small entrepreneurs to hawk water, T-shirts, and other souvenirs. They overran the downtown and made it look tacky—more neighborhood yard sale than prestigious Olympics—and few reaped the promised rewards. Many became frustrated and angry and their rude behavior was the very antithesis of our notions of genteel southern hospitality.

Samaranch, who had always ended each Olympics with the pronouncement that "these have been the best Games ever," was so distressed by the host city's behaviors that he couldn't find a kind word for Atlanta and its citizens in his traditional remarks at the Closing Ceremony. While Athens knew better than to try again to sell its historic right to the Olympic Games, we would be selling its historic love of them, along with the promise that we in Greece would respect and cherish them. It takes a village or, in this case, an entire country. I always sensed that Samaranch was smiling on our endeavor. He had excellent commercial instincts. And what's best for the product might not always be the biggest or splashiest market. Sometimes broadening the market is less important than revitalizing the core product, giving it a rebirth.

We couldn't allow that loving message to be compromised by the squabbling of Greek politicians. In fact, I wanted politicians out of the process. I didn't care about the politics of the people on my team, only that they represented our country's best talent. I needed the IOC to see a fresh, new Greece, a modern and dynamic nation that, in terms of performance and capabilities, was indistinguishable from its continental neighbors. We entertained our guests in true spirit of *philoxenia*: with Greek food, Greek wine, Greek music, and Greek mythology. But our formal presentations were thoroughly modern, rehearsed many times over and utilizing the most sophisticated technology available.

I relied on a core team of professionals. Each knew his or her part and was thoroughly prepared to answer any questions, never letting ego trump team considerations. Our sessions with the IOC members we hosted provided a useful model for how we prepared for the final showdown in Lausanne. That presentation was scripted down to the second and, by my count, we ended up rehearsing it forty-five times before I deemed it ready for prime time. In Lausanne, participants would also have to be prepared to field questions from the IOC delegates, and our Athens presentations—to these very same delegates on an individual basis—proved to be excellent practice.

Keeping the politicians out of the process assured that there would be considerable resentment from powerful circles and that I would, inevitably, face blowback. Much of it was aimed at me in the form of personal attacks about my wealth.

I'm sure most of the top people in government would have preferred some earnest Socialist in frumpy clothes. But I am always myself, and I wasn't going to pretend to be anyone else. As the first woman to lead a bid committee (and the first one to smoke cigars, since I had just taken up the habit), I would be talking to CEOs of major Olympic sponsors, to the international press, to broadcast executives from around the world, and to such royals as Britain's Princess Anne, Monaco's Prince Albert, Spain's King Juan Carlos and Queen Sofía, and the Netherlands' Queen Beatrix. That I was of their world and spoke their language— and I don't just mean English or French—was a major advantage for Athens. I wasn't going to squander it by playing some everywoman role that made the Socialists more comfortable.

The truth is we treated every IOC visitor like they were royalty. We had an intelligence team researching the likes and dislikes of each delegate. If they liked to relax by playing the piano, they were likely to find a baby grand in their Athens hotel suite. Everything we offered them was of the finest quality, from the flowers that greeted them to the pistachios left for nibbling in their room. I could have wined and dined them in fine Athens restaurants, but I preferred to show them the Greek hospitality that makes our people so special. So Theodore and I usually hosted IOC visitors at our home in Athens, letting them look out on the olive trees and smell the magnolia flowers as they dined.

We would serve elaborate meals of Greek specialties. But just in case the delegates compared notes, I never chose the same menu twice. We wanted everyone to feel equally special. I'd join those who shared my cigar habit—we offered the finest Cuban ones—for an after-dinner smoke. Sometimes we'd enjoy festive *bouzouki* music. Whenever Dionyssis Gangas, in particular, heard this stringed instrument, he would leap to his feet and start dancing. Sometimes he would break into a *hasapiko*, which is derived from the Greek word for butcher, reflecting this dance's roots in the common man. At other times it was a *sirtaki*, the dance made famous in the movie *Zorba the Greek*. (As fate would have it, during the Athens 2004 Summer Games, the "Zorba" theme was played during all of the intervals between the various competitions in all of the stadiums across Athens, and all of the spectators—foreign and Greek— would stand and dance.)

Though every evening in our home varied slightly, the afternoon ceremony with each IOC delegate never wavered from the script.

We would proceed from Zappeion to a small forest nearby, where we had created the IOC members park. In it, we had built a small amphitheater, and from its steps, I would recite the story of the goddess Athena, favorite daughter of Zeus, and the olive tree. The legend tells us that Athena and her uncle Poseidon both had a special affection for one Greek city and both had claimed it as their domain. To settle the matter, they competed to see which one could bestow the finest gift on the city. After ascending the Acropolis, Poseidon struck the cliff with his trident, dazzling the onlookers by creating spring waters. But the waters were salty and thus of limited use. Athena then bestowed on the city its first olive tree, a gift of food, oil, and wood. As a result of her triumph, the city was name Athens and the olive tree stood as a symbol of peace.

After the recitation, each delegate would be asked to plant an olive tree. At the end of a huge field stood flagpoles bearing the flags of every "country" that had planted a tree. The honored visitors got to see their flag raised and to hear their national anthem played. The first IOC member so honored was Jim Easton, accompanied by his wife, Phyllis, from the United States. I swear I felt goose bumps every single time.

We weren't Greeks bearing gifts. We were bearing something far more precious, memories (which were preserved with photographs, of course). Before each guest departed, they were presented with a silver-framed photo album commemorating their visit. I checked each frame personally to make sure there were no fingerprints or smudges on the silver.

Our bid campaign had become every bit of the professional operation I had envisioned. But it was not perfect. We endured our occasional mishaps. The most memorable occurred during a visit by an influential

South Korean delegate, Mr. Yu Sun Kim, who was accompanied by his wife. Everything went fine until the tree ceremony. As the flag was being raised, I immediately sensed that we had erred and were raising the flag of the wrong Korea. I glanced over at Mr. Kim and he graciously said, "Never mind." Moments later the wrong flag was coming down and the right flag was going up. I breathed a sigh of relief as we proceeded down the amphitheater steps. When the amphitheater had been built, I had pointed out that one of the steps was steeper than the others. Everyone assured me that nobody else would notice the difference and that it didn't matter anyhow. They were half right. Mrs. Kim didn't notice, but her misstep sent her tumbling hard to the ground.

Fortunately, she was not hurt. And she was as gracious as her husband had been earlier. Nevertheless, I was so distressed about these faux pas that I went to the airport the next morning to see Mr. and Mrs. Kim off personally. I saw them safely into a VIP car driven by one of my most reliable associates, who would take them out to their plane. I hadn't proceeded much farther than half a mile from the airport when my phone rang. It was my associate saying, "It happened three times." That's an old Greek expression that means it's fated. And on this occasion, it was literally true. The third disaster occurred when an airport van struck the wing of the Kims' airplane and they were forced to return to the terminal. I told Theodore, "If Kim votes for us after all this, it will be a miracle."

Even when things went smoothly, it was a grind. We presented our plans in the morning, held ceremonies in the afternoon, and dined and danced in the evening. Unlike the men who could get away with one business suit, I had to have available different outfits for different occasions. I don't know how many times I was racing home for the start of a dinner party and was forced to change clothes in the car. If I weren't quite ready, we would stall, calling the man who chauffeured the various VIPs, Nikos Sismanidis, to suggest he take the scenic route just to give me a few more minutes' grace.

We kept in contact with all of the members after their visits. We sent handwritten thank-you notes to everyone we encountered along the way, a lesson I had learned in business. As an added way of saying "thank you," we sent each of them a copy of their home newspaper from the date of their birth. We also kept them updated on our progress. Our courtship was continuous, an attempt to connect to the human being inside the IOC voter. We wanted to engage everyone. It didn't matter which city a member initially supported.

When the contest eventually reached Lausanne, one candidate would be eliminated after each ballot until a city captured more than 50 percent of the vote. So while delegates might be committed to our rivals on the first ballot, we urged them to support Athens—once their first choice was eliminated—on the second or third ballot. I remember one delegate saying, "I am committed to Stockholm first and Cape Town second." When I heard that, I replied, "Okay, then commit to us third." We monitored the preference, known or presumed, of every single delegate and had a good idea at what point—if ever—he or she might consider casting a vote for Greece.

Stripped down to its essentials, our strategy was straightforward: one day at a time, IOC member by IOC member, NOC by NOC, sponsor by sponsor, broadcaster by broadcaster, journalist by journalist—all governed by an obsessive attention to detail that ensured our preparedness. We never postured as champions; we simply put ourselves out there, without pretensions, as worthy aspirants. We were prepared, but we didn't want our opposition to see us coming. As the Chinese General Sun Tzu understood more than two thousand years ago, "The element of surprise is key."

As we worked hard, presented our plans, planted our olive trees, ate our Greek feasts, and danced to our beloved and diverting Greek melodies, I could sense the momentum growing behind our bid. There was an emerging recognition that, in the wake of Atlanta, Greece might offer a healing balm for the Olympic Games. Nebiolo may have begun to suspect that Rome's prospects of hosting in 2004, seemingly inevitable a year earlier, were fading. Which may account for his actions—and mistakes—when the Sixth World Championships in Athletics were held in Athens August 1–10, 1997, just one month before the scheduled IOC vote in Lausanne.

Those world championships provided us with a chance to showcase our organizational skills and our Olympic plans. We won over fans with a stirring Opening Ceremony created by Vangelis, the Oscar-winning composer of the score for *Chariots of Fire*. We won over journalists by accommodating the two most critical needs of working reporters: a media center that broke new ground in ease of Internet access, and excellent, bountiful varieties of food.

And official visitors could come to Zappeion, where they'd see a mock-up of our proposed Olympic village as well as a full-sized model of the living quarters.

But those world championships were also an occasion for Nebiolo to shine. As President of IAAF, he still commanded center stage. But from that enviable position, he demonstrated a shocking lack of grace and good manners. First, after an early and unimportant session drew only sparse attendance, Nebiolo publicly criticized Greeks for failing to show up and suggested that the Greek people weren't really great sportsmen. The Greek people responded to the insult by filling the Olympic stadium for every remaining session. Nebiolo's second mistake occurred in the privacy of the VIP area of the stadium, which wasn't very private at all considering that so many IOC delegates were camped there between major events. After an Italian woman won Italy's only gold medal of the meet, I walked over to Nebiolo and extended my hand to congratulate him. There was no doubt in my mind or that of any of the dozens of witnesses that he saw my hand before he turned his back on me.

Nebiolo was always more feared than loved. And Greece's flawless performance in hosting a major competition, coupled with his classless acts, may have helped tip the race in our favor. (If so, he would gain a measure of redemption when, in 1999, just a few months before his death, he helped his hometown of Turin orchestrate an upset over favored Sion, Switzerland, to win the 2006 Winter Olympics.)

When I visited Prime Minister Simitis right after the successful completion of the Sixth World Championships in Athletics, I told him—for the very first time—that I truly believed Athens would prevail in the bid for the 2004 Summer Olympics. I could tell from his smile, no longer just tolerant or bemused but bordering on exuberant, that he believed it too.

Chapter 20

A GOLD-MEDAL PERFORMANCE

SHARING A SMILE WITH THE PRIME MINISTER in the late summer of 1997, I reflected on how far we had journeyed together. I understood how taxing it had been for him, in the face of unrelenting opposition from his own people, to appoint me, a wealthy conservative who resided in London, to such a prominent post. And he had proved steadfast, if not always sufficiently forceful, in his support. All the same, his support had not inured me from the machinations of and malicious attacks by the hacks and hatchet men surrounding him.

I had decided that win or lose I had endured enough. I had not only led this effort without break—at considerable sacrifice to me and my family—but had bankrolled it too. I was worn out, exhausted by the constant fighting and the mean-spiritedness of my political enemies. I would proceed to Switzerland and, hopefully, win the bid and the glory for Greece. "I will do my job," I assured Simitis at our final meeting before I left for the IOC confab. "But I'm fed up with all of it. After that, I just want to go home."

What ensued following that conversation only strengthened my intentions. I received a call from Theodoros Tsoukatos, one of the Prime Minister's top advisers, requesting an urgent meeting before I departed for Lausanne. After courteously opening the conversation, he immediately inquired as to my plans after Lausanne. Having just informed his boss of my plans, I didn't understand the question and told him so.

"Well, will you form a new political party?" he asked.

"It never crossed my mind," I said.

"Are you sure?" he said, insultingly. "What do your people in New Democracy say?"

"I don't have any people," I said with growing irritation. "I left Parliament seven years ago. I have a different life now. I didn't do this so that I could run for office. I did it for my country."

Tsoukatos's questions and attitude were particularly galling because my approach had been completely nonpartisan. I had met with every political party along with every interest group as part of an effort to create a broad consensus in support of our Olympic quest. And it had worked. Polls showed that 95 percent of Athenians backed our bid.

But Tsoukatos wasn't really listening to me. He and his cronies obviously couldn't get past the fact that my face was all over the newspapers and television in Greece and abroad. If you were in the news, you had to have a hidden political agenda. It never crossed their minds that I was in the news because I was working so hard to achieve something for our country.

Definitely it didn't cross my mind that I should run again for office after my resignation.

That brief encounter—more than a decade before Greece's economic debacle would become front-page news around the world—is a microcosm of the failure of leadership that has haunted Greece. At a time when Greece was poised for a historic triumph that could rebrand and rejuvenate our country, the politicians' focus was on my possible political ambitions. Greek governments of all political persuasions have made public service and leadership barely an afterthought.

The priority of Greece's politicians had been to maintain the party in power rather than to do what's best for the country. Decisions were made on the basis of one consideration: "Will it help me or hurt me at the ballot box come the next election?" That approach is shameful and the results have been tragic for the Greek people.

Despite my final dispiriting clash with this close associate of Simitis, I remained focused on the mission ahead. I was aware that IOC elections had proved unpredictable in the past and a single stumble could be costly. I wouldn't let up until my job was done, until the Athens 2004 bid team had completed our final presentation to the IOC. Then our hopes and dreams would be at the mercy of the 107 IOC delegates who would cast their votes.

In Lausanne, I kept campaigning right up until the end, courting anyone and everyone I encountered. But there was one meeting that I deemed most critical of all, and it was one that, by IOC rules, I wasn't permitted to attend. It was time once again for Theodore to step in and make another "unofficial" courtesy call. He sought ex-King Constantine's help, this time to arrange a meeting with South African President Nelson Mandela.

Theodore visited Mandela, accompanied by the IOC's South African delegate, at his quarters in the Lausanne Palace Hotel. He would later tell me that Mandela welcomed him warmly. Gentle and soft-spoken, he was not prone to posturing or to the kind of political double-talk that Theodore deplores. Mandela projected a quiet strength and his wisdom and integrity shone through. Theodore told him how much we admired him personally and that we'd been impressed by his country's first Olympic campaign.

Our hope was that the President felt some rapport with the underdogs from Athens and that—if Cape Town was eliminated before Athens—he might throw his support our way. We would have been genuinely happy to do the same for Cape Town. But in truth, while Athens had widespread support from delegates around the world, we didn't control them. Mandela, by contrast, commanded a huge influence over Cape Town supporters, particularly the delegates from the African continent.

It's easy to misjudge such moments—especially in a relatively brief encounter—and to confuse graciousness for support. But at the very least, Theodore felt he had established, on Greece's behalf, a bond with the South African President. As it turned out, Cape Town was the last contender eliminated before the contest came down to Athens vs. Rome. We'll never know if Mandela said anything on our behalf to Cape Town voters. All we do know now is that in the final tally Athens won fourteen of Cape Town's twenty votes.

The connection that Theodore felt with Mandela proved to be genuine. Later that year, during my visit to South Africa, signs were posted everywhere reading, "Congratulations Athens." Cape Town was the only competing city to recognize me and my country in so public a fashion. By contrast, I thought if I were to visit Rome I would have to don armor. I met President Mandela at his home, a special honor for me and a chance to offer my heartfelt thanks for his extraordinarily generous spirit.

Years later, during the 2004 Olympic global torch relay, I was totally occupied with the Summer Games and wouldn't dare leave Athens. Theodore, however, was luckier and traveled on our private jet to many countries where the relay was taking place. He savored the warm welcome of the Olympic torch in Beijing, Cape Town, and Rio de Janeiro. President Mandela was a torchbearer in South Africa, and he invited Theodore to visit the cell on Robben Island where he was kept prisoner for twenty-seven years.

We wouldn't have been Greek if those final days in Lausanne had passed without a political crisis. The Prime Minister and I had agreed that we would keep the involvement of politicians to a minimum, especially since politicians had been overrepresented in Athens's doomed bid for the Centennial Games. Mayor Avramopoulos was required by IOC protocol to speak, but he was brief. Simitis confined his own role to a short videotaped message from our headquarters at Zappeion. But once Athens appeared to have a winning hand, some politicians wanted to claim the spotlight. George Papandreou, the future Prime Minister who was then Foreign Minister, not only insisted on joining us in Lausanne but also demanded to be part of the presentation team. I told the Foreign Minister "no," and refused to rewrite our script. (Remember, we had rehearsed it for weeks and timed it down to the second.)

Outraged by my rejection, Papandreou called Simitis, who apparently told him, "This is Mrs. Angelopoulos's decision." Still not satisfied, he appealed to Samaranch, who had been well briefed and told him, "This is Gianna's decision." (Papandreou was particularly sore that he couldn't gain a place in our lineup when a twenty-six-year-old "kid" he had never heard of was on the panel. That "kid," Michalis Zacharatos, had played a key role throughout the campaign and would become ATHOC's press spokesman during the Olympics. Sixteen years after Lausanne, he continues to work as an associate and adviser to my husband and me.)

Once again, I was reminded how politics makes for strange bedfellows. There they all were with me in Lausanne: the Mayor who had tried to block my appointment and, later, to force my resignation; the

Sports Minister who had become so irate that he had lost all confidence in me; and the Foreign Minister who, when I desperately needed support, hadn't given me the time of day. Fouras even promised that he would shave off his moustache if Athens carried the day.

A political flap was to be expected. But given the amount of effort I always invested in looking my very best in public, I would never have imagined that I would also face a little couture crisis. I had given careful thought to our Athens team uniforms, particularly the color combinations, and had personally selected the men's outfit: dark blue trousers, white jackets with our Athens emblem over the heart, Greek blue shirts, and dark blue ties with a pattern of golden olive wreaths intertwined. Samaranch had been enthusiastic about the idea of matching uniforms for the Athens team, unaware that I didn't have one and certainly couldn't secure one in time for the meeting. But I always travel with more outfits than I need so that I could make my choice depending on the vagaries of the weather or the occasion. And I don't know why, but I always play with the colors white and blue—the colors of the Greek flag.

On this occasion my extensive wardrobe saved the day. I had an Yves Saint Laurent outfit that appeared to match the men's, and once my British dresser sewed on the Athens emblem, everybody from Athens looked like they were on the same team.

Bibi Samaranch, the wife of the IOC President, would tell me later that there was an audible buzz—"Ah, Mrs. Angelopoulos wears the uniform"—when I entered with my team for our presentation. It was only later when her husband murmured his approval of our uniform approach that she informed him that any woman could recognize that mine wasn't exactly a perfect match, that it was from a decidedly finer realm of fashion than the men's in terms of fabric and cut.

The night before the final presentation our team had dined together and, afterward, were sitting around the Beau Rivage Hotel suite where Theodore and I were staying, all trying our very best to relax. Our talking points, from the past year and the next morning, were racing through my mind: "Athens for the athletes"; "Optimism is our way of life"; "Ecology is a Greek concern"; "Greece will be good for the Games"; "The marathon on its original route"; "Greece keeps its promises. We are making progress every day"; "Athens is in motion!"

As nervous as I was, I was genuinely convinced that we had done everything possible to prepare for this moment. And everyone on my team seemed optimistic or, at the very least, was pretending to be for my benefit. I called George Stephanopoulos, who was back in the United States, for one last consultation, and he advised me to smoke my evening cigar and then go to bed early so as to make sure I got a good night's sleep.

I had just lit up a big Cuban cigar when a consultant from a high-powered British public relations firm I had hired strode up to me with an air of self-importance. The firm had proved clueless and, as a result, I had wound up relying more heavily on Stephanopoulos and the other savvy Americans. I had wanted to fire the Brits, but Theodore suggested I keep them around just in case I found some use for them later. It may have been the only dubious advice Theodore gave me during the entire campaign.

The Brit was waving a piece of paper in front of me and saying, "Mrs. A, I have this statement for you to sign off on." I couldn't imagine what statement could possibly require my attention at that moment. He explained that he had prepared a concession statement in case Athens lost the vote the next day.

Everyone else in the room, all of whom knew me far better than this man, began to retreat to a safe distance, eyeing the chairs that could be toppled and the ashtrays that could become weapons. Just as they expected, I erupted. "For one and a half years, I have dreamed of this moment and I have devoted myself totally so that we can win. Tonight I need to believe that we *will* win. How *dare* you come to me now, when I have to be fully prepared mentally and physically, to remind me that we may actually lose and that I should be a gracious loser? Go stick your statement up your ass!" (Years later at a posh London party, I would meet the CEO of the company that sent me that idiot, and the memory so infuriated me that I gave him a piece of my mind. "Your company gave us nothing," I said. I could see hatred in his eyes, but I didn't care. It was the truth.)

On the morning of the presentation, all omens were good. The final presentations were to take place in a hall at the Palais de Beaulieu convention center. While the IOC had discreetly covered the name of that hall, I knew it was the Salle d'Athènes—the Athens Room—so I felt like we had a home-field advantage. Moreover, we had drawn the third hour, the final presentation of the morning right before the lunch break. All the delegates should be wide-awake by that hour and, hopefully, attentive. By the afternoon session, they might be drowsy after a fine Swiss lunch.

Our presentation went off with only one minor hitch. Nikos Kaklamanakis, an Atlanta Olympic gold medalist in windsurfing and a three-time world champion, appeared to lose his voice during his presentation. But Nikos was handsome and charming. And most folks tend to be more forgiving of verbal stumbles by athletes than those of politicians. We also got away with bending the rules by promising something that hadn't been in our original bid plan. The Lausanne meeting was the first time we mentioned our plans for the first-ever international Olympic torch relay connecting all five continents, but everybody seemed to love the idea and nobody noticed or at least commented upon the breach.

As I stood at the podium and introduced our short films and the other speakers, I felt that we were commanding the audience's attention. No doubt we were benefiting from comparisons with Greece's sloppy and hyperemotional performance the last time it sought the Olympics. By contrast, we were disciplined in our timing, on point in our presentations, and, though striking a few sentimental notes, decidedly professional. We didn't just talk about ancient Olympia; we talked about modern Athens— the new airport, the metro system, the improved air quality, and our green commitment to solar, wind, and geothermal energy.

When it came time for me to conclude our presentation, I felt goose bumps as I made Athens's final plea.

> If the athletes are the dreamers, you are the dream makers. With your vote, you can weave wreaths of victory for the athletes from the olive trees we planted together in your park . . . Nowhere in the world is the heart and heritage of a people more bound together with the Olympic Games. Give us this chance today and we will make you proud. We will give you an Olympics that is good for the Games. This is our promise to you and, with three thousand years of history behind us, it is a promise we are destined to keep.

Afterward, Samaranch congratulated us and asked, since I hadn't used a teleprompter, where I had managed to hide an earpiece. He couldn't believe that there was no earpiece, that I not only knew all my lines by heart but also every single line in our presentation. Despite my exhilaration and the enthusiastic reaction of my Athens team, it didn't take long for those goose bumps to turn back into nerves. The long wait—through the IOC lunch and two more city presentations—was excruciating.

At long last, the hour of reckoning had come, and we awaited the IOC judgment. Naturally, we had one last Greek squabble over our seating arrangements. I was told that I should sit between the Mayor and the Sports Minister. But I was not leaving Theodore's side. He had done more for Athens—with no recognition—than anyone else. "Theodore has always been by my side," I said. "We will sit together." And we did.

Then the vote began. We believed that if Athens could stay close to Rome in the early balloting, we could catch the Eternal City in the end. While Rome was a strong first choice for its backers, I was convinced that many more delegates preferred Athens as their second or third choice. I didn't believe that delegates who were supporting underdogs were likely to gravitate to the favorite—particularly to a rich, arrogant favorite like Rome. The vote would be conducted in private and we would know nothing about the proceedings until the IOC President came out and announced the winner.

As it turned out, we did even better than we expected. The long wait through five ballots would not have been as agonizing if we had known we were in the lead from the start. But we didn't have the comfort of that knowledge.

There is no reason, however, that readers should have to wait too. The results of the first ballot were:

Athens	32
Rome	23
Stockholm	20
Cape Town	16
Buenos Aires	16

The tie for fourth place meant a second ballot run-off to see whether Cape Town or Buenos Aires would survive into the third round, and Cape Town prevailed over Buenos Aires, 62 to 44.

In the third round, Buenos Aires's votes would be scattered among Athens, Rome, and Cape Town, which meant that we maintained our solid lead while Stockholm went out. Had I known we were ten votes up at that point, I might have started breathing again.

Athens	38
Rome	28
Cape Town	22
Stockholm	19

My theory would be tested on the fourth ballot. Would the Europeans who had backed the Swedes gravitate to the other European underdog? As it turned out, they did.

Athens	52
Rome	35
Cape Town	20

The final vote came down to Athens and Rome. But we knew none of this as we squirmed in our seats waiting for the final announcement, though for a long time I had sensed that the vote was heading toward this showdown. While we waited, we were shown some sports videos to pass the time. Fouras, who was so nervous he was babbling, thought every frame of the movie was an arcane clue to the final result. "Why are they showing a Turkish athlete?" he wondered aloud. "What do you think that means?" Did I really have to tell him that it meant absolutely nothing? "Calm down," I told him. "Are you a jerk? Istanbul isn't even one of the candidates."

Finally, and mercifully, the IOC officials paraded back into the hall. The voting delegates did not yet know the result, but they at least knew which cities had made it to the final ballot. First into the room were the honorary members, including ex-King Constantine. Did he have something in his eye or was he actually winking at us? Then came the IOC's voting delegates; our Greek delegate Lambis Nikolaou appeared to be making a classic Greek gesture with his hand, moving it from one side to another, meaning something like the French expression *comme ci, comme ça*, or "so-so." I feared he was signaling that disappointment awaited us. Samaranch was the last to enter the hall, and as he approached the podium, I took a very deep breath. I sensed—or maybe it was my intuition—that he was seeking to locate the delegation from the winning city. Was it my imagination or, for just a second, did he look right at me?

Then came the magical words from the dream maker in his classical Catalan pronunciation of the English: "The city that will have the great honor and responsibility of organizing the Games of the XXVIIIth Olympiad is . . . Athens."

Pandemonium swept over us. Theodore actually lifted me up and was twirling me around as if we were dancing. Everybody was hugging, kissing, and dancing. So many people grabbed me and kissed me that I continually had to retrieve my pearl earrings—a special gift that my husband brought me from Japan when Dimitris was born—from the floor lest they get crushed or lost in the mayhem. I could hear Fouras shouting, "I am going to shave my moustache!" My mother was there with our children and told me that Dimitris, who was just five years old, woke up to the raucous celebration and asked her: "Did we get it? Did we get it?"

In Athens, thousands had gathered at Zappeion to watch the announcement on huge video screens. When Greece won, a huge cry went up from the crowd. "*Hellas! Hellas!*" (Greece! Greece!)

For the first time in decades, the Greek people came together as a proud nation, ready to take their proper place on the world's stage.

When we eventually calmed down, the Athens team was ushered onto the stage for the official signing of the host city contract. I became the first bid-committee President given the honor of signing along with the Mayor. I always carry a number of pens—different pens for different occasions—and this one required a very special pen. Actually, Theodore had given me the pen as a gift a year earlier, in Singapore, and his words were: "Keep it to sign when Athens wins!"

When the formalities were over, somebody passed me a Greek flag. I stood at center stage waving it to our nation and to the world. It was like a fairy tale, only better, because it was real. I had done something truly great, something historic, for my country.

The final vote had been Athens, 66, Rome, 41, the largest margin of victory in a competition to host the Games in almost seventy years.

Afterward, when I got a moment to speak to Samaranch alone, he seemed almost as happy as I was. Though he had never shown us any favoritism, I would never forget how helpful he had been from our first meeting and how he had set us on the right course. I had sensed a natural empathy for Athens from many IOC members. Samaranch was clearly delighted to see Greece given this chance.

"Gianna," he said, "you have to be sure you're on the organizing committee."

"That is not going to happen," I told him. "Not after what I went through to reach this moment."

He started shaking his head, indicating he didn't want to hear it. "No, no, no," he protested. "People will trust you."

Later I bumped into the President of NBC Sports, Dick Ebersol. "You know, Gianna," he told me, as we both stood outside smoking a cigar, "Greece needs you to be on the organizing committee because the broadcasters and sponsors trust you."

When I hesitated, he said: "Don't tell me 'no.' I don't trust the others."

And they didn't. History shows that for the following three years nothing happened, and Prime Minister Simitis had to call me back to save the day. The Olympic movement could only trust me.

I couldn't tell Ebersol the truth, that he was right not to trust the others. But there was no way he would understand my decision either. I had had enough of the political warfare and preferred to seek safe harbor at home. In truth, the Greek government had made it no choice at all. Even after the Prime Minister was convinced that we would win, he never mentioned the organizing committee to me or said a word to me about future involvement beyond Lausanne. Though he may have come to value and respect me, he couldn't stand up to all his people who were jealous of me and resentful of my success.

I had beaten Rome at its own game. I had come, I had seen, and I had conquered. *Veni, vidi, vici!* (Perhaps the headline in the *Philadelphia Inquirer* soon thereafter was my favorite: "In Battle to Host 2004 Olympics, It's Athens' Turn to Conquer Rome.")

A huge party followed at the Lausanne Palace Hotel—for which I wore a Yves Saint Laurent suit—where all our delegation and friends from other countries and cities danced into the early hours of the morning. We won the Games on September 5, 1997. Later, I realized that it had been exactly seven years to the day from my resignation from Parliament in which I promised to "find an occasion in the future to again serve my country." And I had. Leave it to the Greek government to put a damper on our celebration. It seemed that they wanted to ensure that I wouldn't return to Greece as some kind of conquering hero. The last thing they wanted was for the Greek people to think that people in service of their country might actually achieve something. Which is why the plane sent to take us home didn't reach Lausanne until two days later. We arrived back in Athens unannounced and, rather conspicuously, too late for the nightly news. My father-in-law was waiting for us at the airport, and I was so moved to see him there that I went up and—out of deep respect—kissed his hand. "Why do you kiss my hand?" he asked. "It is you who have done it."

We were rushed to the Prime Minister's building, where we joined a small VIP reception. The rest of the team was loaded onto a bus that trailed far behind us. My team considered it a deliberate snub and chose to remain on the bus rather than make a belated entrance to a reception where they weren't wanted. Afterward, we all gathered together at Zappeion, where thousands of Greeks waited to celebrate with music and dancing. I danced the Cretan *pentozali* with unabashed pride and joy.

The following year the government would honor me with a ceremony at which I was named Ambassador-at-Large by Foreign Minister Theodoros Pangalos. It was a belated gesture, but one that meant a great deal to me. For a Cretan girl who had dreamed of being an ambassador so as to serve her country, it brought my journey full circle. I had every reason to believe that the honor was the punctuation mark ending the final chapter of my public service. Then again, I have never been a prophet to rival the oracle of Delphi.

Chapter 21

A TALE OF TWO CITIES

SIC TRANSIT, GLORIA!

I had told Prime Minister Simitis the truth when I said I was ready to return to my London home. That didn't mean I was fully prepared for the wide range of emotions that lingered, however. While I shared the thrill of victory with the Greek people—even at a distance of some two thousand miles, their joy was palpable—I also felt the sting of betrayal. Though I had certainly been warned by my friends as well as by Samaranch, it pained me to discover firsthand that my worst enemies were not the Romans or anyone I had competed against but rather those who were supposed to be on my side. And it hurt to be cast aside, like a mother who gives birth and is not allowed to raise her own child.

Returning to London, to the love of my family, proved an excellent balm for the emotional wounds I had suffered in the Olympic wars. And the next few years would prove to be among the most enjoyable of my life. My children were growing up wonderfully and were flourishing in school and in the city. I reengaged with Theodore's business as well as with my work for the Dean's Council at Harvard's Kennedy School.

And Theodore and I were far more active socially than we'd ever been. I do not consider myself a jet-setter; I am totally content being on my own. However, we have always enjoyed the company of important and interesting people. We entertained at home and enjoyed a wide range of friends, from Charles, Prince of Wales, and Camilla, Duchess of Cornwall, to top businessmen and "legends" from around the world. We tried to mix and match our guests: having a Dean of Harvard sit next to a media mogul, or an opera singer sit next to an academic.

We also traveled to visit new friends. The Agnelli brothers invited us to Turin once for the centennial celebrations of FIAT (where we met Henry Kissinger); on another occasion, the Emir of Qatar sought to meet us. In the lead-up to the 2004 Summer Games, I was invited twice to meet with French President Jacques Chirac. Far more quickly than I had expected, I felt revived by my life in London and remarkably content.

In my defense, I tried to keep the Olympics at a distance. The entire inertia about them bled my heart. It was as if the Summer Games were a fantasy I had created, not a reality. Nobody from the government wanted me to have anything to do with the effort. But whenever I visited Greece, the public would show—like a wave—its gratitude and admiration. My poll ratings were sky high. I felt completely torn: How could the public treat me so well yet the government treat me so poorly?

I had far too many friends in Greece, in the IOC, and in the international Olympic community not to be fully apprised of all the news from Athens. And the news was not good.

Athens was not in motion; the dazzling plans we had set forth— our promise to the world—were gathering dust in desk drawers. These undertakings were not optional endeavors. We had signed contracts assuring the IOC that certain measures of progress would be reached by specific deadlines, and the Greek government was their guarantor. "You have to go back and take over," callers would urge me, as if the choice was up to me. "What would you have me do?" I'd ask. "Get down on my knees and beg for the job? Say, 'Please hire me.'?"

It hadn't surprised me that the Greek effort had stalled. Organizing the Olympics, as I would discover later, is a daunting journey that would have strained even Odysseus (or Ulysses as he was known in Latin). The job demanded a unique set of diverse talents. It required bringing together the business and political community to ensure the success of the Games. And it required an instinctive connection with the Greek people so as to keep them emotionally invested in the Olympics during the long seven-year wait for the torch to arrive in Athens. Because volunteers had become the backbone of all previous Olympics in recent memory, Athens 2004 would necessitate—from a country with no culture of volunteerism—thousands of its citizens answering a call to service if the Games we would host were to be a success. Many more Athenians would be asked to sacrifice comfort and convenience during the Summer Games to accommodate the needs of the non-Athenians who would invade the city, and obviously the effort required political consensus. The public had to rise to the challenge of creating what was in essence a new city.

In Olympic parlance, running ATHOC, the organizational committee for the 2004 Summer Games, would be, at the very least, completing a triathlon on top of a marathon. I had run the bid committee and had faced all these issues. It was hard to imagine the ravages of a seven-year campaign. And, quite candidly, even though the Angelopoulos means made me an easy target for the Greek Socialists, I'm not sure that I could have succeeded in my mission without those means.

All of which is to say it didn't come as a shock when Athens failed to hit the ground running. It wasn't until early 1998—six months after the triumph in Lausanne—that Simitis had a President in place for ATHOC. His choice, former New Democracy Minister Stratis Stratigis, had some of the requisite skills demanded by the job, as he was multilingual and an attorney in Athens. But he was also regarded as something of a *bon viveur*—and he told terrific jokes—and his social agenda would eventually prove his undoing. The Prime Minister would later name Costas Bakouris, a successful Greek businessman who had worked in Switzerland, as CEO of the committee. The two-pronged leadership—Stratigis as the public face and Bakouris as the inside man—was recognition of the vast and varying requirements of the job.

But I had always believed in the one-person rule, with one person responsible for building a great team, and from that team would come hundreds and thousands more, and eventually the whole country—Team Greece.

Though I may not have been surprised by Athens's early organizational missteps, I was certainly surprised to get a call—about a year after Lausanne—from Prime Minister Simitis's office. I was informed that he and his wife, Dafni, would be visiting London and were hoping to visit with Theodore and me. Though I had trying relationships with many key players in his government, Simitis and I had maintained a civil one. And I understood why—for reasons of political expediency—he had needed to keep his distance. Though his call was entirely unexpected, I was happy to invite the couple to dine with us at the Old Rectory. I was quite curious as to what had brought the Prime Minister to my door. I couldn't imagine it was purely a social call.

But Simitis proved in no hurry to reveal his business. He took a tour of our home and played with my sons, entertaining them with some tricks he performed with his hands. Later on, when it was just the four of us at dinner in the big dining room (with our unique tapestries and a carpet once owned by Greta Garbo), the Prime Minister began to talk about the Olympic organizational effort. It was quite challenging, he conceded, and wasn't proceeding as quickly or as smoothly as he had hoped. And then I got to experience a little déjà vu from a few years earlier. Only this time it was the Prime Minister calling on me face-to-face rather than the Sports Minister calling me on the phone. Simitis wanted to know if I might consider getting involved with the committee, perhaps from London as a Vice President with international responsibilities. What I thought was: "I led the bid that won the Olympics for Greece and now you ask me to return as a number two? Don't you remember that the only number I like is number one?"

What I actually said was, "I will not accept anything that does not give me ultimate responsibility for the committee decisions yet obligates me to go around trying to explain those decisions and patching up all the problems they create.

"You know me," I continued, though this conversation had made me less certain of that. "There is no way I would do this the way you suggest it."

It would be almost a year before I would hear from the Prime Minister again. This time he phoned and what ensued was a far more unusual conversation. There had been more turmoil in Athens. Already under fire for a lack of progress, social butterfly Stratigis had accepted an invitation to attend the social event of the London season, the wedding of Princess Alexia, daughter of ex-King Constantine. It was a major political gaffe.

To put this in perspective, three years earlier, when I had discreetly permitted the ex-King to set up a meeting for us with Samaranch that Constantine *hadn't even attended*, there had been a major flap in the Simitis government nonetheless. To publicly socialize with Constantine while holding a public role was viewed by the Prime Minister and his government as virtually an act of treason. Simitis felt he had no choice but to demand Stratigis's resignation. "It was simply unacceptable," the Prime Minister told me over the phone just one day before the royal wedding was to take place in London.

Though Theodore and I were to be guests at that royal wedding, I understood the political realities the Prime Minister faced and why he couldn't allow such a provocation to go unanswered. Simitis then shared, just as he had when he visited the previous year, his concerns that the Olympic committee was not doing its job properly and that a new approach was required. For the moment, however, all he asked of me was a favor—a rather unusual favor. "I would appreciate it very much if you would not attend this wedding," he said. The normal response would have been to ask him why not, expecting to hear what the quid would be for my quo. Instead, I took an unusual tack for me. I was silent. And in this silence, he certainly heard my compliance. We both understood that we had begun an elaborate dance, a *pas de deux*, and it might be some time before we took the next step.

If I was intrigued when I hung up the phone, I was ashamed too. Constantine deserved far better than this rude treatment by me. But I felt somehow compelled to acquiesce to the Prime Minister's wishes in order to see how things played out. When I informed Theodore, he was not particularly pleased but decided to go to the wedding without me. We discussed whether I should cancel beforehand or simply let him say I had taken ill at the last moment. But we knew it wouldn't matter, that Constantine, acutely attuned to the politics of Athens, would see through my charade.

So I stayed home. I was both embarrassed with myself and disappointed to miss the festivities, especially as I had bought a beautiful outfit for the occasion (though it was not quite as extravagant as the Gaultier ensemble I would one day put together for the wedding of Prince William and Kate Middleton). When Theodore returned, he said he could tell that Constantine and his family were annoyed about my absence. There were some elements of farce in all of this bad behavior. Stratigis had insulted the Prime Minister by going to the wedding and, as a result, I had insulted the ex-King by not going.

From then on, I paid careful attention to what was going on in Athens with the organizing committee, which still appeared to be not much of anything. The situation was getting more dire by the day. The IOC was evidently quite perturbed. There were even rumors that Samaranch was considering pulling the Olympics out of Athens and moving them to Sydney, which as host of the upcoming 2000 Summer Games would have all the facilities in place for a repeat in 2004. That would be a far greater humiliation for Greece than the failure to win the Centennial Games.

The phone calls urging me to return to the Olympic effort became more frequent. "Are you crazy?" I would say. "I should go and be the scapegoat? You cannot organize an Olympics in four years' time." I even got a call from Samaranch who was clearly despairing. "Gianna, things are not going well," the IOC President told me. "I have told them they are very close to a red light." Despite the distressing calls and my growing anger that the prize I had helped Greece to win was being mistreated, I did not criticize the government or the organizing committee publicly. I kept my distance and my mouth shut.

Nothing happens too swiftly in Greece—or at the IOC, for that matter—and it wasn't until April 2000 that Samaranch took the unprecedented step of going public with his concerns. He labeled the situation in Athens the worst organizational crisis he had faced in his two decades at the helm of the IOC. He said that he had told organizers that a yellow light meant there were many difficulties and a red light meant serious trouble. "We are at the end of the yellow phase," he said, warning that "drastic changes" were required to set Athens on the right course.

In private, Samaranch may even have been advocating for my return. But if he was, I wasn't in the loop. Otherwise, Theodore and I might not have been in Salzburg, Austria, in the middle of an opera festival weekend. People joke that to get a seat at the Salzburg Opera house, someone has to pass away. I was thrilled to be there, enjoying the black tie crowd and the show, but when two people next to us began booing the performance—not uncommon among opera connoisseurs—I wanted to put my Manolo Blahnik heels into them. After the performance, when Theodore and I were dining at the Goldener Hirsch Hotel, our waiter informed me that I had a phone call. On the other end of the line was Lena in Athens. She had been desperately trying to reach me. "The Prime Minister wants to talk with you," she said.

It was loud in the hotel restaurant, so I went out into the lobby for what proved to be a brief conversation. When I told the Prime Minister I was in Salzburg for the opera, he said, "How I envy you." Then he asked, "Were you planning to come to Greece?"

"We don't have any plans to visit to Greece," I told him. "But we will certainly come if you want us to."

"If you could," he said. "It would be best if you and Theodore would come to my offices Monday night. It will be much quieter then, when all the reporters and cameras have gone home for the day."

We returned to London the next morning. Theodore had decided that before we went to Greece the following day, it would be wise to sit down with Samaranch and get his counsel on this matter. We located him in his native Barcelona and flew down for a chat. Samaranch was one of the smartest and shrewdest people I have ever met. He didn't try to overwhelm you with big, flowery speeches, but he packed a lot of wisdom in a few words. The IOC President got to the point quickly: No matter how bad the situation in Greece was—and it was very bad, he said—I had no choice but to accept the challenge. The IOC, the corporate sponsors, the broadcasters, and all the other key players trusted me and had confidence in me. Operating with mutual respect and trust was the only way we could make up for lost time. In fact, I represented their—as well as Greece's—last, best hope.

His encouragement came with a familiar warning, however. He reminded me that Greek politicians, with their internecine rivalries and inclination to blame everyone else for their woes, were their own worst enemies.

On the other hand, he said, I would arrive in Greece at a rare moment when everyone at the table would have the best of intentions. "You have the government over a barrel. Simitis needs you, and to get you he will agree to whatever you want. I urge you to get it all *in writing*."

A little more than twenty-four hours later I was sitting on the couch in the Prime Minister's office, where everything Samaranch had said was being borne out. At first Simitis had resumed our dance. When I asked him if he wanted me to lead the Olympic effort, he responded by asking me if I would accept the job were it offered. Again I repeated my question and this time desperation trumped his natural caution. He not only wanted me to return, he assured me that his government would support my endeavors in every way possible. If I wanted, he would fire the CEO and he would change the committee board too. He would imbue both me, as President, and the committee with new powers that would expedite our procedures. And he would personally intervene to halt the incessant squabbling among his Ministers over jurisdictional powers. He promised to support me "land and water," which is a Greek expression from the time of Herodotus that essentially means everywhere and in everything.

As usual, Samaranch had been right. The floodgates had opened. The only promise the Prime Minister didn't make was to put all his promises in writing. And at that moment, when Simitis was so candid, almost desperate, and at a dead end, I didn't have the heart to demand a written contract. Though I feared what might lie before me—I thought that four years rather than seven might still be a challenge beyond even my abilities—the truth was that I wanted this job as much as Simitis wanted me to take it. When I won the bid for the 2004 Summer Games, it was as if I had given birth to a child. I had bled for that child and now, almost three years later, found it neglected, even abandoned. How could I let it remain orphaned? How could I not try to save my baby? How could I resist the chance to raise it with love and care?

I was not unaware of the irony. To save the child I would have to step away from my own children in London: seventeen-year-old Carolina, nine-year-old Pan, and eight-year-old Dim. For a while, the Games would get more of my care and attention than my own children would. I hadn't planned for this moment. But now that the opportunity had availed itself, I wanted it and I grabbed it. I was back in the Games. The Olympics were a little more than four years away.

The next day the Prime Minister made it official, with a public statement from his office that—at his request—was broadcast on all TV channels. He was effusive in his praise of me, making it clear that I had not sought out this job, that he had asked me to return home because Greece needed me to save the Athens 2004 Summer Games. All of the press followed the Prime Minister's lead and lavished praise on me. I was no longer the imperious leader riding roughshod over the poor, well-intentioned government officials but the savior riding into Athens on a rescue mission.

Soon afterward, I got a call from Samaranch, who was both delighted and amused by the events transpiring in Athens. "How is the honeymoon going?" he asked.

"What do you mean?" I replied.

"You will see. First the short honeymoon after which you will have real life." Then Samaranch got serious. "So, Gianna, whatever he promised you, did you get it in writing?"

I was embarrassed to tell him I hadn't.

"Ah, Gianna," he said, and I could hear despair in his voice. "Be afraid then. Be very afraid of Greek politicians."

He would be proved right about the honeymoon. And he was right about the Greek politicians too. For example, I planned to go to the Sydney 2000 Olympics with the Minister responsible for the Athens games, Theodoros Pangalos, to prove Greece's renewed commitment. Imagine my surprise when he made some poor excuses and never came to Australia. It took an awful lot of diplomacy for me to convince the world that Greece would get back on track for the Games when no government representative was there to back me up. This was particularly ironic because Pangalos had named me ambassador in 1998 and had been our guest at Verona, Italy, enjoying Verdi one week before the Australian trip!

I had let myself be ruled by my heart and I would quickly come to regret it.

I should have gotten everything in writing.

Chapter 22

LAND AND WATER

IT'S HARD FOR PEOPLE TO GRASP just how massive an undertaking a modern Olympics is, how overwhelming the logistical challenges are. After Theodore and I analyzed all aspects of the preparation and organization of the Athens 2004 Summer Games as well as all the stakeholders involved in it, we realized that the Athens Olympic Organizing Committee (ATHOC) would be creating—in just four years—the equivalent of a Fortune 200 company. And when the "company" reached its organizational peak, we would then have to shut it down and say thanks and good-bye to thousands of employees.

Presenting the Olympic Games is a joint effort of the International Olympic Committee (IOC) and the host city's organizing committee, in our case, ATHOC. The IOC is responsible for signing contracts with broadcasters and sponsors. The IOC distributes some of the money collected from the broadcasters and sponsors to the organizations that supervise various sports and to the host city. The host city builds sports facilities according to the international sports federations' specifications, as well as facilities for the athletes and visiting dignitaries and the media. In addition, the host city must agree to provide the infrastructure necessary for the Games, including highways and public-transportation systems. Seven years in advance of the Games, the host city signs the host city contract with the IOC to provide these necessary facilities. (You might recall that I took that formal step of signing the contract in Lausanne in September 1997.)

Each host city determines how it will fund the Games. Some cities, as Atlanta chose to do, take no government funds. In Athens, the Greek government decided and guaranteed that it would build whatever infrastructure would be needed for the Games (sports facilities, airport, tram system, subways, roads, intersections, the Olympic village, and so forth) all by itself.

Other host cities rely on a combination of private and public funds. In addition, the host city generates revenue from ticket sales, local sponsorship, and merchandising. ATHOC's budget for the Games was 1.9 billion euros, roughly $2.6 billion. The IOC gave us $900 million from the sale of broadcasting and international sponsorship revenues. I'm proud to say that we managed to balance our budget. This was due in no small part to the dedicated counsel of ex-judges, accountants, and auditors who sometimes made our lives hell but also ensured that our books were in order.

The following illustration will give you an idea of the scope of the Olympic operation. I first visited Boston in the 1990s when the city was well into what was known as "The Big Dig," the most expensive highway construction project in American history and one that took a quarter of a century to complete. Now try and imagine that at the very same time Boston was digging in, it was also: replacing Logan International with a new airport; adding two new lines to the city's downtown subway system, and two more light railway lines out to the suburbs; widening more than a hundred miles of city streets; repaving Storrow Drive, which winds for two miles along the Charles River; and trying to solve the engineering nightmare of how to maneuver a seventeen-thousand-ton, 269,000-square-foot steel and Plexiglas roof onto Fenway Park, home of the Boston Red Sox. (By the way, Boston's Big Dig was completed five years behind schedule and an estimated $20 billion over budget.)

Now go a step further and try to imagine doing that in a city where every shovel full of dirt is considered part of an archeological dig that might yield hidden treasures. (Having already fulfilled my childhood dream of becoming an ambassador, I was now fulfilling my father's that I become an archeologist—and it was even worse than I had imagined!)

That imaginary scenario in Boston doesn't begin to represent all that confronted me in Athens. The modern Olympics had grown by leaps and bounds. For example, at the 1984 Games, Los Angeles staged 221 sporting events and welcomed 6,800 athletes and 9,800 credentialed journalists. Just two decades later, Athens would hold 301 events and host 10,500 athletes and 21,000 journalists. When the Olympics ended and the attention of most of the world drifted elsewhere, we would have to do it all over again for the Paralympic Games, which brought another 4,000 athletes to Athens. By the time the Athens 2004 Summer Games opened, I would be managing a staff of 13,000, along with 45,000 volunteers, and integrating into the operation 100,000 security personnel while hosting 10,500 athletes, 21,000 journalists, 2,000 officials, and 2,200 guests of the IOC and the Olympic sponsors. We had to construct not only sporting venues but also housing for the athletes and the media. And when I assumed the presidency of ATHOC, the eighteen sports facilities and three-hundred-acre athletes' village were still just lines on paper.

Events in both America and Europe would compound our challenge in Greece's capital. A little more than a year after I began my tenure, the world witnessed the tragic events of September 11, 2001, in America. The IOC had moved far ahead of the world on issues related to security and the threat of terrorism after the murders of eleven Israeli Olympians by the Palestinian terrorist group Black September at the Munich 1972 Olympics. The 9/11 attacks ensured that the massive security apparatus already planned for Athens would become even more massive. While the government bore the responsibility for all security tenders and contracts, ATHOC was charged with integrating security operations into the Games. It was ultimately our responsibility to protect the entire Olympic community and the hundreds of thousands of spectators descending on Athens for the Games.

The European wrinkle was that Athens was the first Olympics that had to comply with the regulations of the European Union as well as the first to host the Games under a common currency, the euro, adding layers of complexity to the procedures required to execute our plans.

All this helps explain why the IOC had extended the Olympic run-up from six years to seven. And yet, there I was, assuming the helm of what appeared to be the Olympic *Titanic* in May 2000, just four years and three months before the day—August 13, 2004—when Athens would welcome the world to the Opening Ceremony. Three months after I took the job, we would be facing a host of IOC deadlines established to monitor our progress. So while my official statement upon assuming the position said, "I am honored," it didn't include what I was actually thinking—"I must be crazy."

After my first visit to ATHOC headquarters and a quick perusal of its operations, I no longer thought I was crazy. I knew it. My old IOC friend Lambis Nikolaou, who had assumed a prominent role on the organizing committee, had assured me that we had secured a first-rate building out of which to operate. My visit there provided the first in a succession of shocks. It wasn't only that it had a tiny, barely visible entrance. Or that inside it was a warren of small, ill-shaped offices that would never accommodate our growing head count as we proceeded toward the Games. Or even that it was located in an area known for its horrific traffic jams. It was the fact that it was built above a Carrefour supermarket. The IOC was highly sensitive about its sponsorships. You weren't allowed to serve Pepsi in the office when the Olympic sponsor was Coca-Cola. Your staff couldn't drive around in Hondas if Hyundai was paying the freight. And you certainly couldn't operate over a supermarket that wasn't an Olympic sponsor.

The next shock was in the numbers. Three years in and we were nevertheless just a bare-bones operation with 165 employees and no clear path forward toward the thousands that would be necessary by the time of the Olympics. While our staff was far too small, the organizing committee's board responsible for making decisions was way too big and unwieldy, with nineteen members. I also inherited another national committee, with more than fifty members who only convened a few times for no organizational purposes; the committee existed for decorative reasons only.

And to top it all off, there was no steering committee to get the job done!

Blueprints that were created for IOC presentations during the bid campaign were in the same boxes—unopened—where we had left them back in 1997. It is one thing to hear about a disaster and another to witness it firsthand. I knew we didn't have a second to waste. I needed to secure a new headquarters, to sack the CEO, to reconfigure the board, and—most urgently—to secure swift passage of laws that would speed up a host of processes, especially those concerning spending authorizations, tenders, and licenses. I also needed to see the Prime Minister posthaste to put my plans in motion.

But when I called Simitis's office, his secretary, Miss Plevrakis, told me she would have to pass on my message because he was unavailable. I waited an hour and called again, and again I conveyed my need to speak to the Prime Minister as soon as possible. "I told him," Miss Plevrakis said. "Well, what did he say?" I asked. "He doesn't give me answers," she replied. An hour later I called again. This time Miss Plevrakis told me he was in a meeting. She assured me that she had passed on both my messages and that she would happily do so a third time, though she was beginning to sound less happy about it. An hour later we were at it again. "Are you sure he cannot come to the phone?" I said. "I am sure," she said. And we kept on like that until evening when, apparently, nobody was around to answer the phone.

I was fuming. I went home and stormed around the house before calling Theodore to blow off some steam. But his words—"Samaranch warned you"—offered very little comfort. I slept badly, and the next morning I started phoning the Prime Minister's office again. Incredibly, this time I couldn't even reach Miss Plevrakis. Instead, I had to settle for her assistant who told me that Miss Plevrakis was busy with the Prime Minister. Then she compounded the insult by inquiring, "May I ask what this is about?"

I slammed down the phone, but this time I didn't wait quite so long. A half hour later I called back and demanded that the assistant to the assistant put me on with the assistant. When Miss Plevrakis picked up, she told me that the Prime Minister was tied up in a cabinet meeting. I told her very politely that it would take me about twenty minutes to drive to the Prime Minister's office. And with such an important meeting going on, there were bound to be journalists and cameramen waiting outside as always. I could wait along with them. They would be surprised to learn that I was hanging around there because I couldn't get in to see the Prime Minister. They might find it surprising to learn that the same man who recently had publicly promised me "land and water" now wouldn't even return my phone calls. "Please inform the Prime Minister of this," I said, and hung up.

Ten minutes later Simitis called. "You asked for me, Mrs. Angelopoulos?" he said. "I asked for you ten times," I replied. "This is important." Begrudgingly, he agreed to squeeze in a visit during his lunchtime. In that moment—in his reluctant manner and resentful tone—I realized that, despite my best efforts and possibly even his honest intentions, we were unlikely to attain the true partnership he had promised in order to lure me back to Athens.

All the same, when I saw the Prime Minister, I patiently explained the problems we faced and what we needed to do. (My emphasis remained on the "we.") We needed to change the structure of the organizing committee and revamp its budgeting process. We required wholesale changes in governmental oversight procedures. We needed new wrinkles in the interpretation of laws governing major construction projects. ("Don't ask me to stop the archaeologists," he said, obviously sharing that frustration.) We needed to rally the public to work harder for our goals. Last but not least, we needed to hire our nation's best and brightest: namely, the people with the requisite expertise to succeed at this daunting Olympic undertaking. And we needed all of it done yesterday or, truthfully, hundreds of yesterdays ago.

I told the Prime Minister that although I understood how busy he was, he simply had to make my issues a priority and himself available. "I don't want to annoy or embarrass you," I assured him, "but I need you to see me whenever I need you. There are so many things to be done that we can only do together." He nodded his acquiescence and, to be fair, he pretty much made good on that commitment.

For the first time, Simitis created an inter-ministerial committee comprising all of the Ministers involved with the Olympics and me to best coordinate all involved agencies. He himself would chair the committee. I remember the first time we convened at the Prime Minister's offices. I placed my Hermes alligator bag in the seat next to the Prime Minister's. Before the meeting started, a Minister moved my bag to the end of the long table. While Simitis was entering the room, he bore witness to me—the dialogue with his Minister was not particularly polite—telling him to "*never again* come close to my bag or my personal documents." The Prime Minister turned to his Minister and said, "Mrs. Angelopoulos's seat will be here, next to mine." Issue ended. From then on, I always sat next to the Prime Minister.

But while he would see me when I requested and, most often, even side with me, Simitis would never change his style and confront his key aides and government officials who were not hewing to his line. That reluctance on the Prime Minister's part ensured that—just as during the bid campaign—my relations with his people would be contentious. And that, in turn, ensured that I would once again become fair game for some of their attack dogs in the press.

Nevertheless, we tried. Theodore came up with the notion of scheduling occasional informal dinners with the Prime Minister and his wife so we could get to know each other better and, hopefully, develop a better working relationship. At one of the first dinners, we were discussing our personal exercise routines. The Prime Minister, who was sixty-four years old at the time, got up early every morning to exercise before walking to his office (and later home as well). That routine apparently permitted him to eat everything he wanted while staying reed thin. Dafni Simitis, who was more full-figured, lamented that she was a slow starter and couldn't go straight to the gym first thing in the morning. I confessed the same—"I cannot perform well at seven in the morning, but I do great at eleven"—attributing my slow start to my low blood pressure. "Wow!" the Prime Minister said. "You mean you are doing all this with low blood pressure?" I could tell what he was thinking, "Given the ruckus this woman creates in my office with low blood pressure, God help us if ever her blood pressure goes up."

In June, Simitis made good on one critical promise and pushed through legislation that would expedite many procedural matters. Swift action was required.

My predecessors had complained, for example, that it took eighteen months just to hire a typist. If they had tried to change the procedures, they couldn't get it done. But even in crisis mode, it took time to locate the talent and then to convince the people to join our crusade. Though our cause was righteous—to spare the nation a humiliation while the whole world was watching—the sales pitch was tricky. We were asking the very best people in the public and private sectors to join us for four years during which, having already given up secure jobs with good incomes, they would be called upon to pretty much forsake their families, their hobbies, and their holidays. That is the nature of a crusade; I'm certain King Richard the Lionheart never promised vacation time.

I've always had one principle when hiring people: "Give opportunities to people no matter how important the position is."

Usually, others prefer to hire professional "legends." I gave the opportunity to literally thousands of people to establish a great "track record" for their next professional steps or leaps. I instructed our human-resources department to hire qualified young women and men even if the position was very important. They protested, "But they're virtually *unknown*!" And I replied firmly: "If they're not good I'll replace them. But if they succeed here, I am giving them the chance to become *very well known*."

For example, thanks mainly to our HR manager, Thanassis "the Cat" Papageorgiou, we gave more than two thousand people who were seeking employment the opportunity to work for ATHOC part-time through the stage program. They could all add this great experience to their CV.

The best example, however, was my appointment of Dimitris Papaioannou, a young and extremely talented avant-garde artist, to become the creative director of the magical Athens ceremonies. The broader public came to know Dimitris only after the Opening Ceremony.

We did, indeed, manage to hire many of the best in Greece. (Though I had to change many personnel during those four years, the following is a list of the people who stayed through to the end.)

"A TEAM"

ATHOC'S STEERING SOMMITTEE

MARTON "THE GENERAL" SIMITSEK, *our chief operations officer*

YIANNIS PYRGIOTIS, *our chief technical officer*

THEODORE PAPAPETROPOULOS, *our chief financial officer*

SPYROS CAPRALOS, *a member of our board*

KEY PEOPLE

LENA ZACHOPOULOU, *my trusted associate*

VENIA PAPATHANASOPOULOU, *an extremely competent, strong, and tough lawyer who headed the President's office and helped me immensely*

NIKOS THEMELIS, ILIAS KOUTROUMPIS, EFSTATHIOS RONTOGIANNIS, GEORGE KOURTIS, *and* ELENI FOTI, *the judges who oversaw our financial operations*

NICOLAOS PAPADIMITRIOU, VASSILIS KOTSOVILIS, DIMITRIS FILIS, ILIAS THEODORATOS, KOSTAS CHOROMIDIS, VASSILIKI SAMPANI, *and* VICKY SOULTANIA, *all excellent lawyers and legal experts*

"BIG" GEORGE BOLOS, *head of marketing and sponsorship*

DIMITRIS TZIRAS, *head of volunteers*

MAJOR-GENERAL VASSILIOS KONSTANTINIDIS, *head of security*

THANASSIS PAPAGEORGIOU, *head of human resources*

DIMITRIS BEIS, *head of information technology*

DIONYSSIS GANGAS, *head of international relations, and liaison for IOC relations*

SERAFIM KOTROTSOS, *head of the press and other media*

MICHALIS ZACHARATOS, *head of communications*

SPYROS LAMPRIDIS, *a consummate diplomat*

THANASSIS KATARTZIS, *an expert on local authorities*

MAKIS ASIMAKOPOULOS, *our sports director*

PANAGIOTIS PROTOPSALTIS, *an expert on transport*

EFHARIS SKARVELI, *who led our operating team at the main operations center*

(OBVIOUSLY THERE ARE COUNTLESS OTHERS, MANY OF WHOM I INTEND TO MENTION IN MY GREEK EDITION OF THIS BOOK.)

When European Commissioner for Regional Policy Michel Barnier assessed ATHOC's human-resources strategy, combining working experience from both the private and the public sector, he wondered how Greece's course might change after the Games should this practice be followed in the future. His admiration fell on the deaf ears of the ruling class. But one of the things that gives me great pride and pleases me the most in the aftermath of the Games is that hundreds of ATHOC's managers have continued their careers in very important positions in Greece and abroad.

Since critics in the government couldn't complain about the volunteers, they complained instead that my staff were overpaid, that they were "Gianna's army." Those critics didn't seem to care that these talented people had left successful careers in the public and private sectors to devote two, three, or four years in service to their country. All were working punitively long hours while sacrificing all kinds of perks, not to mention precious time with their families. Nobody was striking it rich working for ATHOC, but I felt an obligation to make sure that, at the very least, these people—these patriots—weren't punished financially for their commitment to their country.

Nevertheless, many key Ministers and government officials were great allies for the cause of the Games.

KEY MINISTERS AND GOVERNMENT OFFICIALS

KOSTAS LALIOTIS, *Minister for Public Works and the Environment, who was succeeded by* VASSO PAPANDREOU

PETROS EFTHIMIOU, *Minister for Education*

MICHALIS CHRISOCHOIDIS, *Minister for Public Order*

GIORGOS ALOGOSKOUFIS, *Minister for Economy and Finance*

YIANNIS SGOUROS, *Secretary General for Sports*

YIANNIS KOURAKIS, *Undersecretary for Culture and Sports*

KOSTAS KARTALIS, *Secretary General for the Olympics of the Ministry of Culture*

YIANNIS PRAGIATIS, *Ministry for Culture*

TILDA KYRIAKOU, *Ministry for Public Works*

The battle over our new headquarters was a microcosm of the ordeal that accompanied every measure of progress. I had located an old factory in an underdeveloped middle-class section of Athens, Nea Ionia, that was perfect for our operation and could house our entire staff, even at its Games-time peak. The relocation provided an enormous boost to the local economy. I approved the use of Greek eco-friendly materials, creating an attractive, open, worker-friendly environment. After all, this was where we would spend the next three years and where we would welcome the IOC and other VIPs who came to check out the progress of our Athens operation.

I wanted our headquarters to be a showcase that would reflect the beauty of Greece and its people and that would signify the promise of the Olympics on our horizon. But my honeymoon with the press was over and it mocked me as "the empress who thinks it's her own house." It was Greece's house. But only a fool would believe that you could produce state-of-the-art Games without building on a foundation that reflected the same high quality.

I never hid behind an official spokesperson. That wasn't because of vanity or ego or any desire to see my face in the newspapers or on TV. The Greek people deserved to hear the news—quite often, tough news—straight from me undiluted. The Olympics were my team's responsibility and I was willing to stand up publicly and be held accountable. Whenever I was out on the street walking, people would wave and shout out, "Gianna, are we going to do it?" or "Are we going to manage on time?" It was almost always "we"; the public understood that I was on their side and that this was a collective effort.

When I took over as President of ATHOC, a sense of hopelessness was in the air. There was a huge reservoir of self-doubt: Were we in Greece really capable of pulling this off? Greeks of all stripes worried that maybe we just weren't good enough. I was out there alone reassuring the public that we were indeed good enough and that it was okay to have hope for our future. It was important that I deliver that positive message personally because later, as the Games approached, I would call on the public to assume more of the burden of justifying that hope. But with hope came responsibility, I would tell them.

For the duration of the Games, our people, so set in their ways, would have to forget about how they preferred to lead their lives and do what was best for Athens. Forget about driving whenever and wherever you want; take the bus instead. Forget about smoking in public places. In the spirit of *philoxenia*, our deep-rooted Greek hospitality, be courteous and smile at people as if they were guests in your home. Be honest; if you find a lost credit card, locate the person—even if you have to pay for the call. Treat visitors as if they are family.

From start to finish, we needed to show the world an appealing country with a new ethos, a new way of working, behaving, and thinking. If we could successfully rebrand our country, we could transform the lives of the Greek people—not just for the duration of the Games but for the future as well. We had to change the image of Greece from Greek gridlock to Greece on the move.

In some ways, it was reminiscent of the days when I held political office and was willing to talk to anyone and everyone. As Olympic President, I did the same. My team and I went to countless meetings. We visited ministries, NGOs, local and district authorities, educational institutions, commercial and industrial associations, environmental organizations, animal protection societies, the Boy Scouts and Girl Guides, and many more. We briefed everyone on the progress we were making and how new roads, transportation infrastructure, and sports facilities would improve all our lives in the future. We explained how they could become involved in the Olympics and how all their lives, regardless of whether they chose to get involved or not, would have to change during the Games.

I didn't hesitate to ask favors of those who weren't my natural allies. I went to the unions and pleaded for their cooperation, even if they were within their rights to strike or take job actions. "I understand it's your right," I would tell them, "but it's not the right time." Even the anarchists backed off during the Olympics.

I was asking for cooperation and understanding for the common cause, for a shared goal. And I usually wound up getting it because most people respected the fact that I came to them personally to solicit their cooperation.

Even when it was clear we were steadily accelerating our progress, various media stayed on their brutal course. I have a collection of cartoons in which I was cast—often with an unflattering rendering—as Superwoman, as Cleopatra, as Lara Croft, as Iron Lady, as Phantom Lady. There was one journalist on a daily (signing as Pandora) whose comments were especially acidic, branding me *"Fuehrerin"* for my managerial approach and my disputes with the government. The cartoons accompanying those comments would depict me as a queen or an empress on my throne. When I met with Chancellor Gerhard Schröder in the German Chancellery prior to the Games, I sent Pandora a photo of the meeting with a note on the back saying, "Dear Pandora, a souvenir of the *Fuehrerin's* visit to the real chancellery." Pandora took it with good humor.

Whoever I was supposed to be, the characterization remained essentially the same: I was the Olympic bitch—indeed, the Superbitch, a tough and wealthy woman who dictated how everything should be done. Those others reluctantly admitted, however, that I was the doer. One newspaper actually wrote a front-page editorial urging the public prosecutor to indict me and send me to jail, though it didn't bother to specify any charges. Conveniently unwritten was the story about how I had refused the newspaper's owner when he came to my office—all smiles and bearing flowers—and asked me to include one of his large parcels of land in our Olympic development plans. This was the old way of doing business in Greece: using relationships to secure deals that, if not completely corrupt, were untoward and more in one individual's interest than in the national interest. And I wasn't having it. (In the end, I stopped looking at the newspapers, though I had our press office provide me with a digest of what was being written.)

If I was a "bitch" at times—and I was—it was because I had no choice.

I had to get things done with a dispatch that was not customary in our country. There were no precedents for what I was asking of our people. I wanted to create hope, I wanted to get things done, but I first had to create a fear of failure. I had to make everyone—the government, the organizing committee, and the public—afraid that, if they did not heed my urgent pleas, Greece would fail and be the laughingstock of the world.

But personal attacks pained me a lot. I was giving my all to Greece in order to pull off an impossible dream yet I was being pilloried for it. The IOC was breathing down my neck, demanding that I get things moving, yet I was deadlocked with some government officials driven by self-aggrandizement and a need to exercise power for power's sake.

Early in my tenure, especially, I often sat in my office late at night crying, cloaked in the very despair that I was preaching against publicly. Back then, waiting for the government breakthrough that would just give us a fighting chance seemed about as promising as waiting for Godot. If there were one person I could rely upon for his strength, it was the man I had dubbed "the General." COO Marton Simitsek is a tough-minded pragmatist, and there were many nights when he would come into my office and gently say, "President, are we going home?"

I recall one night, though, after another crisis with the government, when he came to my office unusually early.

"President, what are we doing here?" he said. "Maybe we should all just go home."

He was not talking about going home for the night, but home for good. And on many nights I did consider that option.

What kept me going, however, were the hope, the excitement, the expectation, and the belief I could see on the faces of all the people in Greece.

Chapter 23

SUN TZU, MACHIAVELLI, AND ME

THE OPENING CEREMONY FOR THE 2004 ATHENS SUMMER GAMES would begin with a heartbeat. That is, a beat rendered by two drummers, one in the Olympic Stadium and one almost two hundred miles to the west in ancient Olympia, which symbolized our commitment to conduct our Games on a human scale. Four years earlier, that's where I began too. I had to convince Greece that our effort was alive, that despite all evidence to the contrary our heart was still beating and our dream was still possible. Only if Greece believed in that message could we fulfill our destiny.

Sometimes belief can start with a single person, just one person who refuses to take "no" for an answer. I don't believe in the impossible. I have always believed that if you take your passion and transform it into the energy and effort that are required to do whatever is necessary, then nothing is impossible. Sometimes I would overhear one of my staff say,

"Please, God, make it happen." I would get furious. "Stop that b.s.! It's up to us to do whatever is necessary to make it happen. Afterward, if you still want to pray to your God or your Buddha or whomever, well then that's okay."

It is easier to say all this now when we're looking back on our spectacular success as hosts than it was to embrace that belief in the beginning. I can't tell you the number of heartbreaks I suffered along the way, particularly in the early days. To check on our progress I would visit a construction site where there were specific timelines that we had agreed to meet (and that the IOC officials would be checking up on quite soon) and find that the digging hadn't even begun. *Why?* Well, the contractor said he hadn't been paid. *Why?* Well, the government said it didn't have the money. *Why?* Well, the government Minister claimed that the money was supposed to have come from the European Union. And so it went. Greece's newest Olympic sport: passing the buck around and around and around again.

I remember in particular one early visit from IOC officials. Because there were so many construction sites, they didn't have time to visit them all. So instead we showed them a videotape of bulldozers working at the various sites. One of the IOC guys wisecracked, "How long did it take you to move those bulldozers from one hill to another?" I was infuriated by his mockery. Later I told my staff, "Next time we will ask the contractors to use different-colored bulldozers so that these jerks can't make jokes at our expense."

We have an old proverb in Greece that goes like this: "There is no wedding without tears; there is no funeral without laughs."

I have already talked about my ample tears, but there was plenty of laughter too. Jokes, outrageous jokes, were often the only way to handle the huge burdens and continual disappointments without more tears than were already falling. There was no shortage of gallows humor. We just preferred our own jokes to the IOC's.

But through the laughter and through the tears, I was effecting a major change in ATHOC's culture. Greeks have a habit of procrastinating. And they ultimately always tend to reach the same conclusion: "It cannot be done . . ." or "Yes, but . . ." I succeeded in eliminating the "cannot" and "but" from the process. I bore the responsibility so people could choose to do it my way or they could leave. I built up a "can-do" organization. We required that the government do its job and allow us to do our job. The English saying is, "Lead, follow, or get out of the way." I like that approach. Once the Prime Minister pushed through new rules that expedited procedures and armed me with new powers, we at least felt that a lot of obstacles had "gotten out of the way" and we had a fighting chance. But it never ceased to be a fight.

I remember a rare night in Athens in 2001 when I had managed to get home in time to have dinner with my family. Instead, I wound up in a screaming fight on the phone with one government Minister who, typically, had failed to deliver what he had promised when he had promised it. After I slammed down the phone in a rage, Panagiotis, who wasn't yet twelve years old, suggested it might help me if I took an anger-management course. I couldn't help but laugh. "You know, Pan," I said, "I'm afraid this is how it's going to be."

"But, Mom," he said, "it's probably bad for your health." Out of the mouths of babes!

Did I make mistakes along the way? Many. Nobody in the world is trained to do the job I was asked to do. (And believe me, there's a reason that nobody who has ever done it signs on to do it a second time.) A lot of case studies get written after the fact, but there is no university with a graduate program in organizing the Olympics. It is such a vast terrain, requiring elements of an MBA and a law degree as well as studies in government administration, economics, business strategy, organizational behavior, engineering, human-resources management, communications, archaeology, environment, psychology, and a host of other subspecialties.

Mitt Romney has deemed it such a sufficiently large challenge that his successfully running the Salt Lake City 2002 Winter Olympics was one of the reasons he believed he would have been an effective President of the United States. (Those Games, by the way, were only one-tenth the size of the Summer Games we hosted in Athens.)

Nobody before had organized Olympic Games of the magnitude of the ones in Athens, let alone on a reduced timetable in a unified Europe whose legislation required procedures and tenders for every single project. It's less a job than an odyssey in which you are forced to confront a multitude of obstacles, regulatory constraints, and interfering parties—from the Greek bureaucrats to the IOC, from historical protection agencies and archaeologists to the European Union, from environmentalists to the military and defense ministries and agencies from around the world.

Who could guide you through this maze? I had my sources. I have always kept two books by my bedside and regard them as the closest thing to a textbook when it comes to managing and, ultimately, conquering challenges. They are *The Art of War* by Sun Tzu and *The Prince* by Niccolo Machiavelli. Perhaps it seems strange that a book written by a Chinese general more than two millennia ago and a political treatise from the chaotic sixteenth century in Italy could be so relevant to a woman in the twenty-first century. I am also aware that some people regard these books as rather sinister. But I view them as straightforward treatises on strategic planning, critical lessons on how to attain your goals and to protect yourself from the intrigues of others.

Most everybody is familiar with Sun Tzu's pithy pronouncement "Keep your friends close and your enemies closer." The first part is easy and may seem obvious. However, many find the second part to be counterintuitive. Left to my own instincts, I would have kept Lambis Nikolaou, the Greek IOC member and inveterate troublemaker, as far from me as possible. But booting him out would have created a flashpoint for problems with the government and even my key ally, the IOC brass. Instead—to the amazement of Prime Minister Simitis—I named Nikolaou Vice President of the organizing committee. As such, he was nominally in charge of ATHOC whenever I was off duty, which never happened.

Machiavelli resonated with me too. How could I not recognize the wisdom in his admonition that "hatred is gained as much by good works as by evil"? And as I fought back and put ATHOC on the path to success, I certainly embraced his notion that "it is better to be feared than loved, if you cannot be both."

Some people see these books as particularly at odds with a feminist philosophy. Although both men authored their books at a time when men held all the power, I see no underlying gender bias. I don't subscribe to the notion that women manage or should manage in a gentler, more nurturing fashion than men do. Tell that to Margaret Thatcher or Golda Meir. I am a feminist to the extent that I believe women should be free to pursue their ambitions just as men are. Obviously, I did just that in my law and political careers. And when I ran for Parliament, creating the brochure that highlighted all the women who had served in Parliament, I even celebrated that right.

Truthfully, I tend to be biased in favor of women. I believe that women are as talented as men are and, quite often, stronger. Because women give birth, they know both how to give life and how to endure pain. And it was the latter—enduring pain and persevering—that, unhappily, was one of the most critical requirements in our Olympic endeavors. If I was sometimes harder on the women than on the men, it was because I had such high expectations for them.

As President of ATHOC, I hired a tremendous number of women for key positions, the largest number ever for an Olympic organizing committee. I never subscribed to the belief that I was obligated to hire a certain arbitrary percentage of women. I hired people for one reason and one reason only: because they were right for the job. At times I also find myself at odds with feminist dogma because I tend not to be politically correct. I am more pragmatist than doctrinaire in anything and everything I do. I believe that a woman can be most effective by using all her gifts—her strength, her intelligence, her beauty, her charm, and her feminine intuition. Believe me, I used all the weapons at my disposal—except one!—including crying and flattery to manipulate men into doing what was required. At critical points during our Olympic campaign, I wooed and won, as allies, men with whom I would never have deigned to have a cup of coffee otherwise. I would visit their offices and tell them: "You are the only one in Greece who can do this. Your country will owe you an extraordinary debt of gratitude." I provided a photo-op during these visits that would definitely be published or broadcast. Men are easy to manipulate because they are especially vulnerable to flattery and ego stroking.

On the other hand, I also cracked down on young women in my office who wore miniskirts and other casual and, at times, provocative clothing. I hadn't forgotten that I once lived in miniskirts. And I wasn't overreacting to any distraction these women might create in the office. These women were supposed to be part of a team that projected professionalism and the highest standards to all those—and there were many—who came through our doors. And to our visitors, casual could equate to sloppy and unprofessional (except on casual Fridays, if we didn't have an official meeting).

Later, with the Games less than a year away, I dared to suggest to women employees that it was an unsuitable time for them to get pregnant. This was not an issue of women's rights. It was a statement of fact, or at least of mission. We weren't an ongoing enterprise that—after the Games were over—could welcome back a woman after maternity leave. We had a short window in which we were required to perform and we needed everyone doing their all. We had no excess capacity, no fat, in our organization. If a single critical employee couldn't fulfill his or her responsibilities it might make it impossible for ATHOC to fulfill ours. So while we sent flowers and congratulations to women who had babies right around Games time, we replaced them early on, at the moment we knew they would be unavailable to us.

I will confess to another unfashionable habit. I am a control freak. I do not believe that a watched pot never boils. In fact, I am inclined to believe just the opposite: namely, that if employees believe their work is being scrutinized closely they perform at a higher level. I also held secrets closely. With rare exceptions, I told people only what they needed to know to perform their job or task, not the big picture. Our margin for error was razor thin and knowledge is indeed power. In the cutthroat world in which I was operating, knowing everything would have made it too easy for people with private agendas or loose tongues to subvert our plans.

While the grand scheme, the macro-picture, was my province, I also worked incredibly long hours—often into the wee hours of the night—on the micro-picture, tracking developments on every front. Nothing was too minor for my consideration, from questions about the mascots to the choice of colors for the volunteers' uniforms. I thoroughly enjoyed every second of it. Dealing with the micro-issues gave me great pleasure, balance, and peace of mind when I knew I also had to deal with the macro-issues. Eventually, every operational site in our Games plan would reflect my obsessive attention to detail, each resembling a war room with color-coded charts and organizational grids that ranked the relative importance of all the problems we might encounter and who had the responsibility to deal with each. For every possible crisis, we had a plan to handle it, as well as a plan B and sometimes a plan C too.

With me pushing and prodding, macro- and micromanaging, we began to make steady progress. It was not exactly a linear progression. We were dealing with so many diverse projects, constituencies, and agencies at the same time that we could be making progress on one front while simultaneously hitting a dead end on another. Often it was two steps forward, one step back and another step sideways. We had to be prepared to be blindsided. Like when we were digging the new subway lines and stumbled upon relics from Neolithic times. Or when we were about to dredge the rowing venue and our work was called to a halt because European authorities deemed the spot a protected natural habitat. The site was actually filled with dirt and garbage and all the birds had fled long beforehand. We toured it with the Greek Minister of Public Works, Vasso Papandreou (a tough and very able politician), and the EU Environmental Commissioner, Margot Wallström, to show her how our project would protect and enhance the natural fauna and flora in the entire area. Indeed, when we were finished, the water was once again clean and the birds duly returned.

Another—the most heartbreaking—blow to our efforts was, of course, the attacks of 9/11 in the United States. That day I was sitting in my office and, as always, had the TV on without sound. A meeting was in progress when I saw the pictures of the planes and the buildings and the smoke. I yelled to Lena to turn up the sound, and we experienced the same horror as all civilized people around the world did. It may have been the only time in our long and difficult partnership that I actually felt sorry for the Greek government. I knew what was in store for it. Enormous pressure would be brought to bear on Greece regarding security measures, and the price of security would inevitably scale to unimagined heights.

While my committee assumed responsibility for everything once the Games started, the government had the responsibility for all the security tenders and contracts. That didn't keep the problem from intruding into my job frequently, however, and consuming disproportionate amounts of time. Some meetings on security issues were essential. Others were a waste of my time, requiring me to parry the absurd demands of certain Western powers that made it all too clear they didn't trust Greece to protect their people.

Here's an example of what I had to put up with. Shortly before the Games were set to begin, the US Ambassador to Greece, Thomas Miller, informed me that former President George H.W. Bush would be attending the Opening Ceremony. That was no problem; he would be most welcome. What was a problem was that they wanted a large armed security force of US Secret Service agents in the stadium with him. All I could envision was a little Greek boy bursting his balloon and American agents opening fire. I said, "Mr. Ambassador, this is not going to happen." Then I said to my staff in rapid-fire Greek—the Ambassador might have understood a few of my choicer words—"Take this jerk out of here or he will be the first victim." He then took the matter to the new government of the New Democracy party that was more closely aligned with US interests than the Socialists had been. But when the ambassador met with the new Foreign Minister, Petros Molyviatis, he was once again rebuffed. Later, when Molyviatis described the meeting to me, he was actually trembling with anger over what he considered the arrogance and insult of the American demands. "I never lose my temper, but I wanted to take this man by his neck and throw him out," he confessed.

I'd never know where the next headache was coming from—or from whom. I remember an IOC meeting in Prague in June 2003, where Israeli representative Alex Gilady challenged our transportation plan, disputing some of its projections for the Games. Gilady was a powerful figure in the IOC and, though he had not voted for Athens, had always been helpful to and supportive of me personally. So I was surprised when, in front of all the IOC members, he disputed our carefully calculated estimate that during the Games it would require just seventeen minutes to transport IOC delegates from the Hilton Hotel, where they would be staying, to our main Olympic Stadium. It turned out that, in the spring of 2001, Gilady had been in Athens to watch a basketball game between Israeli and Greek teams at the very same time Pope John Paul II was visiting the city. "Do you know how much time it took me to get to the stadium?" he asked. "It took me forty-seven minutes, which means your research is wrong."

Gilady got more and more animated and red in the face as he complained about this impending transportation crisis. I seldom get caught unprepared, but I must have appeared blindsided because one of my people, Yiannis Pyrgiotis, slipped me a note saying, "You must answer him about this." So when Gilady finally wound down, I said: "Mr. Gilady, I do not understand your impatience. You know that Athens will have a transportation plan in place that will allow athletes, the media, and the IOC to go faster than all other traffic. But more important, Mr. Gilady, I know that in August 2004 you will make it in seventeen minutes because then *you* will be the pope in Athens." I knew the "crisis" had been averted when even Jacques Rogge, the very buttoned-up Belgian who had succeeded Samaranch as IOC President in 2001, began to laugh heartily.

Theodore and I had witnessed Rogge's cool demeanor in extremis during what was supposed to be a low-key, get-acquainted dinner on his first trip to Athens as IOC President. The visit came at a time when relations between the IOC and the Greek government were very tense.

It was just one year after the IOC had threatened to remove the Games from Athens, and the committee was continuing to pressure us to proceed more swiftly. With ATHOC moving forward at last, the Greek public was becoming increasingly angry over what they saw as the IOC's bullying tactics.

Following meetings with the Prime Minister and other key government officials, Rogge dined with Theodore and me at his hotel, the Astir Palace. We were chatting amiably when I glanced across the table at Rogge and saw that his face was turning red and he seemed to be having difficulty breathing. I was about to scream, "Get a doctor!" when Rogge rose out of his seat and forced his arms into his belly, somehow performing a Heimlich maneuver on himself. A big piece of lobster went flying out of his mouth and across the table. I don't know whether Rogge, a surgeon by training, saved himself or whether a higher power had intervened. All I know is that for quite a while afterward I was the one who could barely breathe. The words Primo Nebiolo whispered to me on the curb in Monte Carlo echoed in my mind. I thought, "If Rogge had died, you know what they would say in the press: 'Gianna killed him!'"

After honoring us for winning the bid, President Nelson Mandela invited me to his residence and I was struck by his wisdom and his tolerance.

Theodore sitting between two queens. To his right is Queen Margrethe II of Denmark; and to his left is Queen Silvia of Sweden.

Recep Tayyip Erdoğan, the Prime Minister of Turkey, and his wife. Joining us, directly to my left, is Simeon II of Bulgaria.

Queen Beatrix of the Netherlands. I'm carrying on despite a broken stiletto heel.

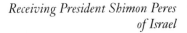

Receiving President Shimon Peres of Israel

Over 165,000 people applied to volunteer—an Olympic record. We selected and trained 45,000 of them for the 2004 Athens Summer Olympics and 15,000 for the Paralympic Games. I am still proud to have been one of them.

Even the students from my former school in Heraklion were there.

Our volunteers' slogan was "I will also be there!"

The opening ceremony, with the President of the IOC, Jacques Rogge

Addressing the world

Let the Games begin

In my volunteer uniform, traveling on our brand-new tramline with the fear-inducing agenda in my hand

All smiles . . .

And laughter!

Talking to British Prime Minister
Tony Blair, with Spyros Capralos

My assistants (from
left to right):
Evelyn Kanellea,
Carolina, and Vassilis
Dimitropoulos

Closing ceremony.
Passing the flag
to Beijing.

Dance, Theodore! It's a party!

Opening the Paralympic Games
on September 17, 2004

Gifts with many different meanings

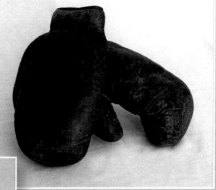

*The red room with so many
Olympic memories*

An honorary doctorate from my alma mater, the Aristotle University of Thessaloniki

Honored by the French government as a member of the Légion d'Honneur

My Carolina's graduation

My two argumentative boys, Pan and Dim, graduate from Harvard and the London School of Economics, respectively.

Waterskiing 2010, 2011

Working at Harvard once again, with (from left to right) *Joseph Nye, Harvard Professor and former Dean of the Kennedy School; Barry Bloom, Dean of the Harvard School of Public Health; Larry Summers, President of Harvard University; myself; Professor Emeritus Dimitrios Trichopoulos; David Ellwood, Dean of the Kennedy School; and Holly Sargent, Senior Associate Dean of the Kennedy School*

Being interviewed at Harvard by White House veteran David Gergen and leadership scholar Barbara Kellerman

Back on my feet, with Dean David Ellwood looking on

1994

Gianna and Theodore introduced to Harvard University

Gianna appointed Vice Chair of the Kennedy School Dean's Council

Gianna welcomes members of the Russian Duma to the Kennedy School

1995

Gianna co-chairs a Harvard Leadership Symposium on "The Greek Paradox" with Professor Graham T. Allison

Gianna welcomes Konstantine Stephanopoulos, President of the Hellenic Republic, to Harvard University

1998

Gianna returns to Harvard after successful Olympic bid process

2002

Gianna and Theodore establish the Angelopoulos Professorship in Public Health and International Development, a joint chair at Harvard School of Public Health and the Kennedy School

2005

President Lawrence H. Summers welcomes Gianna back to Harvard

Inaugural Angelopoulos Lecture on "Global Health Challenges and Policy Opportunities" delivered by Professor Christopher J. L. Murray

Gianna delivers a public address in the John F. Kennedy, Jr. Forum on "The Athens Games: Resolving the Greek Paradox"

JOHN F. KENN

GIANNA *Angelopoulos-Daskalaki*

IN HONOR OF YOUR 50TH BIRTHDAY HARVARD SALUTES YOU!

Harvard wishes me a happy birthday.

With President Clinton

*One of my
children's sweet
collages . . .*

*No mementos mean more to me
than the notes from my children.*

"Parents are the bow . . .

. . . and children are the arrows."

Chapter 24

OMENS AND BUMPS IN THE ROAD

AS THE WRECKAGE OF THE OPERATION I HAD INHERITED was being transformed into something that resembled our original Olympic dream, the people who were responsible for the transformation were suffering from overwork. In the frenzied pursuit of our goals, I myself lost sight of my own physical and emotional needs. I had never concerned myself too much with—indeed I was foolishly oblivious to—the toll that four years of unrelenting work, anxiety, and conflict was taking on me body and soul.

There certainly were plenty of clues that I was paying a price for my commitment. For example, at some point, I—a woman with a lifelong habit of drinking coffee from morning to night—stopped drinking coffee altogether because I no longer required any additional stimulation. Actually, I couldn't handle any more. I had overdosed on "natural caffeine" and I could feel it coursing through my body. That enabled me to work ridiculous hours, but not to get the sleep I needed. I began to think I was bionic. Looking back at those final months counting down to the Games, the only thing that reminds me I slept at all during that time is the memory of having so many nightmares.

I wasn't bionic, however; I had betrayed my body, something that would be proven some months later.

Even worse, I had betrayed my heart. From the start, Theodore had been my greatest ally and booster, the one person I trusted with my secrets, my dreams, my greatest hopes, and my worst fears. But I actually couldn't find time to tend to his emotional needs. I was flying high and he felt he was getting lost in my shadow. Even though I had a sense that he was depressed and that things between us were frayed, I felt helpless to do anything about it. When Theodore tried to broach the subject with me, not an easy thing for him to do, my mind was elsewhere. I couldn't listen to Theodore's frustration. All I could do was vent my own while asking for his comfort, understanding, counsel, and sympathy. Though I heard him clearly, I was struck by the realization that even if I wanted to deal with it, I was incapable of doing so. I was so focused on my Olympic task—and had to remain completely focused in order to succeed—that I couldn't allow myself to be distracted. I simply couldn't deal with what Theodore needed or wanted. I couldn't change a thing . . .

I eventually confronted our problems when I met with a psychologist, a University of Athens professor I knew who somehow got me talking. But what he told me—"To Theodore, you are still his beloved wife, the love of his life, and he wants you back"—only made me furious. "Do you have any idea what I'm going through?" I told him. "I can't even sleep anymore and you expect me to hold his hand to reassure him that I am his beloved wife. I am!" To this day, I feel a chill when I recall what he said next. "Then you are in real danger of having your marriage fall apart. Is it really worth it?"

There were so many things on my shoulders and so many things going through my mind: organizational issues; battles with politicians, the IOC, and the media; and many personal issues. I felt that I was falling emotionally and physically.

Still and all, it took more than that psychologist's warning to command my attention. I was rambling on to Theodore about some problem I would face at some event during the Olympics when he let slip that he would probably not be there. I didn't understand what he meant so I took his words literally, responding that naturally he would be invited and attend. "No," he said. "Probably, I will not be there. This is your show; you don't need me." In that moment, the enormity of what he was saying finally sunk in. And I knew that I needed professional help in order to save what was more important to me than even the Olympics—my marriage and my relationship with my children.

Fortunately, I was not too late. As hard as it was, I invented a modus vivendi . . .

I was hardly alone at ATHOC in my physical and emotional woes. The divorce rate among the Olympic committee staff was some 55 percent. "The General," a powerful physical specimen who had been a top shot-putter as a young man, would say it took him four years after the Games before he fully regained his strength. And Lena, my right hand who on top of all her administrative duties did her best to take care of me, suffered a stroke just two months before the Games. Against doctor's orders she returned to work after only fifteen days of recuperation. The only concession she allowed to her health was that she worked a normal shift. I would have to add three more assistants— my daughter Carolina, Evelyn Kanellea, and Vassilis Dimitropoulos— to fill the void and get me through my never-ending workday. Weeks before the Games, Carolina, already an Olympic volunteer, was at my side constantly. She was invaluable because she understood what

I needed: immediate answers to all my questions. I needed her to be knowledgeable, to be calm, and to present me with straight answers. To me "I don't know" is only an acceptable answer for the briefest period of time. If you don't know the answer you'd better go and find out as quickly as possible.

Back in 2000, during the first stressful months of building the organization, I received a wake-up call from Carolina when she asked me, "Mom, what are you doing there?"

I was tempted to answer her question with technical details and began explaining, "I have just arrived from a meeting with the Prime Minister and—"

"No, Mom," she interrupted, "what are you doing there? Forget about me. I'm going to college. Dad is always traveling. It's my two brothers who need you right now. We are a family that's falling apart."

"Carolina," I told her, "it's complicated and too hard to bring the boys here right now with the house so small—"

"Mom," she interrupted again, "what do you want? The megahouse or the family? You have to bring the boys to you now."

I believe every mother is the cornerstone of every family. In my case, I had another cornerstone, my own mother. The strict Marika Daskalaki proved to be the most supportive, most understanding, most loving, and sweetest grandma I could have ever imagined, for my kids and for me and for Theodore. Her unreserved love and care, I have to say, saved my kids during the endless absences I had to endure. She was the guardian angel of my family. I owe her a lot.

Despite any personal adversity, I never stopped driving everyone just as hard as I drove myself. Some people quit because of the stress. But I believed in leadership by example, and those who stayed saw me giving 200 percent and tried to match it.

I recall hearing a story that when in the midst of World War II

Winston Churchill heard that British Field Marshall Bernard Montgomery had said, "I neither drink, nor smoke. That's one reason why I am 100 percent fit," the Prime Minister immediately replied: "Well, I both drink and smoke. And I am 200 percent fit!"

I stayed the course and I stayed on message. One message, one inviolable rule, had primacy: Stay on budget! I knew that everyone was watching, especially my "allies" who were scrutinizing our operations looking for and hoping for mistakes. Any fiscal errors on our part and they would have real ammunition to use against me instead of the adolescent invective that characterized their personal attacks to that point. This started from the very top, and my CFO, Theodore Papapetropoulos, made sure every single manager became aware of it. I found dozens of ways to say the same thing: "Don't forget about the budget"; "Are we within our budget on this?"; "Don't go one euro over"; "One euro over and they will hang all of us"; "Play it safe and make sure we come in one euro under."

I followed my own edict. I remember our volunteers telling me that while everything was wonderful, there was one slight problem. They were being fed meager meals of sandwiches and beverages, along with two bottles of water. We told them the truth. We had had to dress them, train them, and transport them, and we only had so much money with which to feed them. During the final year, we delayed hiring some employees for months to save on salaries. The rest of us were working 24/7 to compensate. But somehow it came together. ATHOC ultimately finished with a large surplus—123.5 million euros out of a 1.9 billion-euro budget—and I proudly delivered that check to the government after the Games. What we accomplished with our budget is a great success. To me, however, the professional opportunity that we gave to so many people and what we accomplished with our human capital were even more important.

———

In recent years, many people in Greece have criticized the 2004 Olympic Games as being a major cause of the current economic and political crisis. This is wrong. The economic crisis has much deeper economic, social, and political causes, many of which were discussed in the 1995 symposium I cochaired at Harvard and referred to earlier in this book. What is worse, pointing a finger at the Olympics reveals a much deeper social, psychological, and identity crisis in Greece. Playing this blame game has slowly—dangerously, I would say—annihilated all the values that bound Greek society and its traditions together. Greeks smiled in the face of adversity when we struggled to put on the Olympic Games. Today, empty gazes and melancholy prevail.

True, the infrastructure costs ballooned. Truer still, price-gouging and major inefficiencies predated our Olympics. Construction companies were rumored to win contracts based partly on their political ties. They never completed public works on time and on budget.

Indeed, Greece paid a huge price for launching its Olympic effort three years late.

The Games added an enormous number of projects of all sizes to the mix. And depending on when they began, these projects had to be completed in four, three, or sometimes merely two years, without any deadline flexibility. While special laws were passed to expedite the EU's lengthy tender procedures, very few Greek government Ministers had experience dealing with such matters. Many projects became bloated with unnecessary side deals, projects that really had nothing to do with the Olympics but were deemed "Olympic-related" by the government so as to satisfy its electoral constituencies all over Greece. It was all about votes.

Moreover, Greece, being a small country, had only a handful of construction companies that could handle the multitude of projects under such time constraints.

And they took advantage. They seemed to behave in an orchestrated way; they had the government over a barrel and used their position to influence tenders and pricing and to exploit the government's inefficiencies.

It happened that tenders would produce no response until the price went up to a level the companies considered acceptable. The government simply didn't have the experience, the knowledge, the clout, or, perhaps, the political will to stand up to these business coalitions, especially since the media were often party to that orchestration.

We were at the mercy of the construction companies and they didn't have any mercy. All time-sensitive projects eventually required double- and, later, triple-shifts to ensure completion. Suppliers felt free to overcharge for materials and shipping. Cost overruns were huge. And rumors were rife that they were compounded by kickbacks to compliant government officials. As if Greece wasn't already paying enough, the government offered special "bonuses" to the contractors if they delivered their projects on time and to specifications.

The clock was ticking for the Games and the infrastructure costs were already an issue.

I suggested to the Prime Minister that he examine the possibility of private finance initiatives, a method of co-funding public infrastructure projects with private capital. Later the projects would be passed over to private enterprise for a fee. But Simitis would have none of it. "We can't do that," he told me. "What would the public and media say?"

Sadly, the media wasn't saying much about how some of our original plans—the projects as described in the bid file we presented to the IOC—were being altered. Venues were scattered throughout the city and the country with no rhyme or reason except politics. There appeared to be no concern for their viability, as no long-term feasibility studies were conducted. At one point, there was even a ludicrous proposal to build an artificial island off the coast near the old airport and then put a sports venue there. Three new soccer stadiums were planned for cities that already had soccer facilities that could have been renovated to meet our needs.

The IOC, which had been an ally in getting the organizational effort moving, was no help in curbing these excesses. I had disputes with the IOC and international sports federations about budget concerns, but all they were concerned about was getting the best sporting venues and infrastructure built. My mantra for ATHOC had been stay on budget, while every other key player—the government, the IOC, the sports federations—was caught up in a mentality of "spend, spend, spend."

On top of all those issues, there was the impact of the 9/11 attacks; Athens would end up spending some $1.5 billion on security, six times the amount spent at Sydney 2000, the last pre-9/11 Olympics.

In addition to the escalating costs, security issues dealt the Athens Games another major blow. Hysterical Western media, at times driven by special business interests and lobbying groups, portrayed Athens as an unsafe city: wide open, unprepared, and thus ripe for terrorist attack. The characterization wasn't remotely accurate; Athens was more prepared for terrorism and far safer than some previous Olympics had been. But those dire warnings wound up deterring tourists and corporate groups that had been expected to attend the Games, a blow to both our pride and the economy of the Games. These "scare" stories seemed particularly unfair, as they came primarily from the United States, England, and Australia. After all, even before 9/11, America had suffered a terrorist bombing at the 1996 Atlanta Games.

Meanwhile, Greece was doing its job. The West was obsessed with the threat from Al Qaeda and other Islamic terrorists. Greek security forces—thanks mainly to the efforts of Minister for Public Order Michalis Chrisochoidis and Public Prosecutor Yiannis Diotis—arrested the members of Revolutionary Organization 17 November, the terrorist group that had conducted more than a hundred attacks and assassinated twenty-three people in Greece since 1975—among them, as I mentioned previously, my husband's uncle and mentor, Dimitris Angelopoulos.

There would be bumps elsewhere too. One of the most distressing came on the water during the World Rowing Junior Championships held in early August 2003. It was the first of a succession of major test events, competitions designed to ensure that our new Olympic sports venues, along with the ATHOC staff, were up and running—and running efficiently. The International Rowing Federation had chosen the dates, apparently oblivious to the fact that they coincided with a peak period for the turbulent, high Meltemi winds that come out of the Balkans and sweep across Greek waters. These winds created violent conditions that wound up flipping and swamping many of the boats.

I received a call from an annoyed Prime Minister Simitis asking me what had happened. My reply was: "We tried too hard to be the gracious and accommodating hosts and allowed the International Rowing Federation to plan a competition despite the early August winds. On the bright side, Mr. Prime Minister, this event gave us a valuable lesson: 'Don't give in to all demands.' And I assure you that our actual Olympic rowing competition will take place in late August."

After the rowing incident, we knew we couldn't let any sports federation cajole or bully us at the expense of safety.

So I delivered the message loud and clear: I don't like surprises unless I have planned them.

Eventually there came a point when nobody inside or outside the Olympic movement could deny the momentum we had achieved.

Nobody could accuse us of moving bulldozers from site to site because we were building everywhere, creating visible symbols of our progress toward the Games. And by late 2003, every project was essentially on schedule and would be completed on time as long as we maintained our breakneck pace without major delays or disasters. We fortunately averted those, but there were enough bumps in the road to ensure that we never became overconfident.

Chapter 25

"I WILL ALSO BE THERE!"

PEOPLE ALWAYS ASK if there was one moment when I knew with absolute certainty that we would succeed. There was no one moment, but many. Nevertheless, nothing did more to convince me that we were making extraordinary headway and that Greece would ultimately rise to the occasion than our success in recruiting volunteers.

You have to understand that until these Olympics, Greece had no real history or culture of volunteerism. So it wasn't as simple as spreading the word that we were taking applications. We had to "sell" our mission to the Greek people. To do that, ATHOC launched a national advertising campaign promoting Olympic volunteerism. Years earlier at one of our presentations about volunteerism, I came up with the impromptu slogan "I will also be there!" My communications staff picked it up back then and that became our slogan for all our volunteer campaigns.

I personally traveled all around the country preaching the message of a new kind of patriotism, and frankly, I was astounded by the positive response everywhere I went. I remember some people discouraging me from visiting Muslim communities in northern Greece, insisting that it would be a waste of time and that the reception to a female leader might be hostile. I disregarded that advice and have vivid memories of people lining the streets to welcome me and of Muslim women showering me with carnations from their balconies.

I was in a rather unique position to preach about this commitment, of course, since I was, after all, the Athens 2004's first volunteer. I had taken the job as President of the organizing committee to be of service to my country without accepting a salary.

And, just as Theodore and I did during the bid campaign, we wound up paying not only my own expenses but also many ATHOC expenses, such as research and hiring consultants in Greece and abroad, as well as underwriting staff travel.

The Greek people wound up responding to our entreaty for volunteers in numbers beyond our wildest dreams. We shattered all previous Olympic records for volunteer applications. We had to stop accepting them after we received more than 165,000 applications, about four times the number we would require. Two-thirds of the applicants—some 110,000 people—were from Greece, which has a population of only about 10 million, or roughly the same as the Los Angeles metropolitan area. We received applications from 190 countries, many of them from Greeks living abroad or people of Greek heritage. I always feel a special bond with these volunteers, who performed heroically—the shining, smiling, modern face of Greece—during the Olympics and the Paralympics. Throughout the Games, I proudly wore the exact same uniform—no superior cut of cloth this time—worn by every one of our 45,000 Olympic and 15,000 Paralympic volunteers. Years later, people still come up to me and tell me what a thrill it was to volunteer for the Games.

In my heart, I had always believed that the Greek people would rise to the occasion when asked to volunteer. I confess, however, that I was less certain about how we would fare with a new kind of "volunteer" initiative that was just as critical to our success. Come Games time, we needed Athenians to radically change their lifestyle—to sacrifice a lifetime's cherished habits and customs—for the sake of the greater good.

After an inter-ministerial committee meeting, I met privately with Prime Minister Simitis and Minister for Culture and Sports Venizelos and I presented the plan of how the public should be informed of the changes to their daily lives we would be making prior to and during the Olympic Games. These included security and transportation measures; hours when shops and restaurants could be open; more than forty municipalities cleaning the city during the nights (something unprecedented); thousands of supply vans and trucks delivering during the night; smoking restrictions; when and how people should arrive at venues; exclusive use of public transport; and many more important matters.

Venizelos wanted to wait until just before the Games and simply pass a new law that mandated all the changes and prescribed punishments for lawbreakers. I told him and the Prime Minister that his idea was unacceptable. "The Greek people will not accept being told what to do at the last minute."

He insisted, and in an arrogant and pompous manner, without even glancing at me, he said to Simitis, "My plan is the best."

So I said to both of them, "If you insist on this approach, I will resign and you can proceed and pass the law at the last minute."

ATHOC's plan was to begin a campaign more than a year in advance that would educate the public on how their daily lives would be affected prior to and during the Olympics. Likewise, they would learn what would be required of them and, most critically, why. The campaign focused on test events such as the marathon, cycling races, and the triathlon, all of which required major traffic restrictions. We would use multiple vehicles—media, Internet, public meetings, and face-to-face approaches (in cafés, restaurants, shops) in certain neighborhoods near the Olympic venues—to ensure that we informed as many people as possible. In the spring of 2003, we launched our campaign. We held community forums throughout Athens and conducted more than three hundred meetings with 155 different interest groups: customs officials, banks' staff, police chiefs, hospital personnel, truck drivers, taxi drivers, street market vendors, hoteliers, pharmacists, immigrants' associations, groups for special needs people, animal protection groups, forty city authorities, and everybody else in the public and private sectors. In the key neighborhoods near Olympic venues, we even went door-to-door passing out pamphlets that explained what was required of people.

Plus, what was required of the average Athenian, at least by Greek standards, was extraordinary. People couldn't drive in certain places at certain hours. People couldn't park their cars in the streets near the venues, which meant many of them would be forced to park their cars at a considerable distance from their homes. All spectators would have to use public transportation to arrive at the venues, and they would have to abandon the Greek habit of arriving at the last minute. Instead, they would have to arrive hours in advance to clear security.

These changes became so ingrained that during the hours when the otherwise restricted Olympic driving lanes were open to the public, drivers tended to stick to the public lanes, and honked their reproach at those who ventured into the privileged ones.

Taxi drivers didn't hike their prices for tourists. Even Greek VIPs came to accept that nobody was getting free tickets or prime seats.

On a far grander scale than when we had revamped attitudes at

ATHOC, we had to change the mantra of your average Greek from "Yes, but . . ." to "Yes!" Only then could we begin to change how the world viewed Greeks.

The result of our efforts was a testament to how effective leadership can be when the time is taken to ask and explain rather than simply to issue new and unpopular rules and expect the public to comply with them. Compliance with our new regulations would prove to be extraordinarily high and a critical part of our Olympic success. In fact, Athenians did more than we asked of them. It was a lesson in how to effect change. Once the public was informed about the reasons for the new rules, they accepted them and, indeed, embraced them, becoming partners in the success of the Games. It felt very much like a personal vindication.

The average Greeks, the ones who suffer the systemic abuses by the power brokers, had no problems with me. Indeed, just as when I served them on the city council and in Parliament, I sensed that I had earned both their affection and their respect.

Simitis's Socialist government could claim neither. By early 2004, the Prime Minister was acutely aware that he was facing an uphill battle in the next election.

I understood how he felt when he came to me with a bizarre and inappropriate proposal (which was actually Venizelos's idea). ATHOC's plan to make the torch relay a worldwide event—for the very first time, runners would carry the torch on five continents—had created great international excitement. But the Greek portion of the relay, with all the attendant excitement about the approaching Olympics, wouldn't begin until after the national election, too late to help Simitis. So the Prime Minister proposed that we create a much earlier Greek relay that would bring a torch from Olympia to the Panathinaiko Stadium, the site of the first modern Games in 1896, just days before voters went to the polls.

As respectfully as I could, I told the Prime Minister that an additional relay would be impossible. I couldn't turn a sacred Olympic tradition into a political tool for the government—or any political party. I wouldn't compromise the integrity of the Games. The Olympics belonged to the Greek people, not to the Greek government.

In March 2004, just five months before the Olympic cauldron would be lit during our Opening Ceremony, Simitis and his Socialists lost the elections after eleven years of rule, routed by New Democracy in the parliamentary election.

Though I shared a party affiliation with Kostas Karamanlis, the new Prime Minister, and had known him since my first days in Parliament, I felt more than a twinge of regret for my former dance partner, Costas Simitis. Despite all my struggles with his government, I would never forget that it was Simitis who had defied his own party and given me the immense privilege of first leading the bid committee and, later, organizing the Games. It didn't seem fair that now, on the cusp of the Olympics, all the glory, all the speeches, and all the photo-ops would go to his opposition. In my official speech at the Olympic Closing Ceremony, I would ignore protocol by publicly thanking the former Prime Minister as well, acknowledging his pivotal role in bringing the Games to Athens.

The change in governments had no real impact on my job. At that point, so late in the game, we were out of crisis mode and on schedule to meet all our obligations. No elected official in his right mind was going to tinker with a successful plan and risk a failure that could be laid at his feet. Shortly after the election, I met with the new Prime Minister in his office to brief him.

I began, "Mr. Prime Minister—"

"Gianna, please," he interrupted, "call me Kostas."

"Mr. Prime Minister," I continued, "you are one lucky man. Now all the hard work is done. We are 97 percent finished and it is just a little nip and tuck. For you, it should be as easy as taking the cream out of the milk. You can be so proud of the Greek people. We will show the world a brand-new country. If you take advantage of this legacy of our hardworking people, you will wind up running a very successful nation and write history."

I suspect, left to his own devices, he might have taken my excellent advice. But it soon became clear that his advisers were more concerned with who would occupy center stage than with what we had accomplished as a nation. "Why is she the only one we see?" was the refrain in the Prime Minister's office. "You are the Prime Minister, the one chosen by the Greek people," his people were telling him, "but she is always there like the messiah."

All the same, I didn't worry too much, because Karamanlis was smart enough to understand that they couldn't take it from there; they couldn't deliver. But I could. So he shut them up by saying, "Let her finish this."

As I had assured the new Prime Minister, everything was proceeding smoothly. And soon the Olympics were so close at hand the excitement was palpable. But if Greece needed a harbinger of good things to come, that summer—less than six weeks before the Games—provided an extraordinary one. On July fourth, the Greek national soccer team—a 150-to-1 underdog at tournament's start—won the European championship for the first time ever. They defeated Portugal on their home turf in Lisbon by a score of one to nothing.

Theodore and I were in Lisbon for the semifinal victory over the Czech Republic. But on the night of the final, we had to attend a family wedding at the Hotel Grand Bretagne in downtown Athens. That night I was also introduced to George Soros and had a conversation with him about Greece's effort for the Olympics. Throughout the evening, people at the party were streaming in and out of another room to check the score of the game on TV. Theodore had driven the car himself that night because, he complained, he was tired of always being surrounded by people. That was true, though never quite like we would be later that night. When we were ready to drive home, our car was completely engulfed by a mob of cheering people who had streamed into the streets, waving Greek flags to celebrate the soccer victory. People recognized me and began directing cheers at our car. Despite the warnings of our security staff, we opened our windows to wave to the crowd. I was so excited I reached out, clasping hundreds of hands. I knew there was no threat to me or to the diamond. People just wanted to share this extraordinary moment. Some of them began shouting, "Next step, Olympics!" The soccer championship had provided a timely reminder that if you start with a big enough belief, nothing is impossible.

Chapter 26

G FORCE

BY THE SPRING OF 2004, I was convinced we were on track. But the public, both at home and abroad, was anxious: "Is Greece going to make it?" "Will Greece be ready on time?" The refrain I had been listening to for four years, again and again. And we had another test in front of us, a formidable one: how to put in place the huge Calatrava roof over our main Olympic stadium.

That's why three days in May loomed so critical. For the first time, really, the whole world was watching. We were about to stage a spectacular new and unprecedented Olympic event: call it the hydraulic lift and roof plant.

The Olympic stadium roof had come to symbolize more than the Games; it was our grand ambition. It was a 269,000-square-foot steel and glass structure—an arch in two giant sections that would cover the stadium—designed by the world-renowned Spanish architect and engineer Santiago Calatrava. In the design renderings, the roof's soaring beauty—it would peak at a height of more than 250 feet—belied the fact that it weighed seventeen thousand tons. It was as pragmatic as it was elegant; built with a special coating that reflected the sun, the roof would ensure that the stadium remained comfortable despite the summer heat.

And not surprisingly, it was a challenge that provided a focal point for everybody who worried about Greece's ability to execute its Games plan.

I am incapable of explaining the complex hydraulic solution that was supposed to maneuver the roof into place over the Olympic stadium. All I knew was that until we witnessed the roof in its rightful position, nobody at ATHOC, or indeed the entire country, could rest easy. And witnessing that extraordinary feat was something of an excruciating ordeal as the roof moved up into the Athens sky at a glacial pace. I would later learn that the roof was being propelled toward our destiny at a speed of approximately three inches a minute. I would never have guessed it was moving that slow.

After three long days came the magic moment: Wow! The roof was in place above the stadium! The praise was grand: "Roof Is the Toast of Athens," announced the *Evening Standard* on May 11, 2004.

Once the press realized that the roof would hold they busied themselves concocting far worse scenarios than a roofless stadium. Reporters, mostly Brits and Germans, kept trying to sneak into the Olympic stadium, supposedly to demonstrate how lax the security was and how vulnerable we were to terrorist attack. A number of them were caught and detained; one British journalist made it inside and her story played big, as if she had done something very courageous.

I was fed up. They simply ignored the fact that the renovation of the stadium hadn't been completed. Only *after* the renovation would the stadium go into security lockdown, and after lockdown only accredited personnel could enter the perimeter and the stadium.

The ensuing weeks went by in a haze of hard work and frazzled excitement. The finish line was in sight and we were going to sprint through the tape. Typically, there were countless little headaches. How could there not be with thirty-two distinct athletic venues opening around Athens under ATHOC's supervision? And then there were media operations at every venue. Each venue required testing of all its systems to make sure it was up and running to our standards. Nobody in the Olympic movement or the press had forgotten or forgiven the failure of a critical IBM computer system at the Atlanta 1996 Games. Untested before the Games, the system, which was designed to distribute official results to the press worldwide, crashed frequently and was painfully slow. Even worse, it was often inaccurate when it was up.

Per usual, it wouldn't have been Greece if there weren't one more political flap that played out behind closed doors. As the Games approached, Karamanlis's advisers at long last convinced the Prime Minister to be more aggressive with his own Olympic aspirations. Why shouldn't he give the welcoming speech at the Opening Ceremony rather than have me do it? Fortunately, this was not a fight I needed to engage.

The IOC had its well-established protocols, one of which dictated that the President of the organizing committee had the singular honor of welcoming the world on behalf of the host nation. I had the impression that during the Opening Ceremony the Prime Minister was stewing in his seat while the world rejoiced in a new glory that was Greece.

The Olympic Opening Ceremony is such a point of pride for the citizens of the host nation and such a touchstone for viewers all over the world that it is inevitably the most worrisome of all of the Olympics' moving parts. (And that's not even including the security challenge presented by world leaders and royalty filling the VIP boxes.) Early on, I had sought the advice of NBC sports boss Dick Ebersol on how to divide my budget between the Opening Ceremony and the Closing

Ceremony. Ebersol, whose perspective was especially valuable because of his vast Olympic broadcast experience and his deep and abiding love of the Games, responded quickly and unequivocally. "Ninety-ten," he said. "The Opening Ceremony is a showcase for the world. If the Opening Ceremony does not go well, it will be used against you no matter how well the Games go. If the Games go well, the Closing Ceremony doesn't matter so much. It's really just a party for Greece."

We had already won the Summer Olympic Games by pledging to present them on a more human scale. Our Opening Ceremony, starting with a heartbeat, would signal our intention to honor that commitment. And Greece boasted an extraordinary heritage, our gift to Western Civilization and one that we believed would resonate with viewers around the world.

Creating that show—gathering all the people to rehearse in secret, keeping track of all the moving parts—was a task worthy of Odysseus. I had placed the job in the hands of Dimitris Papaioannou, the director of the ceremony, and it proved an inspired choice. Dimitris combined extraordinary creativity and flair with great taste and refinement. He was also blessed with an attention to detail that rivaled my own, an absolute requisite for anyone who hopes to produce this kind of spectacle. I can personally attest to that. I remember standing with him at the stadium exactly one year before the Opening Ceremony—at the exact moment the Games would begin—as he tried to gauge how light from the sky would behave during the production, how it would play off the water and other elements. He wanted to leave nothing to chance.

He even insisted on coming to my home to check out my wardrobe and choose the outfit that he felt was in harmony with the colors and spirit of his production. He chose a simple off-white—almost faded beige—dress that, by virtue of its fabric and flow, looked like it might have been worn on stage in one of the ancient Greek theatrical performances. I would wear no jewelry except those lucky pearl earrings I had rescued from the floor in Lausanne after we won the Games. Dimitris even coached me on how to ascend the steps to the podium for my welcoming speech. He said it shouldn't look like I was climbing a mountain. "People don't want to see a woman who looks exhausted," he explained. "They want to see somebody poised to open the doors to Greece." Dimitris was a superb dancer and he taught me how to move so that my feet were essentially moving independently of my head. The effect, he said, would make me "ascend like a cloud."

We developed a great working relationship, though in the early days he told friends that he wasn't sure he would be able to work with this demanding woman. He complained that I constantly badgered him about financial constraints and repeated over and over again the same question: "Is it feasible?" It was, as Dimitris would demonstrate so brilliantly to the world.

I placed Titos Komninos, an extremely successful Greek CEO, in charge of all other organizational aspects for the ceremony except the production itself. (He was officially our coordinator of the Opening Ceremony.)

Two days before the Games were to commence, I had the special thrill of visiting the Olympic village for a meeting with our staff and volunteers. It was the first time I had donned their uniform, and the volunteers were both surprised and delighted that I had cast my lot with them. I relished the "wows" that coursed through the huge group assembled there. (IOC President Rogge was so taken with the uniform that he requested one for himself.) The uniforms would quickly become the height of fashion in the city, as off-duty volunteers proudly wore them into restaurants and taverns. The only difference in my outfit was that I had a small bag containing the security phone (to be used for extremely important issues) that could connect me directly to Prime Minister Karamanlis or President Rogge. At that moment, I couldn't have imagined how soon I would have to use it. Actually, it was the next day.

The matter involved two Greek sprinters and training partners, Kostas Kenteris and Katerina Thanou, arguably the most illustrious stars on our nation's Olympic team. At the Sydney 2000 Summer Olympics, Kenteris had sprung a major upset by winning gold at 200 meters. Thanou had surprised everyone in Sydney too, winning a silver medal in the 100 meters behind American Marion Jones.

Greeks reveled in the triumphs and embraced the runners as national heroes. Few were aware—I certainly wasn't—that in track and field circles the two were trailed by suspicions. Unfairly or not, suspicion almost automatically attaches itself to any sprinter who has a breakout performance in mid-career—Kenteris was twenty-seven years old in Sydney, Thanou twenty-five—that surpasses all prior achievements. Kenteris repeated his gold-medal performance the following year at the world championships, but the two soon stopped competing on the European circuit, where the prizes are lucrative but the drug testing is rigorous. Shortly before the Olympics, the sprinters had hastily departed Greece for America, somehow avoiding drug testers who had them in their sights in Athens. Though they were required to keep officials apprised of their exact whereabouts, the pair couldn't be located when drug testers showed up at the address they had provided in Chicago.

But once they returned to Athens for the Olympic Games there was nowhere to hide. Or so officials believed. Two days before the Opening Ceremony, the two Greek sprinters missed a scheduled drug test, a major violation of their sport's protocol, and somehow, later that day, wound up in the hospital claiming that they were injured in a motorcycle accident. Nobody could or would explain how the two managed to reach the hospital after this accident. To the IOC, the

IAAF, and the international press, the incident was a charade, a transparent attempt to circumvent drug tests with a tale that defied belief. The apparent betrayal stung Greece, and in response, the Greek press was harsh: "Tell Us The Truth," one local newspaper demanded in large type on its front page.

The truth would remain elusive. The IOC moved swiftly to boot the Greek stars from the Games.

I felt shocked and disappointed and that is why I used the phone.

When I called the Prime Minister to pass on the bad news, he immediately asked, "Can this be managed?" I told him that there was no way this could be kept under wraps. He said, "Okay, let it go." At that moment, he and I felt the same hurt all Greeks would when they heard, on the eve of Greece's proudest moment, that those in whom we had placed the greatest faith had tarnished, had shamed our country.

Beyond the emotional distress, I had a pragmatic problem. At any Olympic Opening Ceremony, the greatest honor for an athlete is to be chosen as the one who, at the climax of the long torch relay, takes the torch on the final leg, raises it to the cauldron, and lights the Olympic flame that will burn atop the stadium throughout the Games. Muhammad Ali had the honor in Atlanta; four years later in Sydney, runner Cathy Freeman set the torch to the cauldron (and went on to become the only person to light the flame and win a gold medal in the same Olympics). The chosen athlete is a closely held secret, but there had been plenty of press speculation that Kenteris would be the one. And this was, unfortunately, one of those rare occasions when press speculation was correct.

With Kenteris out of commission and out of the Olympics, we had to make another choice—and swiftly. We needed to find somebody who was telegenic and who could command the stage for what is, without doubt, the most dramatic moment of the evening. In other words, somebody with style and more than a little flair. Eventually we made our choice: Nikos Kaklamanakis, an Olympic gold medalist and three-time world champion in windsurfing whose good looks and charm had served Greece so well seven years earlier during our bid presentation in Lausanne.

There was only one disadvantage in picking Nikos. The five other athletes were already on hand for rehearsals because they knew they were part of the festivities. At that critical moment, one day before the Opening Ceremony, nobody knew exactly where Nikos was or how to reach him. Then there was a series of frantic calls to try and find his father, who might have the answer. When we finally located his father, he told us that Nikos was out on the water training on his windsurfing board and there was no way to communicate with him. At my urging, his father went out on a boat to try and flag him down. When he finally caught up with Nikos and handed him a phone, I could barely hear him over the sounds of the wind and the sea. But I didn't need to hear Nikos. I just needed him to hear me. I told him he was about to star in our show and that he needed to get his butt off the water to where we would be waiting to speed him to the stadium for his first and only rehearsal—twenty-four hours before showtime!

When I got home that evening, my daughter brought me some fresh almonds and walnuts, but I had no appetite. Theodore chided me that I had to eat something to keep up my strength. "Don't speak to me like my father," I told him. "Besides, tomorrow I want to feel light." I actually slept well, though I awoke very early. Everyone had counseled me to stay home and rest up for the big night. So, naturally, I got up and proceeded to the stadium where I could find all kinds of things to worry about. I no longer had to worry about Nikos; he was in place and I had no doubt he could run the required two hundred meters, get up the steep stairs without tripping, and apply the flame to the cauldron. What concerned me, though, was whether the computer technology would work flawlessly. There would be critical moments throughout when we were all subservient to the computer.

There had been some famous glitches in Olympic cauldron lighting. In 1992 in Albertville, there was a premature conflagration before the torch even touched the cauldron. And in 2000 I had been in Sydney when, for a few seconds, the giant cauldron essentially stalled on its designated course. I remember how everyone seemed to be holding their breath. The Israeli IOC delegate, Alex Gilady, who was seated a few rows in front of me, turned to look at me and tapped the side of his head with his finger. I took that to mean: "You see what can happen. Learn from that." Sydney officials later determined that some ham radio operator briefly jammed the signal. In Athens we were relying on computers to generate the artistic dazzle, and I couldn't help but wonder what would happen if the signals were somehow jammed. What were our plan B and our plan C? But everybody kept reassuring me: "Don't worry, everything will be all right. If the technology fails, we can do everything manually." With all the tasks assigned, all I had to worry about was my speech (and a possible broken heel, I was thinking!).

I had declined a teleprompter, certain that I could memorize and deliver my speech in three languages: the official Olympic languages of English and French, as well as Greek, naturally. I had practiced diligently and wasn't worried about stage fright, which had never been my problem. My worries were about things like a broken heel on my shoe that would make my ascent to the podium treacherous if not impossible. That had been an obsessive concern of mine ever since I had broken a heel during a ceremony welcoming Queen Beatrix of the Netherlands to Athens. Through a very long ceremony, I was forced to pull off the gymnastic feat of balancing myself on one foot despite a cramping leg.

Ever since I have carried an extra pair of shoes to every event. But that precaution wouldn't help if the heel snapped while I was climbing the steps mid-ceremony. Then again, I wouldn't be climbing; rather, I would be ascending like a cloud. I could only hope it wasn't a dark cloud.

Departing the stadium Thursday evening, after the final rehearsal, I bumped into one of the more prominent members of the Greek Olympic team, a former Olympic high jump medalist Niki Bakoyanni (no relation to the Mayor). She had a worried look on her face when she approached me, as if she had something really serious on her mind. It turned out that she was even more worried about the next evening's events than I was—and I was very anxious. "Madame President," she said, "I have to confess something."

I was puzzled, but encouraged her: "Go on."

"I just came from my astrologer."

After a long pause, I prompted her, "And . . ."

"And my astrologer told me something very bad is going to happen tomorrow."

I didn't laugh at the young woman because everybody had worries. For that moment, I set aside all my own and put on my best Games face. "Don't be concerned; everything is going to be okay. But there is one thing you have to do."

"Yes, what is it, Madame President?" she asked nervously.

"Find another astrologer."

Chapter 27

GAMES ON!

ON AUGUST 13, 2004, the opening night of the Twenty-Eighth Olympic Games, Athens was a flurry of excitement. Huge crowds thronged around the stadium. People from all over the world had descended upon this country and they were buzzing with anticipation in all their many languages.

I recall, as I was arriving at the stadium, looking out at the huge crowds of Greeks arriving at the same time. They looked so happy and so proud and so carefree. I felt a twinge of envy. I was happy and proud, but not exactly carefree. This was to be my moment, the one to which I had devoted so many years of my life, and I wasn't sure I was going to get to enjoy it.

Besides all the worries, I had responsibilities to the VIPs—"Madame President, you must greet him," "Madame President, you must greet her"—and was saddled with a nervous Prime Minister to boot, who needed constant reassurance because he looked out and saw a stadium that was half empty rather than one that was half full. "Gianna, why is it half empty?" asked Kostas Karamanlis nervously. I patiently explained that every seat had been sold, but because the people were coming by public transportation, as we had requested, and because of the high security, he was going to have to endure a slow, steady procession of fans before the stadium was filled.

"Are you sure it will fill?"

"I am sure, and it will start to the exact second. We control everything."

In the command center, our "war room," were COO Marton Simitsek, Creative Director Dimitris Papaioannou, Opening Ceremony Coordinator Titos Komninos, and Venue Manager Thanassis Papageorgiou. They were all fully alert.

Truth be told, I was ready to cede control for just this one evening. Though I knew every second of the production, I wanted to surrender myself to the moment and experience it, like all the others, in my heart. Before the broadcast began, we had Nikos Aliagas (a famous Greek TV presenter who has made an exceptional career in France) warm up the crowd. During this time, he performed a small sketch with two workers pretending to be putting the last nails into the stadium. The crowd loved it!

Once the ceremony began, I tried to soak it all in: the percussive heartbeat countdown; the collective gasp of delight at the sight of the sea of water filling the stadium; the four hundred drums and bouzoukis and their players that ringed the sea; the dueling drums from the stadium to Olympia, connecting (via video) three thousand years of Olympic tradition; the comet that crashed into the stadium floor, igniting the Olympic rings of fire; the enthusiastic reactions of the people in attendance; and the theater of our extraordinary civilization—and its

contributions to the world—from ancient to modern times. Dimitris
Papaioannou's vision of Greece's place in the world was fully realized.

One of the modern miracles was that more than half a million
gallons of water were drained from the stadium floor within three
minutes to make way for the parade of nations and athletes. According
to Olympic protocol, I walked out into the stadium alongside IOC
President Jacques Rogge and the President of the Hellenic Republic,
Costis Stephanopoulos, for the presentation of the Greek flag and the
national anthem. I was consumed by joy. If you look back at the pictures,
the two men wore rather solemn and ceremonial expressions; I, on the
other hand, was simply beaming, an emotional blaze radiating through
my face. When I returned to my seat, everyone I passed—Queen Sofía
of Spain, King Albert of Belgium, Tony and Cherie Blair, Shimon
Peres of Israel, President Horst Köhler of Germany, Zanele Mbeki,
the First Lady of South Africa, Frederik, Crown Prince of Denmark,
and dozens of royals and heads of state—congratulated me. But when I
sat down next to the Prime Minister, he remained expressionless. After
four arduous years of struggle, doubts, and victories, it seemed that
everyone in the world was thrilled to be in Athens, everyone except
the Prime Minister, that is.

The stirring parade of nations climaxed with the entry of Greece
to a thunderous welcome. In every Olympics, the Greek team marches
first in the parade in honor of having hosted the first Olympics. The
host team marches last. As both the historic and the current host,
Greece marched last for the first time in Olympic history. I stood on the
podium in the shadow of an olive tree to officially welcome the world
to the XXVIIIth Olympiad, to Athens, and to Greece. Such passions
were stirring in my soul. I felt as if my very blood were rising through
my body and might just explode through my head. That little girl from

Crete who had such big dreams had never, in her wildest imagination, conjured up anything approaching that surreal moment.

I didn't want to think about the seventy-two thousand spectators who filled the stadium seats, the fifteen thousand athletes from 202 nations who filled the stadium field, and an estimated two billion viewers around the world who would tune in to watch part or all of the ceremony. Instead I thought about where we had started out and how far we had come. Instead I thought about all the Greek people who had contributed so much, enabling me the privilege of standing there to declare: "Greece is here! We're ready! Together we write a new and wonderful chapter in the history of the Games. Olympic Games, welcome home!"

In the stadium, the ovation would turn thunderous as forty-seven-year-old Nikos Galis, revered as the man who transformed Greece into a European basketball power, trotted into the stadium carrying the Olympic torch. He handed the torch to sixty-two-year-old Mimis Domazos, who captained Panathinaikos FC for more than fifteen years and is regarded as Greece's greatest soccer star. It was then passed to thirty-nine-year-old Voula Patoulidou, who became a national hero when she won gold in the 100-meter hurdles at the Barcelona 1992 Summer Games, the first Greek woman to capture an Olympic medal. Next came Kakhi Kakhiashvilli, the thirty-four-year-old Georgian-Greek weightlifter who had won three consecutive gold medals: the first in Barcelona competing for the post-Soviet "Unified Team," and the next two in Atlanta and Sydney for Greece. Then the torch was handed off to Ioannis Melissanidis, who as a nineteen-year-old at the Atlanta 1996 Centennial Games stunned the gymnastics world with his gold medal in the floor exercise.

And then Nikos Kaklamanakis, our windsurfer and last-minute savior, was standing there holding the torch, looking as if he had been readying for this moment his entire life. As he ascended the stairs toward the stadium roof, the giant cauldron—designed, like our Athens Olympic torch, to resemble an olive leaf—bent down to meet him. He gently laid the torch inside its lip and, as the cauldron lifted skyward, it burst into flame. Cheers, fireworks, music composed by Shostakovich (our amazingly gifted musical director, George Koumentakis from Crete, had selected the music for the entire ceremony and composed some parts himself) all erupted to bring a glorious evening to its close.

I had to do a press conference afterward and was a bit puzzled as to what I should say. The spectacular ceremony had spoken for itself; any words I could add would not do the evening justice. Then I remembered some advice George Stephanopoulos had offered me before we won the Games in Lausanne. He said it was the same advice he gave Clinton before he won his first presidential election. After you've won, he told me, "Tell them whatever you want." And that night I said what I felt: Greece had without a doubt won over the world.

When at long last I got home, it was almost the mirror opposite of the previous night when I couldn't eat but had slept surprisingly soundly. Starving, I devoured moussaka, salad, figs, and dessert, but I was simply too exhilarated to sleep. The music, the fireworks, the cheers were all still ringing in my ears. Even if sleep wouldn't come, I could wrap myself in the comfortable blanket of triumph.

The next morning I went to the shooting event, where the first gold medal would be awarded. For obvious reasons, nobody would entrust me with a gun. So I was armed only with my emergency phone and my contingency plans. And for seventeen days I carried them around without ever needing them. It is a measure of the remarkable performance by our team and our volunteers that not only was there never any crisis, there were never any serious problems either.

I continued to have routine daily meetings at 6:30 AM with the IOC

Coordination Commission, but no emergency meetings were ever held. After three days, the IOC conceded that things were going so well that the early-morning meetings were unnecessary, so we stopped holding them, something that hadn't happened in the previous Olympics. Everything proceeded like clockwork, a performance exceeding anybody's expectations for Greece—even, if I am to be honest, mine. I thought we would be very good. But we were great, virtually flawless. With no reason for me to remain tethered at all times to my office or the operations center, I was freed up to also be a fan. I put everything bad that had happened before the Olympics behind me and set out to enjoy, indeed to revel in, the extraordinary events for which I had worked so hard and suffered so much.

Some of them had extra meaning for me. We had not won the Games based on our Olympic legacy alone, but once the Games were ours, we could imbue them with that glorious connection to our heritage. After three millennia, women got to compete at the birthplace of the Games. The shot put competition was staged amid the ruins of ancient Olympia. The marathon was run from Marathon. One cycling race was competed in the shadow of the Acropolis. And Panathinaiko Stadium was the site of the archery competition. It was emotionally stunning to bear witness to how Greece's storied past spanned three thousand years to reach out and touch its present.

I may have been the gold medalist among spectators. Besides attending those "historic" sports events, I saw track and field in the Olympic stadium, gymnastics, basketball, tennis, the triathlon, weightlifting, swimming, synchronized swimming, diving, rowing, and softball. At the softball game, I actually got to throw out the first pitch, something that—because softball is not really a Greek game—required a lot of practice. ATHOC's competition managers at each venue kept me well apprised of any event at which there might be the chance for a Greek medal. Happily, that was more often than anticipated as Greece won sixteen medals—six gold, six silver, and four bronze—in ten different sports, and I was there to celebrate most of them. Among those medalists was our Opening Ceremony hero Nikos, who added a silver medal to his Atlanta gold.

The late American filmmaker Bud Greenspan became famous for the lyricism and emotional wallop of his Olympic documentaries, chronicling the games from Los Angeles in 1984 to Vancouver in 2010. In Athens, he had plenty of dramatic material to choose from. A dry recitation won't do it justice, but let me just note a few of the highlights and "firsts."

China won thirty-two gold medals—only three fewer than the United States, at the top of the chart—signaling the dominance that would come four years later in Beijing.

American swimmer Michael Phelps would win six golds and two silvers, another harbinger of extraordinary things to come in Beijing and London.

Israel, Chile, and the Dominican Republic all won first-ever Olympic gold medals.

America's NBA stars would lose an Olympic basketball game for the first time, and then, quite shockingly, endure a second and a third loss, as Argentina won the gold medal.

The great Moroccan distance runner Hicham El Guerrouj won the 1,500 and 5,000 meters, the first runner to pull off that double since the famed "Flying Finn," Paavo Nurmi, eighty years earlier.

And forty-two-year-old German kayaker Birgit Fischer won her eighth gold medal in Athens, her sixth Olympic appearance!

It was such an unexpected pleasure for me to be able to watch so many of these events and to be able to smile and cheer just like all the other Greeks there. And it was a healing experience. I received so much affection, appreciation, and admiration from my fellow Greeks as I made my way around the Games that it served as a balm for the emotional wounds of the Olympic wars. People kept coming up to me just to thank me for delivering this treasure to our nation. Some would actually tell me how they didn't like me at first, but they had changed their mind when they saw how I stood up to the politicians. "You've got balls," I remember many saying. "We're proud of you and what you've done."

All those words helped more than they could ever know. Especially because there was one accident that I worried could take on a life of its own.

It is Olympic protocol for the President of the organizing committee to host a private reception for the VIPs on the evening of the first day of competition. Just like when we courted the IOC delegates, Theodore and I decided there was nothing more authentically Greek than to host the people at our home. It was a star-studded cast of guests from around the world—with royals, heads of state, IOC elite, and, naturally, my "friends" in the Greek government. We assembled an absolutely gorgeous setting with a beautifully decorated gazebo set on the lawn as the centerpiece. The meal was fabulous and everything was proceeding perfectly until . . .

We had decided that we should cap the evening, just like at the Opening Ceremony, with a celebratory fireworks display. The display had been set up in the distance, on a hill beyond a large stand of trees, and the fireworks operators had rehearsed without any problems.

To this day, we are not exactly sure what went wrong. But as everybody stood and watched the fireworks go off, flames engulfed one of the pine trees on the ridge near the launching point. By the time the fire department responded, several trees had been lost. As guests left, offering comforting words, all I could think was that it was not the way I wanted to end a perfect beginning to the Games.

Theodore and I have seen to it that today the trees once again stand tall and there is no evidence of the fire, except for the memory of that near-disaster that is burned into my mind!

Although it did cause a small brouhaha in the Greek press, nothing had changed that night as far as the world knew. I was still being hailed as the savior of the Olympics, the maestro of this extraordinary Greek surprise.

Nevertheless, as the Olympics wound to their end, I became preoccupied with what President Rogge would say at the Closing Ceremony as his epilogue for the Games. His predecessor, Juan Antonio Samaranch, had famously declared every Olympics during his long tenure "*the best* Games ever." (That only became noteworthy in Atlanta when he omitted those words from his summation.) Rogge, whose Athens 2004 Summer Games were his first as IOC President, had already indicated that he would not adopt Samaranch's "best Games" tradition and would say something unique about each Olympics. I was extremely anxious to know exactly what that "something" would be for Athens.

But when I asked Rogge for a copy of his speech in advance, he refused. He told me, smiling, "Gianna, you will hear it when everybody else does."

Fortunately, one of my most reliable employees, Michalis Zacharatos (whose extreme sacrifices made him a casualty of the 55 percent divorce rate), who was serving as ATHOC's press spokesman during the Games, came to the rescue. He can be quite charming and is also smart enough to use some of that charm on the secretaries. As we all know, in a lot of large organizations, the secretaries do much of the work and tend to be underappreciated despite knowing an awful lot about what is going on. Michalis told me he had learned from the secretary who had typed Rogge's speech that, while she couldn't remember his precise words, he was going to say something very positive about Athens.

That didn't quite mollify me. I wanted to know exactly what he was going to say. Later, Michalis sidled up to me with a big smile, leaned his head very close to mine, and whispered to me rather conspiratorially. He had apparently spoken to a journalist whose wife was a friend of somebody in the IOC who knew what Rogge would say. Michalis did not tell me—at least not right then—that he had learned it fourth-hand or that it came from a source he regarded as self-aggrandizing and not entirely reliable. He pronounced with every confidence that Rogge would pronounce the Athens 2004 Summer Olympics "unforgettable dream games."

The next day we, along with all the other privileged parties, secured a copy of Rogge's speech, which confirmed the superlative that the IOC President would bestow on our effort. But when I met the President on Sunday before the Closing Ceremony, I didn't let on that I had unearthed his precious secret prior to receiving the official copy. When Rogge relented and shared with me what he would say, I pretended to be surprised, but I didn't have to pretend to be overjoyed. I could have heard it said a thousand times. I was so relieved that he would sing Greece's praises to the whole world and thrilled that my Olympics would end on such a high note.

Unforgettable Dream Games!

Chapter 28

LAST DANCE

BEFORE WE COULD GET TO ALL THE SINGING AND DANCING to close and celebrate the Athens 2004 Summer Games, there was some official business that had to occur. I received the Olympic Order in Gold for my service and, for the final time, was privileged to address the world. I ignored protocol and first thanked Theodore and my children, who would never get the recognition I had, but whose sacrifice had made Athens 2004 possible. And I infuriated the government once more by thanking not only its current leaders but also former Prime Minister Costas Simitis. Throughout the Games, the government had refused to acknowledge his contribution, but I would never forget who had given me this chance to fulfill my destiny and all the efforts he had made in support of the Games. Nor that it was Simitis who had devoted eight years to our Olympic effort only to see a new government enjoy a breeze of a five-month run-up to the Games, then try to hoard all the glory.

But all that was just political foreplay. Since this evening's finale was truly meant first and foremost for Greece, my most important message was aimed at a Greek audience. I had learned all too well the lessons of "the Greek Paradox," and I knew how easy it would be, especially in the absence of genuine political leadership, for Greece to squander its Olympic legacy. So after speaking in English and French, I switched to Greek to make an urgent plea to my countrymen and women, a message of hope—"the new face of Greece"—tempered by the admonition, "Keep the flame for creativity, effort, and victory burning in our souls."

As I mentioned in the prologue, near the very end of that night's celebrations I began to dance the *hasapiko*. I wasn't aware that cameras were focused on me, though had I been, I wouldn't have cared. It was Greece's moment and my moment and I was going to relish it until the last note of the last bouzouki was sounded. The joy was real, but, as it turned out, short-lived. Some in the press scolded me—"How dare she"—over what they characterized as an indecorous and narcissistic exercise in self-promotion, one that could have been fueled by my post-Olympic ambitions.

It was preposterous. I had endured enough. I didn't want any part of a system where officials chose to serve themselves rather than the people. I could no longer compete with people whose weapons of choice were betrayal and the savaging of reputations. I had no illusions left. Seven years earlier I had won the Olympics for Greece and went home. I was ready to step out of the limelight and go home to be with my family and—for the first time in years—rest, rest, and rest some more.

But while the focus of the world may leave the Olympic Games rather swiftly, the President of their organizing committee has other obligations. The Paralympic Games lay ahead in September and those too would be a dazzling success. There was no rush to submit ATHOC's final financial statement—Sydney 2000 hadn't yet finished its report by then. But I told the accountants I wanted the final report finished—"with everything explained clearly and without a single euro out of place"—in less than a year. Impossible, our accountants insisted, which is always the wrong answer for me. "I'm impatient," I told them. "I want to finish the story." By the following March, we had completed our report, returning, as I mentioned earlier, a surplus of 123.5 million euros to the government and closing its books on the Athens 2004 organizing committee.

Almost immediately after the Games ended, I felt a little strange. Nothing I could articulate, but I was not quite myself. Sometimes I felt cold and at other times I would break out into a sweat. My temperament had become a little erratic. I had explosions of temper and, afterward, I would have no idea why I had been so upset about that matter.

In November 2004, the key staff of ATHOC and I traveled to Beijing for a working visit during which organizers of the previous Olympics offer the facts, insights, and wisdom they have accumulated to the organizers of the next Games—what the IOC calls the "transfer of knowledge program."

When I arrived in Beijing, my symptoms got worse. I felt feverish, and my whole body ached. I arranged to have a massage and the hotel sent an elderly masseuse. She touched me and sensed something was not right. "Oh madame," she said, "you are very ill." I was furious that she was talking such nonsense and I was dismissive. I said she needn't worry; I had but a slight fever, and it was going away. The truth was that I had survived so many years on long hours, little sleep, and erratic eating habits I had convinced myself I was pretty much invincible.

The Chinese masseuse proved to be right and I was wrong. Dangerously wrong. A month later, our family gathered for our first Christmas and New Year's holidays at our home in the mountains in Gstaad, Switzerland. I was thrilled to have everyone gathered together for our first extended vacation in more than four years. But from the first very day, I didn't feel right—certainly not well enough to go out skiing. Not even to go outside. I thought perhaps I was having difficulty adjusting to the altitude—something that had never happened before.

But the next day I stayed in bed and barely had enough energy to say hello to the children when they returned from skiing. The following day all I did was sleep. My husband arranged for a doctor to come and take some blood tests. What I didn't know at the time was that the day after he examined me he informed my husband that he could not take responsibility for my treatment and that I needed to be hospitalized immediately. "Your wife is seriously ill. Her blood is like water."

At the hospital in Lausanne, I was so weak I could barely move. Over the next day, doctors conducted a battery of tests. When Theodore told me they wanted me to stay in the hospital, that I had some potentially serious medical problems, I refused. I told him that I wanted to go home and see in the New Year with my family. We argued and somehow I summoned the strength to find my driver, whom I ordered to take me back to our chalet. But even though I returned home, I wasn't really there. I had no strength and felt as if I had no inner core. My emotional pitch, usually so animated—I'm either laughing or yelling—was totally flat. I was frightened that I had turned into someone else completely, a person I didn't recognize.

The following day the doctors called my husband with the test results and an ultimatum. "Tell your wife that if she won't come in by herself immediately, we will send an ambulance to pick her up and bring her here." I went, and for almost a week I lay there lifeless. I told Theodore—I cried when I told him—that I didn't want him or anybody in the family to see me like that. Not him, not my mother, not my sister, and especially not our children. Only Lena, my faithful friend who flew in from Athens to be with me, was allowed in my room. More than a week later, when it was time for the children to return to school, Theodore insisted that I let them visit me in the hospital. Lena helped me change into some silk pajamas and a red robe, and, for the first time since I left home, I put on some makeup. Then I put on a brave face. Leave it to the youngest to be so perceptive. When Dimitris saw me, he said: "That's good. Mommy is wearing her makeup."

Soon after, I was capable of rational thought. But the thoughts were not comforting. "Maybe this is the end for me. Maybe they won't be able to save my life. But I am not going out of this life without the kind of fight I have put up throughout my life." So I picked up all the pieces of myself and decided to tap all the strength I had found to fight for my country and use it again, now, to fight for myself.

It was a long struggle, but slowly I improved. Later in the month I was well enough to spend an occasional night in a nearby hotel. Be that as it may, I saw only Lena and I spoke only to Theodore, who was having some health problems of his own—with his heart—and had to remain in Athens, and to my children. I wasn't ready to talk to anyone else.

But there are no secrets in this world. Word always gets out. Often it's not because of whom you talk to, but because of many to whom you don't talk. Silence from me was like throwing up a red flag. After I refused enough calls, including from the President of the Hellenic Republic, people began to wonder if something might be seriously wrong. They knew that it would take something serious to knock a woman as vigorous as me out of circulation. Inevitably, rumors reached me that I was on my deathbed.

But if the rumors had ever been true—and obviously I had confronted that possibility—by the time others heard them they no longer were. I was worried, however, that I might never be completely well or completely myself again. I desperately wanted my old life back. By February 2005, I wanted at least to be in Athens for Dimitris's birthday on the seventeenth since I had already missed Theodore's and Panagiotis's birthdays in early February. I had spent more than six weeks in the hospital; the doctors announced I was strong enough to make the trip home to Athens under strict medical supervision. I don't know how the news got out—maybe from airport sources that knew the Angelopoulos jet was heading to Switzerland and returning almost immediately—but the word was that the plane would be returning to Greece with my "coffin."

I was unaware of this dire report when I arrived home. I was so excited to be there that I insisted on taking a short walk so I could just soak in my neighborhood. People were staring at me as if they had seen a ghost. Only later did I understand why they seemed stunned to see me. Clearly they were thinking, "Oh my god, she's alive!"

As Mark Twain famously said, "The rumors of my death have been greatly exaggerated." When people felt they could talk to me about what I had endured during my illness, they frequently asked if, in crisis, I had found religion. I'd tell them I hadn't and that I wasn't looking for it either. I would never seek a deathbed conversion in hopes of eternal salvation. "The people in heaven would be too boring for me," I'd sarcastically joke. "I'd much prefer hell, where I know I will at least have some interesting conversations." When they heard that, they knew I was really back and my old self again.

Chapter 29

NEW PATHWAYS AND PARADIGMS

AFTER RETURNING TO ATHENS FROM LAUSANNE, I wanted to reinvent my life. I had to learn how to live again, how to accept and even embrace a brand-new life.

For five years, I had been at the center of everything, surrounded by people and consumed by my work and my mission. I had a thousand things to do and a million things on my mind. Now I had none of that.

I had plenty of time to think about where the Olympics had left Greece and me. I had had my fill of Greek politics and Greek politicians. What pained me most was to hear their disdainful attitude toward what we had learned and earned through the years on the way to delivering those "unforgettable dream games."

———

Although ATHOC had no responsibilities beyond the organization of the Games, I was very mindful of legacy considerations and made several workable suggestions to the government. All were ignored by both governments: first by the Socialists and later by the conservatives of the New Democracy.

I would ask the Ministers, "What is your plan for the 'next day' after the Games?"

They would typically reply, "That's our job. You deal only with ATHOC."

The government had closed its books on the Games. Since it couldn't deny our Olympic success, it simply ignored it, a conjurer's trick to, essentially, make the Games disappear from public consciousness and memory. Our state-of-the-art control center, which could have become a national command center for any emergency situation, was dismantled, moved, and reassembled as a run-of-the-mill computer filing and information storage center.

The new athletic venues went largely unused and were allowed to deteriorate. Our showcase Olympic village lay derelict and abandoned. The absence of long-term planning by the government resulted in the waste of some extraordinary resources. Instead of building on the legacy, the government let it fade away and let the country drift back into the easy and familiar old ways that constituted business as usual. Nobody in the government or even the opposition resisted or seemed the least bit concerned where this might lead.

Unlike after the bid campaign, when the Simitis government made me an Ambassador-at-Large, the Greek conservative government of New Democracy—the party I once belonged to and ran for—did not publicly honor or acknowledge my Olympic effort. Only the President of the Republic, Costis Stephanopoulos, singled me out by bestowing on me Greece's highest civilian honor, the title of Commander of the Order of Merit. Regrettably, I could not receive it in person because I had taken ill in Switzerland.

The politicians had the opportunity to build on an extraordinary legacy. Instead, they ignored it. We passed them the baton and they dropped it. I would prefer to pretend that none of the harsh treatment had bothered me personally. But the words still stung, the wounds still lingered, and the rejection still hurt. To comfort me, a friend put together a notebook filled with stories of all the famous Greeks, beginning with ancient times, who had been betrayed, ostracized, cast aside, or even poisoned. I found myself in some very good company, with people like Socrates, Ioannis Kapodistrias, Phidias, Harilaos Trikoupis, Alcibiades, Eleftherios Venizelos, and countless others. Trust me, it is not a short list.

Gradually, as my health improved, I reclaimed my life. It was a very quiet and private life, but I didn't mind that. There were so many things for which I had had no time—reading, practicing yoga, listening to opera, swimming and water-skiing year-round in the Aegean—that I could now enjoy again. For periods as long as two weeks, I never left the house. I could exercise in the open air and was perfectly content. I even found time to study some books about cooking and to master a few recipes. One time when I visited Pan in Boston, I insisted—to his amazement—on cooking dinner for him and his friends. When I came out wearing an apron and a Hermes headscarf, his jaw dropped. When I produced *filet au poivre* flambéed in cognac, he could only say, "Wow!" After the first taste, Pan cheered, "Bravo, Mom!"

During all the years I worked toward Athens 2004, Lefteris Kousoulis, a trusted friend who—besides offering savvy political counsel—liked to play amateur psychologist, would occasionally check in on me to see how I was doing. Unlike everybody else who asked me that question, he wasn't concerned with Olympic progress. He was asking how things were going with my family. I was all fired up about the Olympics and he would ask in his calmest voice: "How is Theodore? How are the children?"

I would get irritated. "Don't you see what I have on my plate?" Then I'd start talking about this project and that project and all the ups and downs of my Olympic undertaking.

One time he just cut me off. "Gianna," he said, "I know your plate is full, but keep in mind that the day after all of this is over, you will be alone with your family. Don't jeopardize that."

He was right.

Thus, most important of all during this period, I reconnected with Theodore, giving him the attention that he needed and so deserved. For myself, I wasn't willing to undertake anything new. I wanted to process the past, nurture myself through the early stages of healing, and learn to relax in a fashion that had eluded me throughout my life. Theodore, as he has always been, was understanding and very supportive. "Take your time," he said. "It will come."

I probably was avoiding "garden variety people." But it was because I was embarrassed to face them. When we had asked people in Greece to make sacrifices and change their daily habits, it was not just for the seventeen days of the Games but in order to change all our lives for the better, for years to come. I had given people hope and, as a result, they had high expectations. It was hard to look them in the eye when, by this time, I knew that we all had been betrayed, that the Greek government had no intention of delivering on the kind of future we had once envisioned for our country. I reread my speeches from the Olympics period and I felt shame.

In that frame of mind, I felt I had no choice but to reject dozens of invitations from all over Greece—from universities, civic authorities, NGOs, volunteer organizations, and many others—to speak on the Olympic legacy. There was nothing honest I felt I could say to them about the Olympic aftermath. I did agree, however, to speak to a forum at Harvard University's John F. Kennedy School of Government on how—almost a decade after I had organized the colloquium "The Greek Paradox"—we had demonstrated that such a paradox did not have to be an eternal condition.

I also accepted an invitation from former IOC President Juan Antonio Samaranch to address a conference in Barcelona on sports culture, where I was also honored for my contribution to the Olympic movement. The most surprising honor, however, came from the Greek Socialists. George Papandreou, who had replaced Simitis as party leader, had invited me to his party's convention, which was held at an Olympic venue. Though the party faithful knew I wasn't and never would be one of them, I received a standing ovation from the five thousand delegates.

Before I became ill, Theodore had flirted with the notion of investing in media. By the end of 2004, he was so distressed by this failure of leadership that he began negotiating to buy a media company—a newspaper and a TV station—so that we might have a platform from which a message of national unity could be preached to try and reinvigorate the Olympic legacy. It didn't work out. The negotiations fell through.

By 2006, when one of the few newspapers with close ties to conservatives was up for sale, we bought it. We also established a radio station. We thought we would offer a distinctive voice among the largely leftist media. And unlike other media owners who used their public influence to boost their private economic interests, we had long before chosen to divert our business interests away from Greece.

At the time we assumed stewardship of the paper, the New Democracy government was undergoing, or at least attempting, a political shift. Traditionally a conservative party, New Democracy was trying to move toward the center in order to more effectively challenge the leftists that had long been dominant in Greek politics. Our intention with the newspaper was to encourage the government in its efforts to be more centrist, open-minded, and progressive. Furthermore, we hoped to invigorate the political debate that, in Greece, too often revolved around personalities rather than ideas. It didn't work out. The government believed there was no reason to engage a paper that was already on its side.

We complained repeatedly to the government, and eventually Prime Minister Karamanlis agreed to sit down with somebody from our paper. It wouldn't be a formal interview, but more of a *tourlou*, which is a Greek dish in which you throw all the vegetables in the pot and, hopefully, come up with a tasty stew. In this case, we hoped that a wide-ranging discussion might provide fodder for any number of stories. I sent our editor, Yiannis Papoutsanis, to talk with the Prime Minister at the Maximos Mansion.

When Yiannis was finished, he called me immediately at home. I could tell he was very stirred up, but he wouldn't talk to me over the phone. It is common to hear Greeks say that someone is listening to every conversation, so we distrust the phone. "I have to come over and meet you in person," he said. He told about the meeting in his own fashion, slowly, just as it had unfolded. The Prime Minister was in his armchair and Yiannis was perched on the end of a sofa adjacent to him. As the discussion was winding to an end, Yiannis asked the Prime Minister to pick the single moment of his tenure that he would treasure the most once he left office.

It was what journalists call a "softball" question, one that shouldn't challenge any politician let alone a veteran like the Prime Minister. It gave him a chance to show his human side while sharing something that was genuinely precious to him. Yet the question seems to have stymied Karamanlis. He pondered it for quite a while before leaning over to Yiannis and twice clapping him on the leg, which suggested he was about to confide something both intimate and of consequence. "My happiest moment," he said, "will be the moment when I leave this place."

Yiannis was absolutely shocked. It didn't surprise me quite as much, except perhaps that the Prime Minister would admit it. The Greek people had given him a historic opportunity to lead a nation prepared to work differently, with a fresh ethos; competent people who were eager to continue to present a brand-new country to the world. He resented the idea of leading them.

We bought the newspaper with a lot of grand notions and high expectations that we could once again make a difference in Greece. But it didn't take us long to discover that we were mistaken. We had entered an alien culture and good intentions weren't enough. Almost everyone seemed to have his own agenda and appeared largely indifferent to the goals and ambitions of ownership. The journalists proved less than enterprising. A lot of them seemed to be sitting around not doing much of anything. No matter how hard I tried to provide leadership, I couldn't gain control of the overall operation. I always wound up feeling frustrated.

The newspaper proved to be a bad move for us, as we never succeeded in becoming a key part of the public discourse. We had no real choice but to close it, which we did in June 2009. We gave generous severance packages to all of the staff at the newspaper. That was something, I am sad to report, that had never been done in Greece before.

Additionally, when we sold the newspaper titles and the radio station, all revenues were distributed among the employees.

Mistakes are unfortunate, but they are more unfortunate when you don't learn from them. I learned a lot from this one. While I held fast to my belief that I had a lot to offer, I knew it was time to look beyond Greece. I needed to embrace a cause in an arena where true commitment and a passion for action were truly respected.

The answer for me was to go back to the future, to break out of the constraints on my thinking and imagination that Greece imposed, just as I had done when I had left the country almost two decades earlier. I needed once again to take a broader, more global view of the issues I cared about, just as I had done more than a decade earlier when I got involved with Harvard's Kennedy School. The Olympics had fallen into my lap in the first place because I had international credentials and international credibility. And while our Olympic success may have been above all a Greek triumph, it was an international one as well.

When I got involved with Harvard's Kennedy School, I was always inspired, moved, and motivated by its motto: "We are shaping the leaders of the world."

It was that motto, along with my more recent involvement with one of the great leaders and visionaries of our time, former President Bill Clinton, who reinvigorated my thinking about public service and the role I could play through Harvard and its Kennedy School.

After eight challenging years in the White House, Clinton had earned the right to take it easy. He could have written his book, given a few speeches, sat on a few boards, and played a lot of rounds of golf. Instead, the former President took his formidable leadership skills and reinvented himself as a problem-solver in a new domain. He founded the Clinton Global Initiative and set about creating new paradigms for the twenty-first century that have demonstrated how change can be accomplished without relying exclusively on government. He had the vision to recognize that NGOs and private-public partnerships and a host of ad hoc alliances might address problems more effectively. I share this mantra as well.

His message resonates with my pragmatic side. It is not enough to foment lofty intellectual discourse on how government should work. It is far more important to go out and get something accomplished, even if it is on a very small scale. Create something more than an idea; feed somebody, house somebody, inoculate somebody, or educate somebody. Ideas become far more credible—as well as fundable and marketable—once somebody has demonstrated that they actually work.

Clinton's example inspired a new program that I established at Harvard's Kennedy School, the Angelopoulos Global Public Leaders Program. The Kennedy School has always brought in veteran leaders to share past experiences with the students, our future leaders. The Angelopoulos program offers a twist. What we want is to bring to Harvard successful leaders who have completed their terms in their countries. These people are too valuable to be put out to pasture. We want to give them a place and some time where they can explore new avenues so that, just as President Clinton did, they can once again serve the public by confronting the global challenges of our time.

I am proud that, a decade ago, I provided a model of leadership for my country, one that unified a fractious nation behind the public interest. But governments, especially with today's severe budgetary constraints, are often too inefficient and too politically insecure to utilize their power on behalf of the common good for any sustained period.

Bill Clinton has inspired me to find a new path, and I hope that through my public-leaders program I can in turn inspire others to join me on that path. Public service was my dream as a child and my life's work as an adult. I have returned to that arena a little bruised but a lot wiser for my experiences. I am convinced not only that I can I make a difference but also that I can make a difference in the lives of extraordinary leaders who will then make a difference in the lives of many more people.

A GREEK DRAMA

AS I LOOK BACK ON THE GLORIOUS NIGHT of the closing ceremony of the Athens 2004 Summer Olympics, when I urged my countrymen and women to keep showing "the new face of Greece" and to "keep the flame for creativity, effort, and victory burning in our souls," it becomes clear that the call went unheeded.

By early 2013, Greece's economy was in a nosedive: Unemployment had reached 27 percent. More than half of the population under the age of twenty-five was out of work. Businesses failed by the thousands. Hundreds of thousands of households fell into poverty. GDP had decreased by more than 20 percent in four years.

The country I love, the country in which I live, has been turned upside down. Those who were comfortable have seen their lives contract as they sold their car and sold their home. Families have pulled their children out of university because of the exorbitant cost. Young Greeks are going abroad for opportunity, a brain drain that could hobble Greece long into the future.

No statistic signifies the devastation more than this: By mid-2012, Greece, which once had the lowest suicide rate in Europe, had the third highest.

This situation and Greece's global image form a tragic antithesis to the pride and joy Greeks felt during the 2004 Summer Olympic Games. Today, even the most troubling aspects of "the Greek Paradox" seem minor by comparison.

Over decades, there were many causes that contributed to the crisis, but I am convinced a lack of decisive leadership deepened and compounded all of them.

What I learned heading our Olympic effort is that leadership is about confronting the issues head-on, about inspiring people to try to find solutions to the problems that keep us from achieving our goals.

The graver the situation, the tighter the timeline, the greater the importance of leadership.

A leader shows and paves the way and has a vision; a leader exercises discipline and leads by example; a leader does not shy from hard, hard work; a leader is willing to sacrifice; a leader instills a "can-do" problem-solving approach and always has plans A, B, and C available.

As I said in an address to the Clinton Global Initiative in April 2012,

I've been thinking a lot about leadership recently, as I've seen my own country go from the "high" of a successful Olympic Games, to the "low" of the current crisis.

And the more I thought about it, the more it confirmed my belief that the Greek people have great capacity. After all, we were the ones who were able to do in four years leading up to the Olympics what other countries could barely do in seven.

What we lacked—during the years when no progress was made on the Games, and in the years that the country has slipped into decline—is leadership. Leadership that is tough, and honest, and inspirational. Leadership that allowed the Greek people to envision a future for themselves that they may not have envisioned by themselves.

To me, that is the definition of leadership: to help people see a future and to see their own role and their own power in achieving it.

From Athens, to Arkansas, and to the Arab Spring, leaders who can do that are a vital resource. And they are a renewable resource.

Greece has suffered from a lack of leadership.

Successive governments blamed the previous ones for the gravity of the crisis; parties blamed other parties; and analysts blamed the bloated public sector and tax evasion. The Greek public was led to blame the European Union and Germany in particular; the European public responded by blaming their own stereotypical images of the lazy and profligate Greeks.

Taking their cue from all of that blame shifting, some thought it would be politically useful to blame even the Olympics themselves.

When the cost of the Athens 2004 Games began being mentioned as a factor that affected Greece's debt, I was appalled. I shouldn't have been surprised, though. When fingers are being pointed, facts tend to fall by the wayside. And what began as a whisper campaign among those who opposed hosting the Games in the first place started to find purchase in the mainstream media.

By 2009, when the crisis erupted, Greece had amassed a public debt of 365 billion euros. According to the government's own accounting, however, the investments made in the Summer Olympics by the government amounted to only 6 billion euros—less than one-sixtieth of the total debt of 2009!

As I have noted earlier, the organizing committee's budget of two billion euros, which was my direct responsibility, returned a surplus of 123.5 million euros at the Games' end.

What's more, politicians inaccurately added to the costs of the Olympics much of the costs for several major infrastructure projects that were previously planned and budgeted: a new airport, a new ring road, and a suburban metro system, among others. (Never mind many other projects that were christened "Olympic" projects simply to get them funded and fast-tracked by the government.)

Yes, the major infrastructure projects were useful for the Games, but more important, they were necessary for the economic functioning and everyday life of the citizens of a modern country.

Indeed, one of the reasons that Greek governments of differing political stripes had sought to host the Games was to spur critical investments for economic prosperity. This is why many countries throughout the world compete to host the Games.

Even as the poisoned perception of the role of the Games in Greece's economic woes spread, it wasn't until January 2013 that we heard the economic benefit of the Games openly acknowledged by the Greek government.

On January 15, a member of Parliament named Yannis Panoussis asked Finance Minister Yannis Stournaras what, at the end of the day, the Games actually cost.

Stournaras began running through the numbers. He started with a total expenditure of 8.5 billion euros. From that, he subtracted ATHOC's roughly two-billion-euro budget, because it wasn't paid by the state, but rather funded out of television rights, sponsorships, and ticket sales.

He then cited another two billion euros that financed work done for the Unification of the Athens Archeological Sites or for the modernization of Athens hospitals (matters that were related to the Games, but loosely).

He also made reference to additional investments, such as of the Olympic Ring road or the revamping of the Coastal Front, and then explained how tourism and additional economic activity from the Games brought in a further 3.5 billion euros to state coffers (mainly from the value-added tax), resulting in a net cost of some one billion euros.

This sum, he continued, was more than compensated for by additional economic benefits from the Games.

Remember, the growth rate for Greece in the years up to the Olympics and in the three years following was one of the highest in Europe, averaging 4.5 percent per year.

In the discussion that ensued in Parliament, Panoussis and Stournaras addressed the fact (one that I have addressed previously in these pages) that, beyond the dereliction of the Olympic venues, the legacy of the Games, in which modernized processes coupled with the people's can-do attitude to overcome any challenge, was abandoned.

Yes, people who are concerned about Greece's situation should point their fingers at the Olympics. But they should do so for an entirely different reason.

During the 2004 Summer Games, Greece had become a totally new country, acknowledged by everybody around the world.

Greece was a place that had won the Games not by right but by merit, and that sense of being governed by rules rather than relationships had started to infuse the culture of the country.

We created a vision for the Greek people that they may not have had for themselves but that they came to embrace. It was a vision of a competitive, modern, willing-and-able nation.

On the strength of that vision, we were able to create a mentality—in the organizing committee and the volunteer movement—that permeated through the administration, the judicial system, the local authorities, the public sector, and the citizens of Greece.

People took it upon themselves to solve problems. When I saw our staff, volunteers, and spectators smiling, I knew they weren't doing so because they had been told to smile; they were smiling at a bigger role they were seeing—for themselves and for their country.

We banished the inefficiency that holds back the capabilities and talents of Greeks individually and collectively.

Everyone, whether they were a government official, an executive, a blue-collar worker, or a homemaker, believed that they had a role to play—even if that role was just being a spectator—in making the Olympics a success. And they acted on that belief.

The Greek people adapted to and, in many cases, came to embrace the changes we asked them to undertake.

In this common effort, we had resolved the paradox that Greeks overseas achieve great success while Greeks in their own country seem to accept failure.

If something of the "common cause" spirit we had built back in the days of our Olympic endeavor had survived, then that same spirit could have helped the people of Greece to solve the present difficult situation.

Instead, so much of what we were able to create was completely and unnecessarily dismantled, including the volunteer movement we had built. We had tens of thousands of dedicated individuals—a corps larger than either the Greek navy or air force—who had demonstrated a willingness to serve their country.

To paraphrase President John F. Kennedy, Greece had people who were asking not what their country could do for them but what they could do for their country. What other great national projects could those patriots have been asked to undertake?

Had these patriots and their sense of duty and selfless commitment been nurtured or enhanced, or simply kept intact, it would have been key to the spirit of solidarity that is so vitally needed now as Greece faces a crisis of almost unimaginable proportions.

EPILOGUE

SO, I HAVE GIVEN YOU MY STORY. A life story I could never have imagined but actually lived.

A rebellious girl who dreamed of a life for herself beyond the rocky shores of her native Crete.

A young lawyer who defied expectations to win a seat on the Athens city council.

A woman who found herself in a fairy tale romance, a *coup de foudre*, with one of Greece's most admired businessmen.

A new kind of public figure who battled state bureaucracy and inefficiency to successfully invite the world to see a new Greece during the 2004 Olympic Games.

If you had told that little girl in Crete who dreamed of becoming an ambassador that she would one day be the face of her nation to the world, she would not have believed it.

If you had told that young lawyer that she would one day represent her nation in Parliament, she would not have believed it.

But this has been my journey. It is a journey I never could have predicted I would take. And one that I wouldn't trade for anything.

My nation has likewise been on a long journey. And I truly believe that my nation's future, like the future for that little girl in Crete, can be bright.

Leading up to the Athens Summer Games, we managed to overcome every challenge that was placed in our path: endless procedures for belated projects, permits covered in red tape, a sense that "We can do it tomorrow" instead of "We need it done yesterday."

We were able to achieve in four years what was supposed to be done in seven.

It can be done.

The Greek Paradox can be resolved.

The Greek people have the capacity for change.

It is the Greek leaders who saw the Games not as a pinnacle but as a threat to the established order.

We must continue to expand the grassroots movements that are springing up in Greece to bring support and relief to those in need.

We must break the shackles of inefficiency that have created a culture of dependency.

We must overcome the deficit of confidence, get results, and only then confront our partners, not by begging but by believing in our own capabilities and skills.

Most important, we must seek out leadership at all levels of governance: leaders who will explain to the people the truth no matter how harsh it is; who will represent us with honor and pride and not with condescension; who will not fear responsibility; and who will nurture expectations and cancel envy.

And we must begin yesterday.

Only then, like the basil seeds that I distributed during my first political campaign, will Greece once again flourish and grow.

Only then will the world rediscover Greece for what it truly is.

Change is so desperately needed. A daring new start that will relegate past practices to history, permanently, and usher in an era with less Greek Drama and more Greek Triumph.

Yes, things must change. And that change begins with each and every one of us.

A fellow Cretan, Nikos Kazantzakis, once wrote: "You must love responsibility. You must say: 'I, I myself will save the world. If the world perishes, I will stand to blame.'"

ABOUT THE AUTHOR

GIANNA ANGELOPOULOS is an Olympic organizer, former ambassador of the Greek state, lawyer, former parliamentarian, and best-selling author. In 1986, Ambassador Angelopoulos was elected to the Athens Municipal Council. In 1989, she was elected to parliament, and won reelection the following year.

Following her marriage to Theodore Angelopoulos, Gianna resigned her seat in the Parliament to focus on family and business. In 1996, the prime minister of Greece appointed her to lead the country's successful campaign to host the 2004 Olympic Games. In 2000, when slow progress and gridlocked bureaucracy put Athens in danger of losing the Games, she was asked to assume the presidency of the Athens 2004 Organizing Committee and save the project.

Throughout her career, Mrs. Angelopoulos has played leading roles is several leading global institutions.

At Harvard University, Mrs. Angelopoulos has served as vice-chairman of the Dean's Council of Harvard's Kennedy School of Government since 1994 and now also serves as a member of the Advisory Board of the Center for Business and Government. She established the Angelopoulos Global Public Leaders Program to bring distinguished leaders to the HKS to share lessons learned with students and plan for their next phases of contribution to the common good.

Mrs. Angelopoulos was also a member of the Clinton Global Initiative and is the founder and sponsor of the Angelopoulos CGIU Fellowship Program, a competition that has selected and nurtured seventy-five young Greeks with entrepreneurial projects that benefit the country. She is a proud parent of three grown children and two beautiful granddaughters.